Mizan Series 2

MUSLIMS AND US POLITICS TODAY

The Mizan Series
General Editor, Michael Pregill

The Mizan Series is published by the Ilex Foundation in partnership with the Center for Hellenic Studies. The series supports the central mission of the Mizan digital initiative to encourage informed public discourse and interdisciplinary scholarship on the history, culture, and religion of Muslim societies and civilizations.

www.mizanproject.org

Also in the Mizan Series

Muslim Superheroes: Comics, Islam, and Representation,
edited by A. David Lewis and Martin Lund

MUSLIMS AND US POLITICS TODAY

A DEFINING MOMENT

Edited by
Mohammad Hassan Khalil

Ilex Foundation
Boston, Massachusetts

Center for Hellenic Studies
Trustees for Harvard University
Washington, D. C.

Distributed by Harvard University Press
Cambridge, Massachusetts and London, England

Muslims and US Politics Today: A Defining Moment
Edited by Mohammad Hassan Khalil

Published by Ilex Foundation, Boston, Massachusetts and The Center for Hellenic Studies, Trustees for Harvard University, Washington, D.C.

Distributed by Harvard University Press, Cambridge, Massachusetts and London, England

Production editor: Christopher Dadian
Cover design: Joni Godlove
Printed in the United States of America

On the cover: photo illustration featuring photos from Wikimedia/Creative Commons of state senator Patricia Torres Ray, (then) state representative Ilhan Omar, and (then) state representative Peggy Flanagan leading the Women's March in St. Paul, Minnesota, January 2017, by Fibonacci Blue (top); Minneapolis City Hall "Eviction Rally," Black Lives Matter, December 2015, by Tony Webster (center); and Khizr and Ghazala Khan, speaking with VOA's Urdu service in Washington, DC, August 2016, by B. Allen (bottom). Background photo: mobile phone with blurred image of protesters, Shutterstock ID 391401886.

Library of Congress Cataloging-in-Publication Data

Names: Khalil, Mohammad Hassan, editor.
Title: Muslims and US politics today : a defining moment / edited by Mohammad
  Hassan Khalil.
Description: Boston, Massachusetts : Ilex Foundation ; Washington, D.C. :
  Center for Hellenic Studies, Trustees for Harvard University, 2019. |
  Series: Mizan series | "Distributed by Harvard University Press,
  Cambridge, Massachusetts and London, England." | Includes bibliographical
  references and index.
Identifiers: LCCN 2019016944 | ISBN 9780674241343 (alk. paper)
Subjects: LCSH: Muslims--United States. | Muslims--United States--Politics
  and government. | Islam and politics--United States. | United
  States--Ethnic relations.
Classification: LCC E184.M88 M85 2019 | DDC 305.6/970973--dc23
LC record available at https://lccn.loc.gov/2019016944

CONTENTS

Mohammad Hassan Khalil
Introduction.. 1

PART ONE: MUSLIMS AND THE AMERICAN STATE

Kambiz GhaneaBassiri
Religion-State Relations and the Politics
of Religious Freedom in Muslim America 9

Mucahit Bilici
Muslims and the American Constitution:
From the First Amendment to the Second?.................................... 27

Edward E. Curtis IV
Blood Sacrifice and the Myth of the Fallen
Muslim Soldier in US Presidential Elections after 9/11 48

PART TWO: ANTI-MUSLIM POLITICS

Salah D. Hassan
Muslim Presence: Anti-Muslim Politics in
the United States and the Rise of Muslim American Culture.......................... 69

Evelyn Alsultany
Real Time with Bill Maher and the
Good Muslims of Liberal Multiculturalism 83

Juliane Hammer
Muslim Women, Anti-Muslim
Hostility, and the State in the Age of Terror 104

PART THREE: MARGINALIZATION AND ACTIVISM

Alisa M. Perkins
Muslim Detroit after Orlando: The LGBTQ Question, Rituals
of Inclusion, and Coalition Building across Racial and Religious Lines 127

Sally Howell
Rights versus Respectability: The Politics
of Muslim Visibility in Detroit's Northern Suburbs 149

Mohsen Mostafavi Mobasher
Politics, Immigration, and Ethnic Mobilization:
The Predicament of Iranian Immigrants in the
United States since the Iranian Revolution 169

PART FOUR: RETHINKING MUSLIM POLITICS

Donna Auston and Sylvia Chan-Malik
Drawing Near to God's Pleasure:
A Dialogue on the Black Muslim Political Tradition
and the Moral-Ethical Imperatives of American Islam 185

Junaid Rana
The Idea of a Global Muslim Left 201

Index of Names 217

Contributors

Evelyn Alsultany is an associate professor of American Studies and Ethnicity at the University of Southern California. She is the author of *Arabs and Muslims in the Media: Race and Representation after 9/11* (New York University Press, 2012). She also co-edited two books: *Arab and Arab-American Feminisms* (Syracuse University Press, reprinted in 2015), which received the 2012 Arab American Book Award for Non-Fiction, and *Between the Middle East and the Americas: The Cultural Politics of Diaspora* (University of Michigan Press, 2013), a book that received Honorable Mention in the 2014 Arab American Non-Fiction category of the Arab American Book Award in 2014.

Donna Auston is a doctoral candidate in the Department of Anthropology at Rutgers University and a community activist. She has been researching and writing about the history and experiences of American Muslims for many years, with particular focus on African American Muslims. She lectures regularly at universities and other venues, and has appeared on television and radio outlets discussing topics such as Islamophobia, faith and feminism, media representation of racial and religious minorities, and, most recently, race and policing.

Mucahit Bilici is an associate professor of sociology at John Jay College and CUNY Graduate Center. He is the author of *Finding Mecca in America: How Islam Is Becoming an American Religion* (University of Chicago Press, 2012).

Sylvia Chan-Malik is an associate professor of American and women's and gender studies at Rutgers University. She is the author of *Being Muslim: A Cultural History of Women of Color and American Islam* (New York University Press, 2018).

Edward E. Curtis IV is professor of religious studies, adjunct professor of American studies and Africana studies, and Millennium Chair of the Liberal Arts at Indiana University-Purdue University Indianapolis. He is the author of *Muslims in America: A Short History* (Oxford University Press, 2009); *Muslim Americans in the Military: Centuries of Service* (Indiana University Press, 2016); *Islam in Black America: Identity, Liberation, and Difference in African-American Islamic Thought* (State University of New York Press, 2002); *Black Muslim Religion in the Nation of Islam, 1960-1975* (University of North Carolina Press, 2006); and *The Call of Bilal: Islam in the African Diaspora* (University of North Carolina

Press, 2014). His other books include *The Columbia Sourcebook of Muslims in the United States* (Columbia University Press, 2008); *New Black Gods: Arthur Huff Fauset and the Study of African-American Religions* (Indiana University Press, 2009); *Bloomsbury Reader on Islam in the West* (Bloomsbury, 2015); and *Encyclopedia of Muslim-American History* (Facts on File, 2010).

Kambiz GhaneaBassiri is a professor of religion and humanities at Reed College. He is the founding co-editor of the Islam of the Global West book series published by Bloomsbury Academic and the author of *A History of Islam in America: From the New World to the New World Order* (Cambridge University Press, 2010). A scholar of Islam in America and the Middle East, he has been selected as a Carnegie Scholar (2006) and a Guggenheim Fellow (2012), and served as one of five national scholars for the National Endowment for the Humanites' and the American Library Association's Muslim Journeys Bookshelf.

Juliane Hammer is an associate professor of religious studies and the Kenan Rifai Scholar of Islamic Studies at the University of North Carolina at Chapel Hill. She is the author of *Peaceful Families: American Muslim Efforts against Domestic Violence* (Princeton University Press, 2019); *American Muslim Women, Religious Authority, and Activism: More Than a Prayer* (University of Texas Press, 2012) and *Palestinians Born in Exile: Diaspora and the Search for a Homeland* (University of Texas Press, 2005), as well as co-editor of *The Cambridge Companion to American Islam* (Cambridge University Press, 2013) and *A Jihad for Justice: The Work and Life of Amina Wadud* (2012).

Salah D. Hassan is an associate professor of postcolonial studies and Arab American and Muslim American studies at Michigan State University. He is the founder of the Muslim Subjects website, which was funded by a grant he received from the Social Science Research Council in 2011. He is the co-producer of two documentary films on American Muslims, *Migrations of Islam* and *Death of an Imam.*

Sally Howell is an associate professor of history and director of the Center for Arab American Studies at the University of Michigan-Dearborn. She is the author of *Old Islam in Detroit: Rediscovering the Muslim American Past* (Oxford University Press, 2014), which received the 2015 Arab American Book Award for Non-Fiction; co-author of *Citizenship and Crisis: Arab Detroit after 9/11* (Russell Sage Foundation Press, 2009); and co-editor of *Arab Detroit 9/11: Life in the Terror Decade* (Wayne State University, 2011).

Mohammad Hassan Khalil is currently the director of the Muslim Studies Program, an associate professor of religious studies, and an adjunct professor of law at Michigan State University. His books include *Islam and the Fate of Others: The Salvation Question* (Oxford University Press, 2012), *Between Heaven and Hell: Islam, Salvation, and the Fate of Others* (Oxford University Press, 2013), and *Jihad, Radicalism, and the New Atheism* (Cambridge University Press, 2018). He is the principal investigator of the Muslims of the Midwest digital archive project, which in 2014 was awarded a Humanities Without Walls grant (funded by Mellon) and involves ten researchers at five Midwestern research universities.

Mohsen Mostafavi Mobasher is an associate professor of anthropology and sociology at the University of Houston-Downtown. He is the author of *The Iranian Diaspora: Challenges, Negotiations, and Transformations* (University of Texas Press, 2018); *Iranians in Texas: Migration, Politics, and Ethnic Identity* (University of Texas Press, 2012); and co-author of *Migration, Globalization, and Ethnic Relations* (Pearson, 2003).

Alisa Perkins is an anthropologist and assistant professor of comparative religion at Western Michigan University. Her current research project is an ethnographic study of Muslim American civic engagement in the Detroit-metro area. She is the author of *Muslims in Metro Detroit: Gender and Religious Boundaries in Urban America* (New York University Press, forthcoming) which was funded by grants from the Wenner-Gren Foundation for Anthropological Research, the National Science Foundation, and the Philanthropic Educational Organization.

Junaid Rana is an associate professor and associate head of Asian American studies at the University of Illinois at Urbana-Champaign. He is the author of *Terrifying Muslims: Race and Labor in the South Asian Diaspora* (Duke University Press, 2011), winner of the 2013 Book Award in Social Sciences from the Association for Asian American Studies. He is co-editor of *With Stones in Our Hands: Writings on Racism, Muslims, and Empire* (University of Minnesota Press, 2018).

Introduction

Mohammad Hassan Khalil

O N THE AFTERNOON of Friday, June 10, 2016, before a global audience, various luminaries eulogized the most famous American Muslim of all time, Muhammad Ali. The televised audience also witnessed Islamic invocations, recitations from the Qur'an, and, if they listened carefully, gleeful shouts of *Allahu akbar* ("God is the greatest") from many of the thousands of attendees who packed Louisville's KFC Yum! Sports Arena for the memorial service. In the words of then president Barack Obama, Ali "will always be America."

A mere two days later, Americans awoke to the tragic news that a young American Muslim, Omar Mateen, had perpetrated what was then the deadliest mass shooting in US history when he took the lives of dozens of innocents at Orlando's Pulse nightclub. His proclaimed affiliation to ISIS and the various claims of his homophobia and anger problems were all over the news. Then presidential candidate Donald Trump tweeted that the shooter reportedly shouted *Allahu akbar* during the horrific rampage. And Obama condemned what "was an act of terror and an act of hate."

To be sure, this has been a volatile period in American Muslim history. And this volatility has become more pronounced as the number of reported hate crimes against Muslims has risen parallel to the election and now presidency of Trump. Trump himself has maintained that he is not an Islamophobe. Back in September 2015, he told CNN's Jake Tapper, "I love the Muslims. I think they're great people."[1] Three months later, however, he called for "a total and complete shutdown of Muslims entering the United States until our country's representatives can figure out what the hell is going on."[2] And in March 2016, he told CNN's Anderson Cooper, "I think Islam hates us."[3] Although such statements did not deter a minority of American Muslims from supporting Trump in the 2016 presidential election, many found these words and their generally welcome reception among Trump's supporters to be profoundly unsettling. And yet, interestingly, parallel to Trump's candidacy and presidency, Muslims have played unprecedented roles of influence in US pol-

1. Lee 2015.
2. Johnson 2015.
3. Schleifer 2016.

itics – from Gold Star parents Khizr and Ghazala Khan's televised statement at the 2016 Democratic National Convention to the increasing prominence of 2017 Women's March organizer Linda Sarsour to the election of Somali American Ilhan Omar to the Minnesota House of Representatives in 2016 and the United States House of Representatives in 2018.

To help make sense of this new chapter in American Muslim history, a symposium on "Muslims and Contemporary US Politics" was convened at Michigan State University in April 2017. Various leading scholars who study American Muslims were invited to examine new ways in which these Muslims are (a) being represented in contemporary US politics (with "politics" here being defined as broadly as possible); (b) themselves being affected and shaped by contemporary US politics, in regard to their subjectivities and agendas; and (c) engaging politics on individual and community levels. All of the chapters of the present volume can be traced back to the MSU symposium.

The contributors were each invited to approach the topic as they saw fit. As such, although this volume treats various critical issues involving Muslims and contemporary US politics, it was not intended to be exhaustive in its approach. Furthermore, and as the contributors quickly discovered at the symposium (during lively round table conversations), this project was not intended to offer a unified vision. Indeed, as readers will notice, each chapter represents a unique perspective and approach (though by no means a complete spectrum of views). This is even reflected in the terminology used in each chapter. For instance, Muslims residing in the United States are variously called "American Muslims," "Muslim Americans," "US Muslims," and, simply, "Muslims."

The volume is divided into four parts. Part One, "Muslims and the American State," consists of three chapters. In Chapter One, "Religion-State Relations and the Politics of Religious Freedom in Muslim America," **Kambiz GhaneaBassiri** grapples with a paradox in American Muslim politics: on the one hand, the state, at varying points in American history, has tried to define the role and place of Islam in the public square and in international affairs for varying political purposes; on the other, because of the First Amendment, it has also recognized different Muslims' right to interpret and institutionalize their religion in America as they see fit. These opposing approaches to Islam, GhaneaBassiri argues, have shaped the contemporary political activity of American Muslims.

In Chapter Two, "Muslims and the American Constitution: From the First Amendment to the Second?," **Mucahit Bilici** explores how Muslims appropriate and use the American Constitution as both an object of veneration (a sacred object for self-defense à la Khizr Khan) and a sacred text of citizenship (as observed in the rise of "Second Amendment Muslims" in America). As Bilici observes, Muslims have adopted the Constitution's language (often quoting phrases such as "life, liberty, and the pursuit of happiness") and freedom of speech; however, now we are at an interesting turning point, a movement from the First Amendment, or the democratic politics of American citizenship – "don't hurt us," "accept us," "we want to speak" – to the Second Amendment – Muslims thinking about gun ownership as both an act of self-protection and an assertion of American citizenship.

In Chapter Three, "Blood Sacrifice and the Myth of the Fallen Muslim Soldier in US Presidential Elections after 9/11," **Edward E. Curtis IV** notes that in the two most consequential US Presidential elections after the 9/11 attacks, the blood sacrifice of two fallen soldiers named Khan (Corporal Kareem Khan and Captain Humayun Khan) occupied the symbolic center of nationalist mythmaking. According to Curtis, these US Muslim military members became mythic – that is, superhuman – as their blood was imagined to be an almost magical elixir that could redeem the nation. The mythic Muslim soldiers that are discussed here were real people, but narratives of their sacrifice were appropriated and transformed in a public discourse about the meaning of communal belonging and national identity in the post-9/11 era. Curtis concludes by analyzing the limits of the success of the myths of the fallen Muslim soldier, as some critics challenged the authenticity of such narratives while others disagreed with the underlying premise that Muslims could or should be incorporated into the nation.

Part Two, "Anti-Muslim Politics," consists of three chapters. In Chapter Four, "Muslim Presence: Anti-Muslim Politics in the United States and the Rise of Muslim American Culture." **Salah D. Hassan** presents briefly the landscape of organized anti-Muslim politics in the United States, which was established well before the rise of Trump as the Republican presidential candidate and has played a role in shaping public opinion and US foreign policy. Hassan maps the linkages between anti-Muslim politics and anti-Muslim think tanks. He concludes by discussing some organized responses to this anti-Muslim discourse.

In Chapter Five, "*Real Time with Bill Maher* and the Good Muslims of Liberal Multiculturalism," **Evelyn Alsultany** examines how the left perpetuates racism and Islamophobia. Through conducting a discourse analysis of segments of *Real Time with Bill Maher* and the debates that ensued in op eds, Alsultany outlines the ways in which liberal discourses perpetuate logics that justify the exclusion of Muslims from rights, citizenship, and humanity. While Islamophobia is often understood as perpetrated by the right, this chapter will examine how the left uses tactics similar to those of the right in promoting anti-Muslim racism and its implications for Muslim Americans.

In Chapter Six, "Muslim Women, Anti-Muslim Hostility, and the State in the Age of Terror," **Juliane Hammer** explores the addition of the Muslim terrorist woman, modeled on the wife of the San Bernardino attacker, to Islamophobic discourse, and the ways in which she has made Muslim women less savable and more threatening. She then analyzes the ways in which both of the Trump administration's executive orders banning Muslims from entering the United States have targeted women as much as men and thereby implicitly cast women as equally threatening terror suspects to men. Lastly, she notes the curious turn against American Muslim women activists like Linda Sarsour, who have been the targets of vicious right-wing attacks and threats because of their vocal advocacy on behalf of Black Lives Matter, minority rights, and gender rights.

Part Three, "Marginalization and Activism," consists of three chapters. In Chapter Seven, "Muslim Detroit after Orlando: The LGBTQ Question, Rituals of Inclusion, and Coalition Building across Racial and Religious Lines," **Alisa Perkins** focuses on how Muslim Americans are participating in debates related to LGBTQ visibility with a focus on activism in the wake of the Orlando shootings. On the basis of ethnographic research, Perkins reveals the complexities of these debates, especially in a context of anti-Muslim sentiments. She also explores the significance of the vigil as a unique and powerful American cultural form.

In Chapter Eight, "Rights Versus Respectability: The Politics of Muslim Visibility in Detroit's Northern Suburbs," **Sally Howell** traces the efforts of several Muslim communities to establish mosques in the face of stiff opposition in the suburbs of Macomb County, a space defined by white flight and conservative working-class outsiderism. Muslim congregations have deployed a mix of "respectability" strategies to overcome this frequently vituperative resistance, but they have found the Department of Justice to be their most consistent ally. Howell argues that in the Trump era particularly, "rights" politics are more effective than "respectability" politics.

In Chapter Nine, "Politics, Immigration, and Ethnic Mobilization: The Predicament of Iranian Immigrants in the United States since the Iranian Revolution," **Mohsen Mobasher** traces the immigration policies on Iranian immigrants in the United States since the 1979 Iranian revolution (his analysis includes two of Trump's recent executive orders), and describes the various ways Iranians have sought to protect their civil liberties and oppose discriminatory policies. In so doing, Mobasher highlights the differences in approach taken by first- and second-generation Iranian-Americans.

Part Four, "Rethinking Muslim Politics," consists of two chapters. In Chapter Ten, "Drawing Near to God's Pleasure: A Dialogue on the Black Muslim Political Tradition and the Moral-Ethical Imperative of American Islam," **Donna Auston** and **Sylvia Chan-Malik** engage in a dialogue on US Muslim politics, paying special attention to Black American Muslim politics and gender justice. While issues of foreign policy, terrorism, national security, and Islamophobia tend to dominate US Muslim political concerns, the attitudes of Muslim leaders toward Black Lives Matter, for instance, are often ambivalent or oppositional. But if US Muslim communities seek to advocate for expansive and inclusive conceptions of justice, Auston and Chan-Malik argue, then they must adopt an intersectional approach that accounts for race, gender, class, and sexuality.

In Chapter Eleven, "The Idea of a Global Muslim Left," **Junaid Rana** sketches how the notion of a Muslim left might be conceptualized in contemporary US politics. He does this by drawing on the internationalist views and critiques of white supremacy offered by two twentieth-century activists: Malcolm X and Dada Amir Haider Khan.

Taken as a whole, the present volume does not provide neat conclusions. Rather, it seeks to offer insights, provocations, and various points of departure for future discussions and debates.

Works Cited

Johnson, J. 2015. "Trump calls for 'total and complete shutdown of Muslims entering the United States.'" *Washington Post*, December 7. https://www.washingtonpost.com/news/post-politics/wp/2015/12/07/donald-trump-calls-for-total-and-complete-shutdown-of-muslims-entering-the-united-states/?utm_term=.e8c32f24244e.

Lee, M. 2015. "Trump to CNN: 'I love the Muslims.'" *CNN*, September 20. http://www.cnn.com/2015/09/19/politics/donald-trump-muslims-controversy/index.html.

Schleifer, T. 2016. "Donald Trump: 'I think Islam hates us.'" *CNN*, March 10. http://www.cnn.com/2016/03/09/politics/donald-trump-islam-hates-us/index.html.

Part One

Muslims and the American State

Religion-State Relations and the Politics of Religious Freedom in Muslim America*

Kambiz GhaneaBassiri

WHEN DONALD TRUMP delivered his inaugural address on January 20, 2017, certain observers noticed something moving. Peeping bleakly amidst the "carnage" was an immiserating meme taken from the Batman film *The Dark Knight Rises*. In that film, the supervillain Bane frees thousands of criminals from prison as he announces, "We take Gotham from the corrupt, the rich, the oppressors of generations who have kept you down with myths of opportunity, *and we give it back to you ... the people*." In his inauguration address, President Trump marks his Presidency as the day that "we are transferring power from Washington DC. *and giving it back to you ... the people*."[1]

In the flurry and the fury of the new Trump administration, most of us did not grasp the import of this political manifesto compressed into a meme known on the Internet as the "Baneposting" meme. What was missed was a diagnostically noteworthy implication of these eight words.[2] The official inauguration of the 45th presidency of the United States of America ventriloquized, of all things, a Batman comic book villain's declaration of total war in *The Dark Knight Rises*. Donald Trump's co-writers Steve Bannon and Stephen Miller inserted the "Baneposting" meme verbatim into the inaugural address to stir the insurgent alt-right, an audience who recognized their own meme.

There is no question that this ventriloquism was programmatic and successful. As one journalist observed, already during Trump's presiden-

* I wish to express my gratitude to Mohammad Khalil for his helpful feedback on an earlier iteration of this chapter and to Atéha Bailly and Kamala GhaneaBassiri for their assistance with copyediting and finalizing it.

1. Trump 2017a. To get a sense of the circulation of this particular Baneposting meme, see the following exemplary videos: Anonymous 2017, "Trump=Bane? And we give it back to you ... the people"; and Anonymous 2017, "Trump Bane|And We Give It Back To You, the People."

2. This chapter grew out of a series of discussions with Steve Wasserstrom. Because of time constraints and the demands on both of us, these conversations did not result in the co-authored op-ed we had hoped. Although I took those conversations in a different direction in this chapter, I remain indebted to Steve for bringing the "Baneposting" meme to my attention and for allowing me to use his phrase "eight words."

tial campaign, the alt-right began "citing Bane as their lodestar,"[3] and when Bane's words were knowingly or unknowingly mouthed by President Donald Trump, alt-right members immediately recognized them with delight. Within hours of the speech, not only was the meme published on YouTube,[4] but Andrew Anglin, founder of the white supremacist website the *Daily Stormer* (named after "the gutter Nazi propaganda sheet known as *Der Stürmer*"),[5] also celebrated it in an article tellingly titled "Meme Magic: President Trump Channels Bane in Inauguration Speech." "Dearest brothers," Anglin declared, "in 2017,... all of our memes will become real. This is the power of a people who have learned to channel the magic of memes using the tubes of the internet: we are unstoppable."[6]

The day after the inauguration, Anglin wrote, "The media is saying that Trump's BANEPOST speech 'put the world on notice,' and that is the fact. Everyone is going to do what we want them to do, or they're going to be invaded and brutally conquered, or simply nuked. And that INCLUDES Merkel's Germany."[7] Who is this "everyone" who must fear Trump's America as the people of Gotham stood in terror of Bane? The answer is found in the picture Anglin inserted at the end of his article: another internet meme in the form of a selfie a Syrian refugee in Germany, Anas Modamani, took with Chancellor Angela Merkel.[8]

Herein then lies the underlying political manifesto of Trump's eight-word Baneposting meme: the world must fear America so that America can have its way with the world. The magic of this Internet meme, however, does not lie in its ability to bypass standard modes of political speech so as to evade the gatekeepers of democratic politics – the media, technocrats, pundits, and politicians. Its magic lies in its uncanny capacity to mask the bypassing of standard politics as populism. Who exactly are "the people"

---

3. Michel 2016.

4. See footnote 1 above.

5. Southern Poverty Law Center n.d.

6. Anglin 2017a. After lambasting Heather Heyer, who was fatally run over by a car while protesting a white supremacist rally in Charlottesville, Virginia, on August 12, 2017, the *Daily Stormer* was removed from its original web host's server. Following several failed attempts to find a new web host server (see Blake 2017) it has landed, at the time of this writing on October 16, 2017, on the following URL: www.dailystormer.ai. The articles that I cite from the *Daily Stormer* could be found on this new site by replacing .com in the references I provide with .ai. Given the hateful and incendiary nature of the site, it is likely that the *Daily Stormer*'s domain name will continue to change by the time this chapter is published. For this reason, I refrained from changing the original URLs for the articles I cite from the site.

7. Anglin 2017b.

8. This image was widely distributed on the Internet. It can be seen in a 2015 article in the *Nation*: https://www.thenation.com/article/merkels-refugee-policy-is-political-calculus-not-humanitarian-generosity.

to whom President Trump, a multimillion dollar socialite who peddles in luxurious consumption and who lost the popular election by nearly three million votes, presumes to return power?

It is instructive that "you … the people" attending Trump's inauguration in support of his election and to whom his presidency claimed to return power are different from the people who actually make up American society in all its diversity. Trump's "popular nationalism" is constructed against the reality of the nation. It thus must construct the nation it wishes to govern.

As I write these words in fall 2017, it is too early for any sound assessment of Muslim American politics in light of Trump's presidency. Given that American Muslims are not new to anti-Muslim rhetoric and political agendas, it is unlikely that we will see major changes in their political participation in US society.[9] More likely, American Muslims' political participation will intensify and gain more limelight as their struggle for inclusion and civil rights comes to be seen as part of a larger struggle for defining America's national character and the rights of all its citizens regardless of race, religion, ethnicity, gender, and sexual orientation.

As Denise Spellberg's meticulous research into discourses on Islam among the Founders has shown, for much of US history Muslims have been included in state discourses on religious freedom and national identity. The criteria for assuring that the US Constitution adequately recognizes the religious liberty of its citizens include that there be no religious test for civic and political participation in the United States and that the wall between church and state be impervious enough that even "Papists may occupy that chair [of presidency], and Mahometans may take it."[10] It took some time – well into the nineteenth century – before there were no established churches in all of the states that made up the American republic, but nonetheless, as Spellberg shows, "the mention … of Muslims as potential citizens of the United States forced the Protestant majority to imagine the parameters of their new society beyond toleration. It obliged them to interrogate the nature of religious freedom"[11] and to divorce faith, at least theoretically, from civic participation.

From our twenty-first-century perspective, it is mindboggling to think that white Protestant men thought America was a religiously tolerant society when many did not consider women, native Americans, blacks, Chinese

9. See, for example, Anonymous 2010, "Paladino TV: I'll Stop the Mosque"; Anonymous 2012, "Adam Hasner Speaking about Radical Islam and Sharia Law"; Anonymous 2012, "Bachmann Muslim Brotherhood Ad"; and Ali et al. 2011.

10. Elliot 1888, 4:200. Cited in Spellberg 2013, 183.

11. Spellberg 2013, 4.

Americans, and so on, their equals. In the case of black Africans and native Americans, the notion that they even had a religion was suspect. Nonetheless, the idea championed by Thomas Jefferson – and later enshrined in the First Amendment – that any law "establishing religious freedom ... comprehend, within the mantle of its protection, the Jew and the Gentile, the Christian and Mahometan, the Hindoo, and infidel of every denomination,"[12] had a significant impact on the way in which the white Protestant majority came to politically define America.

During the revolutionary years, the French colonist Hector St. John de Crèvecoeur famously asked, "What, then, is the American, this new man?" And he, just as famously, responded: an American is an amalgam of European nations who left the religious prejudices of that continent behind to create a new tolerant society where "a Catholic, who ... believes in trans-substantiation" is neighbors with "a good honest plodding German Lutheran" next to whom "lives a seceder." Crèvecoeur's experiences in the American colonies led him to define citizenship in terms of how individuals behaved in the nation rather than what they believed: "How does it concern the welfare of the country, or of the province at large, what this man's religious sentiments are, or really whether he has any at all? He is a good farmer; he is a sober, peaceable, good citizen."[13]

Later, the Presbyterian leader and early historian of religion in America Robert Baird attributed the evangelical fervor in mid-nineteenth-century America largely to the de-establishment of religion. In a popular survey of religious life in America for a European audience, he wrote:

> The Christian – be he Protestant or Catholic – the infidel, the Mohammedan, the Jew, the Deist, has not only all his rights as a citizen, but may have his own form of worship, without the possibility of any interference from any policeman or magistrate, provided he do not interrupt, in so doing, the peace and tranquility of the surrounding neighborhood. Even the Atheist may have his meetings in which to preach his doctrines, if he can get anybody to hear them. It is a remarkable fact, that the United States is the only country in all Christendom where perfect religious liberty exists, and where the government does nothing, by "favor" or otherwise, to promote the interests of any one religion, or of any one sect of religionists, more than another.[14]

12. Jefferson 1853, 45.
13. Crèvecoeur 2013 (orig. 1782), 31, 35.
14. Baird 1856, 645. In the 1844 edition of the book, Baird mentions Texas alongside the United States as "the only countries in all Christendom where perfect religious liberty exists" (318–319).

For Baird, the political assurance of religious liberty made the United States exceptional in comparison to European states in general and Catholic countries in particular. Whatever theological disagreements Christians in America may have had at this time, Baird wrote, "they would all acknowledge, without a moment's hesitation," that religious sects, "when tempted by power," resort "'to the practice of religious persecution; but to the credit of Rome it must be said that the baptism of fire is almost exclusively *her* sacrament for heretics.'"[15]

Baird's singling out of the Catholic Church reveals how the guarantee of religious freedom was never a neutral enterprise in the United States but rather a political mechanism for assuring "peace and tranquility." The idea was that religions, and more specifically Protestant denominations, can all flourish if they are free from the yoke of an established religion. Religious freedom thus served to promote American exceptionalism. It undergirded a political consensus among people of varying religious backgrounds and, as such, was instrumental in shaping a common American national identity in the early history of the republic.

When one considers all the changes American social and political structures have undergone since the 1780s, the longevity of the idea that religious freedom makes America unique and serves as a basis for political unity is nothing less than spectacular. It speaks to the foundational role ideas about religion have played in managing diversity in American politics. A century after enthusiasts for religious freedom, such as Baird, touted the exceptional nature of religion-state relations in the United States, President Dwight D. Eisenhower evoked the centrality of the principle of religious liberty to American national identity during the height of the Cold War. Speaking to American Muslims and representatives of Muslim-majority states at the opening ceremonies of the Islamic Center of Washington, DC, in 1957, he said,

> I should like to assure you, my Islamic friends, that under the
> American Constitution, under American tradition, and in American
> hearts, this Center, this place of worship is just as welcome as could
> be a similar edifice of any other religion. Indeed, America would fight
> with her whole strength for your right to have here your own church
> and worship according to your own conscience. This concept is indeed
> a part of America, and without that concept we would be something
> else than what we are.[16]

15. Citing Rev. George B. Cheever, of New York, Lecture on Bunyan's Pilgrim's Progress; Baird 1856, 645.

16. Eisenhower 1957.

Baird, writing as a religious leader, primarily addressed fellow Protestants. In fact, the full title of his book was *Religion in America; or, an Account of the Origin, Relation to the State, and Present Condition of the Evangelical Churches in the United States*; for him, evangelical denominations constituted religion in America. State officials who had to govern citizens of different religious persuasions, however, did not take definitions of religion for granted. They were more keen on defining the type of religious understandings that that state would tolerate, lest the wrong understanding of religion enter into the political system. Jefferson, for example, reduced religion to individuals' subjective opinions when he successfully advocated that in the American republic "our civil rights have no dependence on our religious opinions."[17] In the post–World War II era, as America became more religiously diverse and the white Protestant establishment slowly gave way to an American civil religion,[18] religious belief for the state was not a matter of individual "opinion" but a matter of faith in "the peaceful progress of all men under one God," through "our common goals" of civilizational advancement and world peace. Thus, in his speech at the Islamic Center of Washington, DC, Eisenhower folded Islam into American politics at a time when the United States took on the role of "the leader of the free world" by focusing on how Muslims

> for centuries contributed to the building of civilization. With their traditions of learning and rich culture, the countries of Islam have added much to the advancement of mankind. Inspired by a sense of brotherhood, common to our innermost beliefs, we can here together affirm our determination to secure the foundations of a just and lasting peace.[19]

That state definitions of religion have not been neutral in US history is also evidenced in the state repression of groups like the Moorish Science Temple and the Nation of Islam in the mid-twentieth century. These groups challenged the state's authority by pointing to its racist laws and institutions. They were thus not seen as being "really" religious.[20] Rather, they were labeled as "militant" and "subversive" movements in the guise of religion. The Federal Bureau of Investigation, Sylvester Johnson explains, created a training manual in 1955 entitled *The Muslim Cult of Islam* to train its agents for surveillance of the Nation of Islam. The manual interpreted the teachings of

17. Virginia Bill of Religious Freedom 1786, cited in Jefferson 1801, 326–327.
18. Bellah 1967.
19. Eisenhower 1957.
20. Curtis 2002.

the Moorish Science Temple and the Nation of Islam as racist propaganda of ill-prepared southern black migrants who blamed whites for their failure to attain success in northern urban centers. It "went on to characterize the essence of this 'Muslim cult' as teaching hatred and violence." As Johnson has argued, the state compared this "cult" with "authentic Islam" to show that "the true religion of these Black subjects ... was not an acquired religion of Islam ... but an essentially limbic religion of primitivism that stemmed from the racial constitution of Blacks."[21]

The political consensus achieved in America through the principle of religious liberty has depended on an understanding of religion that accommodates the state. As the enactment of sweeping civil rights legislation in the 1950s and 1960s demonstrated, the state's mechanisms of governance are subject to significant change and could become more inclusive, but despite these changes the association of religious liberty with American national identity has remained intact. By way of example, Warith Deen Mohammed, who took over the leadership of the Nation of Islam from his father Elijah Muhammad in 1975 and converted it to Sunni Islam, regarded the passage of civil rights legislation as a national "invitation" for blacks to join "mainstream America." This invitation, according to Mohammed, allowed for African American Muslims to "hold the American flag high" and celebrate the fourth of July as "Patriotism Day."[22] For Mohammed and his followers, the guarantee of religious freedom (along with other civil rights) was instrumental in their self-understandings as citizens and their relationships to the state.

While the instrumentalization of religious liberty for the purpose of building political unity has been a steady feature of Muslim American politics, after 9/11 it became a national priority. American Muslim activists appealed to religious liberty to assert their civil rights, and in doing so embedded themselves further in the civic life of the nation. During the 2010 congressional election cycle, for example, when Park51, a multi-story mosque and community center proposed for construction near Ground Zero in Lower Manhattan, became a matter of national controversy, American Muslims stepped onto the national stage through various media outlets and called for unity around the principle of religious freedom.[23] President George W. Bush and President Barack Obama have also appealed to the First Amendment in addresses to American Muslims, in order to define America's national character and the conceptions of Islam that would fit within it.

21. Johnson 2015, 377–380.
22. Mohammed 2008, 120.
23. See, for example, Ahmed 2010.

Six days after al-Qaeda's attack on the World Trade Center and the Pentagon, President George W. Bush spoke to the nation from the Islamic Center of Washington, DC. He sought to quell vigilantism by clearly expressing his disapproval of acts of violence against American Muslims and people mistaken to be Muslims, which saw a sharp rise after 9/11.[24] He did so by reminding the nation that American Muslims are "tax-paying citizens" who "make an incredibly valuable contribution to our country ... [as] doctors, lawyers, law professors, members of the military, entrepreneurs, shopkeepers, moms and dads." He also stated, "Islam is peace" and "a faith that brings comfort to a billion people around the world," and he followed his understanding of Islam with a reassurance to American Muslims that their religious practices would be tolerated in the United States: "Women who cover their head in this country must feel comfortable going outside their homes. Moms who wear cover must be not intimidated in America. That's not the America I know. That's not the America I value." He ended his speech by celebrating the American nation as "a great country" where "we share the same values of respect and dignity and human worth" and where Muslims "love America as much as I do."[25]

Bush's seven-minute address to the nation aimed to achieve calm in the nation by painting an image of America that appealed to a longstanding national narrative – a narrative that posits religious liberty as a formative force in shaping American identity and politics. He also defined the type of religion and civic activity that the state expects from its citizens. And lastly, he posited that the political values through which the United States balances religious liberty and national unity are not only formative in defining the nation's character but are the very basis of its "greatness." The language of "greatness" here harks back to the notion that the United States is exceptional because, out of all the nations in the world, it gets the relationship between religion and state right. President Bush clarified what he meant in a longer speech he delivered on June 27, 2007, on the occasion of the fifty-year anniversary of the opening of the Islamic Center of Washington, DC:

> The freedom of religion is the very first protection offered in
> America's Bill of Rights. It is a precious freedom. It is a basic compact
> under which people of faith agree not to impose their spiritual vision
> on others, and in return to practice their beliefs as they see fit. This
> is the promise of our Constitution, and the calling of our conscience,
> and a source of our strength.[26]

24. Bakalian and Bozorgmehr 2009, 1–6, 125–155.
25. Bush 2001.
26. Bush 2007.

Bush went on to state: "The greatest challenge facing people of conscience is to help the forces of moderation win the great struggle against extremism that is now playing out across the broader Middle East." He defined extremists as those "who seek to use religion as a path to power and a means of domination." According to this definition, religion, when used as a path to power, cannot be conceived as religion proper. It is labeled as "extremism" – an aberration of religion that is not subject to state protection. This is not because there are no religions that seek power, but because conceptualizing religion in a way that permits people to exercise power through religion will disrupt the delicate balance between state power and religious liberty through which the United States, since its founding, has sought to establish political unity amidst its diverse population.

The free practice of religion in America has always been accompanied by state efforts to define what is an acceptable form of religion. Once we recognize this, the question to ask, as Nadia Marzouki has argued, is not the one that is often asked of political discourses about Muslims in America: How do Muslims become "good Americans"? Rather the question to examine is: How do Americans "come to take responsibility (or not) for this original founding hypothesis" that if the state gives individuals of diverse religious backgrounds the freedom to practice their religion they will become loyal, patriotic citizens?[27]

At a historic speech delivered at the Islamic Society of Baltimore on February 3, 2016, President Obama offered a concise answer to the question of how Americans ought to take responsibility for this "founding hypothesis." In this speech, Obama thanked American Muslims for their work in improving their communities and the nation as a whole. He clearly meant to counter the Islamophobic rhetoric of then-Republican presidential candidate Donald Trump who, a couple of months earlier, had called for a ban of all Muslims entering the United States.[28] In his speech, Obama referred to this as "inexcusable political rhetoric." He went on to acknowledge that "[w]e're one American family," but the image of America Obama painted was more complicated and nuanced than that of Bush. He acknowledged the centuries-old presence of Muslims in the United States as well as the persecution of religious minorities, despite the nation's founding ideal of religious freedom. He aimed to counter stereotypes of Muslims by educating non-Muslim Americans about some "basic facts" about Islam. He began,

> [L]et's start with this fact: For more than a thousand years, people
> have been drawn to Islam's message of peace.... Whoever wants to

27. Marzouki 2017, 11.
28. Diamond 2015; Pilkington 2015.

enter paradise, the Prophet Muhammad taught, "let him treat people the way he would love to be treated." For Christians like myself, I'm assuming that sounds familiar.

The President went on to speak of the diversity found among Muslims and admonished Americans that fighting bigotry and negative stereotypes of Muslims falls on everyone's shoulders. He called for making the "good works" and "talents" of "the Muslim community in all its variety" visible. "Our television shows should have some Muslim characters that are unrelated to national security," he said to an applauding audience. He called on American Muslims, in return, to "let [their] light shine" by celebrating their achievements in the United States and serving as an example to the rest of the world's Muslim population in the "battle of hearts and minds that ... is taking place right now." He explained,

> American Muslims are better positioned than anybody to show that it is possible to be faithful to Islam and to be part of a pluralistic society, and to be on the cutting-edge of science, and to believe in democracy. And so I would urge all of you not to see this as a burden but as a great opportunity and a great privilege to show who you are.... Because when you do you'll make clear that this is not a clash of civilizations between the West and Islam. This is a struggle between the peace-loving, overwhelming majority of Muslims around the world and a radical, tiny minority.

Like President Bush, President Obama regarded those who use religion as a path to power as corrupters of "true" religion and purveyors of bloodshed. He said, "There has to be global pressure to have the vision and the courage to end this kind of thinking and this approach to organizing political power." Furthermore, Obama, like Bush, concluded by referring to how the founding ideals of the United States struck the right balance between religious liberty and state power even though, historically, their implementation has been imperfect:

> We are blessed to live in a nation where even if we sometimes stumble, even if we sometimes fall short, we never stop striving for our ideals. We keep moving closer to that more perfect union. We're a country where, if you work hard and if you play by the rules, you can ultimately make it, no matter who you are or how you pray. It may not always start off even in the race, but here, more than any place else, there's the opportunity to run that race.

In sum, Obama called for American Muslims specifically to affirm the exceptional nature of American political values by showing the world how they strike the best possible balance between religious liberty and state power. In doing so, Obama, like George W. Bush and Dwight Eisenhower, sought to bring Muslims within the confines of American national interest and identity.[29] But he went further than presidents before him by depicting America as a project in the making – a nation still working to realize the egalitarian ideals embedded in its foundation. And he called on American Muslims who are currently subject to prejudice and discrimination to overcome this "burden" by helping the nation realize its founding ideals.[30]

While Obama had intended to counter the Islamophobic rhetoric of Trump's 2016 presidential campaign, the benefit of hindsight reveals how he misconstrued the appeal of Trump's anti-Muslim rhetoric. Insofar as Obama pointed to commonalities between Islam and Christianity and highlighted the unacknowledged contributions of American Muslims to the nation, he sought to show that American Muslims are not much different from other Americans, and Islamic and American values are not as inherently contradictory as anti-Muslim polemics claim. Those who found Trump's anti-Muslim rhetoric appealing, however, were not interested in whether Muslims could fit into American society or if their values are compatible with America's liberal democracy. In light of Trump's policy speeches as president, it seems clear that they were preoccupied with the changing racial, ethnic, and religious makeup of the nation.

Not only did Trump ventriloquize a comic book villain in his inauguration address, stirring white nationalists, but he depicted an eerily dark picture of the nation, a picture contested by reality. During the Obama administration, the United States climbed out of a deep recession, lowered its unemployment and violent crime rates, and was beginning to see a rise in wages that had been stagnant for over a decade.[31] Trump depicted these as "victories" of "the establishment" and "the government" that did not benefit "the people." He claimed,

> For too long a small group in our nation's capital has reaped the
> rewards of government while the people have borne the cost.
> Washington flourished – but the people did not share in its wealth....
> Their victories have not been your victories; their triumphs have not

29. President Bill Clinton similarly introduced state practices that sought to include Muslims within the political and civic life of the nation. For example, in 1996, he and First Lady Hillary Rodham Clinton began the practice of hosting a reception for Eid al-Fitr, which marks the end of Ramadan, at the White House.

30. Obama 2016.

31. Jackson 2016.

been your triumphs; and while they celebrated in our nation's Capital, there was little to celebrate for struggling families across our land.

To give his dark vision of America an aura of reality, Trump did not rely on data about the economy or the state of the nation; rather he used racialized language to appeal to his supporters and corroborate their feelings:

> For too many of our citizens, a different reality exists: Mothers and children trapped in poverty in our inner cities; rusted-out factories scattered like tombstones across the landscape of our nation; an education system, flush with cash, but which leaves our young and beautiful students deprived of knowledge; and the crime and gangs and drugs that have stolen too many lives and robbed our country of so much unrealized potential. *This American carnage stops here and stops right now.*[32]

Trump's solution for stopping this "carnage" was simple – put "America first." He argued that the United States was "enrich[ing] foreign industry,… subsidiz[ing] the armies of other countries,… defend[ing] other nation's borders," and improving their infrastructure, all at the expense of Americans. He exclaimed, "We've made other countries rich while the wealth, strength, and confidence of our country has disappeared over the horizon."

By any measurable standard, this statement is false. The United States stands today as the richest and most powerful nation the world has ever seen. Yet, for many of Trump's supporters, who are predominantly white and Christian,[33] his depiction of American carnage *feels* true because of the increased diversity they perceive in the nation. By depicting a grim picture of the United States while calling on Americans to "make America great again,"[34] Trump nostalgically recalls an America where non-whites and non-Christians did not have the legal, social, and political status they have today. Insofar as this image of America contradicts the reality of the nation's laws and the diversity of its population, it is imaginary. And insofar as Trump's anti-Muslim rhetoric and policies succeed in depicting "Radical Islam" as an ideological threat against which Americans must unite, they bridge the gap

---

32. Trump 2017a (italics added).

33. According to a *New York Times* exit poll during the 2016 presidential elections, whites were the only race whose majority voted for Trump (58 percent). The majority of Christian voters (58 percent of "Protestants and other [non-Catholic] Christians" and 52 percent of Catholics) voted for Trump; see Huang et al. 2016. A 2016 CNN exit poll similarly found that 57 percent of whites, 59 percent of Protestants, 50 percent of Catholics, 56 percent of Mormons, and 54 percent of "other Christians" voted for Trump; see Anonymous 2016, "Exit Polls."

34. This was Trump's 2016 campaign slogan.

between the diverse reality of America in the twenty-first century and the America of Trump's imagination, which he wishes to remake.

The touting of an existential threat from "Radical Islamic Terrorism" plays a central role in Trump and his supporters' attempt to rebuild America in the exclusionary terms of its European and Christian heritage. In a speech delivered in Warsaw, Poland, to kick off the second foreign trip of his presidency, Trump explicitly evoked religious nationalism to uphold Poland as a model for "Western Civilization." Referring to Pope John Paul II's visit to Poland on June 2, 1979 – the first time a pope visited a communist country – he said,

> A million Polish people [who had gathered for the visit] did not ask for wealth. They did not ask for privilege. Instead, one million Poles said three simple words: "We want God." In those words, the Polish people recalled the promise of a better future. They found new courage to face down their oppressors, and they found the words to declare that Poland would be Poland once again.... The people of Poland, the people of America, and the people of Europe still cry out "We want God."[35]

Trump went on to compare "the specter of communism" that confronted "the West" with "radical Islamic terrorism," which he defined as "another oppressive ideology – one that seeks to export terrorism and extremism all around the globe." He then went on to identify America with Europe of yesteryear:

> We are the fastest and greatest community. There is nothing like our community of nations. The world has never known anything like our community of nations. We write symphonies. We pursue innovation. We celebrate ancient heroes, embrace our timeless traditions and customs, and always seek to explore and discover brand-new frontiers.

He employed gendered stereotypes of Islam to symbolically exclude Muslims from "the West" by exclaiming, "We empower women as pillars of our society and of our success." And if there was any doubt that "we" referred to white Christians who must unite in the face of an existential threat from "Radical Islam," his next statement put those doubts to rest:

> What we've inherited from our ancestors has never existed to this extent before. And if we fail to preserve it, it will never, ever exist again. So we cannot fail.... As long as we know our history, we will

---

35. Trump 2017b.

know how to build our future.... The fundamental question of our time is whether the West has the will to survive. Do we have the confidence in our values to defend them at any cost? Do we have enough respect for our citizens to protect our borders? Do we have the desire and the courage to preserve our civilization in the face of those who would subvert and destroy it? ... Our freedom, our civilization, and our survival depend on these bonds of history, culture, and memory.

It is difficult to see how Trump could speak of bonds of history, culture, and memory that white Christians in Europe and the United States share while standing in the heart of Europe where several decades ago millions of Europeans and Americans fought and killed one another in some of the bloodiest wars in history. It is also difficult to see how the violent heritage of colonialism and slavery in Europe and the United States could be the basis for building the future of "the West," given the diverse and cosmopolitan make-up of nearly all major European and American cities today. By evoking the perceived threat of a Muslim enemy, Trump conjures a sense of coherence and unity in the West that is historically and sociologically nonexistent.

Perpetuating the constructed notion that Islam is a radical ideology that poses an existential threat to the United States does much work politically to build the nativist ideology and nationalist loyalties through which Trump seeks not only to govern but to redefine America. "The bedrock of our politics," Trump told Americans on the day he was sworn in as president, "will be a total allegiance to the United States of America, and through loyalty to our country, we will rediscover our loyalty to each other."[36] The threat of Islam buttresses not only American nationalism but also popular support for extravagant military spending in order to keep the so-called enemy outside of "our" country's borders.

Obama, in his address to American Muslims, recognized the imperfection of America's past and called on Americans to work to contribute to the realization of its founding ideals. Trump's presidency thus far has depicted an America in dire straits and addressed Islam through nostalgia for white Protestant cultural hegemony. Despite their obvious and substantive differences, however, neither were concerned with actual Islamic teachings. In fact, state discourses on Islam and Muslims in America, from the constitutional era through the Cold War era to the present, have all had very little to do with Muslims' beliefs and practices and everything to do with the political mechanisms of exclusion and inclusion in the United States' democracy.[37]

36. Trump 2017a.
37. While it could be argued that state discourses on Islam are shaped by the acts and beliefs of those individual Muslims or militant Muslim groups who have fatally attacked Ameri-

The US Constitution's guarantee of religious freedom has historically been accompanied by debates about what constitutes a religion. Today, this question is most saliently asked about Islam, and it belies a deep-seated anxiety about the fragility of democracy in the United States. There has been a longstanding fear in America that the inclusion of the wrong type of beliefs, ideas, or peoples in America's democracy could undermine its institutions from within. This notion that democracy has the seed of its own undoing embedded within the freedoms it affords its diverse citizenry has always meant that its borders need to be carefully policed. It has meant that everyone other than white, property-owning, Protestant, heterosexual men – whose humanity and citizenship the state took for granted at the time of its formation – have had to prove their ability to participate in American politics and society as equal citizens. And it could be argued that much of Muslim political activity since 9/11 has focused on defending Muslim civil rights on the one hand and allaying the majority's fears about the participation of Muslims in American politics on the other.[38] Through both of these processes, American Muslims have become more integrated into American civic life and politics.

Today, American Muslims, who were once politically invisible, have stepped into the fringes of the political mainstream, and their experiences in getting there are demonstrative of how relations between religion and the state in the United States simultaneously act as a force for integration and religious pluralism as well as for alienation and religious nationalism. In either case, what is clear is that the state guarantee of religious freedom is by no means politically neutral; rather, the politics of state-religion relations is the very foundation upon which Americans negotiate their national identity.

---

cans in the United States, these Muslims comprise a miniscule percentage of Muslims in the United States or the world. They do not pose the existential threat that Trump and his supporters feel they do. The imbalance of power between the United States and these groups is vast and undeniable. It is thus safe to assert that polemics about Islam are, at best, only tangentially related to what Muslims in America actually believe or do.

38. For an overview of such efforts, see Bilici 2012.

Works Cited

Ahmed, P. 2010. "What Would Our Founding Fathers Say about the 'Ground Zero Mosque'?" *The Huffington Post*, August 23. http://www.huffington-post.com/parvez-ahmed/what-will-our-founding-fa_b_686742.html.

Ali, W., E. Clifton, M. Duss, L. Fang, S. Keyes, and F. Shakir. 2011. "The Political Players." In *Fear, Inc.: The Roots of the Islamophobia Network in America*, 119–123.

Anglin, A. 2017a. "Meme Magic: President Trump Channels Bane in Inauguration Speech." *Daily Stormer*, January 20. https://www.dailystormer.com/meme-magic-president-trump-channels-bane-in-inauguration-speech.

———. 2017b. "Trump's Full Speech at the Armed Services Ball." *Daily Stormer*, January 21. http://www.dailystormer.com/trumps-full-speech-at-the-armed-services-ball.

Anonymous. 2010. "Paladino TV: I'll Stop the Mosque." *YouTube.com*, August 5. https://www.youtube.com/watch?v=zLLrd79aOqI.

Anonymous. 2012. "Adam Hasner Speaking about Radical Islam and Sharia Law." *YouTube.com*, September 1. https://www.youtube.com/watch?v=pVEN91CLKzc.

Anonymous. 2012. "Bachmann Muslim Brotherhood Ad." *YouTube.com*, September 18. https://www.youtube.com/watch?v=Upf5emI9hPQ.

Anonymous. 2016. "Exit Polls." CNN, November 23. http://www.cnn.com/election/results/exit-polls.

Anonymous. 2017. "Trump=Bane? And we give it back to you ... the people." *YouTube.com*, January 20. https://www.youtube.com/watch?v=pSH3xWNUWi4.

Anonymous. 2017. "Trump Bane|And We Give It Back to You, the People." *YouTube.com*, January 21. https://www.youtube.com/watch?v=ppkYuAGp4DQ.

Bakalian, A., and M. Bozorgmehr. 2009. *Backlash 9/11: Middle Eastern and Muslim Americans Respond*. Berkeley, CA.

Baird, R. 1856 (orig. 1844). *Religion in America*. New York.

Bellah, R. 1967. "Civil Religion in America." *Daedalus* 96:1–21.

Bilici, M. 2012. *Finding Mecca in America: How Islam Is Becoming an American Religion*. Chicago.

Blake, A. 2017. "Daily Stormer, Neo-Nazi Website, Loses Icelandic Web Address in Latest Domain Spat." *The Washington Times*, September 29. http://www.washingtontimes.com/news/2017/sep/29/daily-stormer-neo-nazi-website-loses-icelandic-web.

Bush, G. W. 2001. "'Islam Is Peace' Says President," September 17. https://georgewbush-whitehouse.archives.gov/news/releases/2001/09/print/20010917-11.html.

———. 2007. "Remarks by President Bush at Rededication Ceremony of the Islamic Center of Washington," June 27. https://2001-2009.state.gov/p/nea/rls/rm/2007/87430.htm.

Crèvecoeur, J. H. S. J. 2013 (orig. 1782). *Letters from an American Farmer and Other Essays*. Edited and introduced by Dennis D. Moore. Cambridge, MA.

Curtis IV, E. E. 2002. "Islamizing the Black Body: Ritual and Power in Elijah Muhammad's Nation of Islam." *Religion and American Culture* 12:167–196.

Diamond, J. 2015. "Donald Trump: Ban All Muslim Travel to U.S." CNN. com, December 8. http://www.cnn.com/2015/12/07/politics/donald-trump-muslim-ban-immigration/index.html.

Eisenhower, D. 1957. "Remarks at Ceremonies Openning the Islamic Center." The American Presidency Project, June 28. http://www.presidency.ucsb.edu/ws/index.php?pid=10824&st =muslim& st1=.

Elliot, J. 1888. *The Debates in the Several State Conventions on the Adoption of the Federal Constitution, as Recommended by the General Convention at Philadelphia, in 1787.* 5 vols. Philadelphia.

Feder, J. L. 2016. "This Is How Steve Bannon Sees the Entire World." BuzzFeed News, November 15. https://www.buzzfeed.com/lester-feder/this-is-how-steve-bannon-sees-the-entire-world?utm_term=.asJyyB4d2e#.wr7QQymo38.

Fox, L. 2012. "Michele Bachman Sticks to Accusations about Muslim Brotherhood." *U.S. News and World Report,* July 19. https://www.usnews.com/news/articles/2012/07/19/michele-bachmann-sticks-to-accusations-about-muslim-brotherhood.

GhaneaBassiri, K., and S. van Geuns. 2017. "Trump's 'Muslim Ban': A Symptom of White Nationalism in U.S. Politics," *E-International Relations,* August 1. http://www.e-ir.info/2017/08/01/trumps-muslim-ban-a-symptom-of-white-nationalism-in-us-politics.

Huang, J., S. Jacoby, M. Strickland, and K. K. R. Lai. 2016. "Election 2016: Exit Polls." *New York Times.* https://www.nytimes.com/interactive/2016/11/08/us/politics/election-exit-polls.html.

Jackson, B. "Obama's Numbers October 2016 Update." *FactCheck.org,* October 9. http://www.factcheck.org/2016/10/obamas-numbers-october-2016-update.

Jefferson, T. 1853. *The Writings of Thomas Jefferson: Being his Autobiography, Correspondence, Reports, Messages, Addresses, and Other Writings, Official and Private,* vol. 1. Washington, DC.

———. 1801. *Notes on the State of Virginia with an Appendix.* Boston.

Johnson, S. 2015. *African American Religions, 1500–2000: Colonialism, Democracy, and Freedom.* New York.

Marzouki, N. 2017. *Islam: An American Religion.* New York.

Michel, C. 2016. "The Bane of the Alt-Right." Blogpost of C. Michel, June 12. https://medium.com/@cjcmichel/the-bane-of-the-alt-right-e9e537167b2c.

Mohammed, W. 2008. "Historic Atlanta Address." In *The Columbia Sourcebook of Muslims in the United States,* edited by E. Curtis IV, 116–120. New York.

Obama, B. 2016. "Remarks by the President at Islamic Society of Baltimore," February 3. https://obamawhitehouse.archives.gov/the-press-office/2016/02/03/remarks-president-islamic-society-baltimore.

Pilkington, E. 2015. "Donald Trump: Ban All Muslims Entering US." *The Guardian*, December 7.

Spellberg, D. 2013. *Thomas Jefferson's Qur'an: Islam and the Founders*. New York.

Southern Poverty Law Center. N.d. "Andrew Anglin." https://www.splcenter.org/fighting-hate/extremist-files/individual/andrew-anglin.

Trump, D. 2017a. "Inaugural Address." January 20. https://www.whitehouse.gov/inaugural-address.

———. 2017b. "Remarks by President Trump to the People of Poland." July 6. https://www.whitehouse.gov/the-press-office/2017/07/06/remarks-president-trump-people-poland-july-6–2017.

Muslims and the American Constitution: From the First Amendment to the Second?

Mucahit Bilici

> We are honored to stand here as parents of Captain Humayun Khan and as patriotic American Muslims. Donald Trump, you're asking Americans to trust you with their future. Let me ask you, have you even read the United States Constitution? I will gladly lend you my copy. In this document look for the words "liberty" and "equal protection of law."
>
> Khizr Khan, Gold Star father and Muslim American citizen, speaking at the 2016 Democratic National Convention

> The two men drove to an isolated parking lot off Highway 45, a midway spot between their adversarial existences, to try to settle their differences. "Meet me at the Dairy Queen," David Wright, 44, had suggested. Ali Ghouri, 29, obliged. They each brought a friend, and they each brought a gun.
>
> Wright climbed out of a Ford Lobo, wearing a black sleeveless T-shirt and baggy blue jeans tucked into cowboy boots. Ghouri stepped out of his Toyota Corolla. He had spiked hair and wore a red shirt that matched his red Converses.
>
> The first time they met was five months ago, when Wright led a group of men to Ghouri's mosque and accused them of supporting terrorists. Wright and the few dozen who came with him were armed with "Stop the Islamization of America" signs and assault rifles.
>
> Ghouri, going against the wishes of mosque leaders, walked up to the protesters with a defiant message: "I have a weapon. You have a weapon. I'm not scared of you."
>
> "A Showdown over Sharia," *Washington Post*[1]

> With word and deed we insert ourselves into the human world, and this insertion is like a second birth.
>
> Hannah Arendt, *The Human Condition*

1. Samuels 2017.

Introduction

A threshold moment arrived on July 28, 2016, when a Pakistani immigrant and Muslim citizen of America, Khizr Khan, accompanied by his wife, appeared on stage at the Democratic National Convention and publicly chastised then-Republican candidate and now president Donald Trump for not being a good American. Khan's presence there resulted from the opening created by the contest between America's two political parties and from the patriotic sacrifice of his son, an Army captain who had given his life in service to his country. His gesture that night, pulling a copy of the Constitution from his pocket and holding it up for all to see, was perhaps the highest-profile act of citizenship by an immigrant Muslim American to date. In a book of memoirs he later published, Khan would recount that moment and enlarge upon his relationship with the Constitution as a sacred object:

> I had carried that Constitution with me for years. It was dog-eared and creased, marked with notations and highlights. I had studied it, and I had long cherished the words, the ideas, embodied within. To celebrate it publicly, to hold it up as a reminder of what America is supposed to be, seemed the most patriotic thing I could do.[2]

Muslim citizenship in America should be understood as an ongoing process – a sequence of moments in which certain elements gain salience. Each moment is punctuated by the necessities of the times, the pressures of the environment, and the maturity of Muslims themselves as Americans. This is especially so for Muslims of immigrant background, with whom this analysis is primarily (though not exclusively) concerned. (The African American Muslim experience with respect to the American Constitution and the law more broadly has its own distinctive trajectory.) This chapter delineates an emerging dimension of American Islam: Muslims' deepening engagement with the American Constitution. American Muslims have for some time championed certain key phrases of the Framers (such as "life, liberty, and the pursuit of happiness") and have come to treat the Constitution itself as an object of veneration (and protective talisman, in Khan's case). I argue, however, that Muslim appropriation of the American Constitution has now gone beyond such emblematic uses. While Muslim interest in the Constitution was once mostly concentrated on the First Amendment and the basic freedoms of religion and speech, now more and more sections of the Constitution are coming under the Muslim purview. This trend can be encapsulated in some Muslims' unexpected embrace of Second Amendment rights. What

2. Khan 2017a, xii.

are the implications of this development for Muslim citizenship in America? And in what ways does this coming-of-age bring the complex relationship between violence, sovereignty, and citizenship into the picture?

By way of an answer, I will first explore the conditions that are shaping the space of possibility for Muslim citizenship in an age of widespread Islamophobia, and then engage in a discussion of Muslim appropriations of the American Constitution, both symbolically and in terms of principle. In this latter part, I broach the question of Muslim violence in its relation to American citizenship.

The New Public Islamophobia

Hate crimes against American Muslims have spiked to their highest levels since the aftermath of the 9/11 attacks. According to the Pew Research Center's 2017 survey of American Muslims, 75% of Muslims believe that there is a lot of discrimination against Muslims in the U.S.[3] While some of this rise is due to the intermittent occurrence of terrorist attacks, it is also connected with the rhetoric and anti-Muslim politics of Donald Trump and his supporters. Scholarship on Islamophobia shows the extent to which anti-Muslim fringe organizations have found widespread acceptance in the political mainstream.[4] The disproportionate amplification of acts of Muslim terrorists (mostly abroad) and deliberate and sustained efforts on the part of what has now become an "Islamophobia industry"[5] have collectively shaped the public perception of Muslims as dangerous and monstrous.[6] Are Muslims, the average American citizen might well ask, really part of "We the People"?

The post-9/11 backlash plays a major role in the ways in which Muslim men and women answer that question.[7] For the answer cannot simply be a subjective affirmation on the part of Muslims. It requires an intersubjective institution of this affirmation in the public sphere; and this means political and civic confrontation. I should note that the burden of this question looms particularly large for Muslim women, who are often more recognizably Muslim and therefore an easier target,[8] and whose otherness claim is doubly reinforced by racism and male dominance, a phenomenon captured by the question of "gendered Islamophobia."[9]

---

3. Pew Research Center 2017.
4. Bail 2015; Ali et al. 2011.
5. Lean 2012.
6. Alsultany 2012; Ernst 2013.
7. Bakalian and Bozorgmehr 2009.
8. Cainkar 2009.
9. Hammer 2013, 109. It is no coincidence that in his response to Khizr Khan's speech,

Recent studies have noted that Muslims surpass atheists as the most unpopular group in the United States. Muslims who are citizens of the state nonetheless continue to be seen and treated as aliens by the nation. In the current fraught moment, the constitution of Islam as a legitimate American religion remains a fragile process.

"Our most effective weapon against terrorism is YOU," reads a billboard on a busy highway in New Jersey. It continues: "If you suspect it, report it." And, further: "Anonymous calls accepted." At mass transit sites in New York and elsewhere, signs constantly remind us, "If you see something, say something." Such widespread delegation of the power to identify threats has important consequences: a power that is unofficially and anonymously exercised over others is being given to ordinary citizens. Their target is any suspect person, activity, or object. This partial delegation of the powers of surveillance to the public deepens the securitization of everyday life. Commenting on a case of mistaken identity by a passenger who reported a suspicious person, a commercial airline pilot bemoaned "security protocol that is too rigid – in the sense that once the whistle is blown everything stops without checks – and relies on the input of people who may be completely clueless."[10]

As the author(ity) of security shifts, in part, from the state to the public, the criteria for identifying a threat shift as well, from reason to sentiment. In place of – or in addition to – the state's rational or rationalized Islamophobia, we now see the empowerment of the public's cultural or sentimental Islamophobia, and Muslims are faced with new demands for legitimacy, tests of loyalty, and a need for legibility. You can defend yourself before the law with reason. But how do you defend yourself before a sensitive – and incensed – public?

American Muslims' legal citizenship risks being eclipsed by popular exclusion. At times, the state's legal protections seem challenged by the vindictive impulses of populism. Occupying this liminal space – outside the nation and yet inside the state – puts a severe strain on Muslims. With the culturalization of citizenship, lay definitions of citizenship and state definitions of citizenship may easily collide. Membership now involves more than law. It places phenomenological demands on the psyche and calls for cultural conversion. More and more aspects of Muslims' selves come under public

---

Donald Trump chose to focus on Ghazala Khan's "silence," implying that she perhaps was not allowed to speak (presumably by her oppressive Muslim husband). In response, Ghazala Khan published an op-ed piece in the *Washington Post* and explained why she chose not to speak at the convention (G. Khan 2016).

10. Rampell 2016.

scrutiny. Unlike the rational state, the sentimental public demands loyalty to the nation in various extra-rational forms, including sight, smell, speech, silence, appearance, and comportment. In other words, the rhetoric of citizenship is no longer about *logos* alone but extends also to *ethos* and *pathos*.

What does the public want from Muslims? They have to prove their loyalty to the nation before a public that demands transparency of Muslim existence. Islam and Muslims have to become legible.

To the extent that Islamophobia is no longer simply an attitude held by some Americans but has been equipped with the power of an informal security apparatus – one that is arguably being reinforced from within the highest levels of government – Muslim responsibility and loyalty to the United States becomes more complex and fragile and shifts toward the psychic.

Indeed, the federal government, while demanding vigilance from its citizens, sometimes feels the need (or did, at least, under the Obama administration) to intervene to protect Muslims from the public's excesses. In Bensalem, Pennsylvania, a Muslim congregation had long pleaded with township officials to allow the construction of a mosque. They paid for expensive traffic studies, repeatedly explained Islamic practices, and revised design plans multiple times, only to face rejection. Eventually the Justice Department stepped in, charging that the township zoning board had violated land use laws by denying the congregation's application, while it had granted zoning exemptions for other religious construction projects. As a member of the congregation told a reporter, "We were just asking for our mosque and we just wanted to be treated like everyone else."[11]

This, then, is the problem Muslims face: not being (or not being seen as being) like everyone else. The desire to become ordinary and unnoticeable has become an issue of survival. This I call the problem of *Muslim opacity*.

Opacity

In the United States, there has been an upsurge in cases of mistaken identification of terrorists by the public. These unofficial sightings have resulted in people (Muslim and otherwise) being kicked off planes, suspended from school, and humiliated in public. At the root of all these misidentifications is a sense that what the Muslim presents is "not what one normally expects" in a given setting.

The world of aviation is especially rich in such cases. Consider but a few examples:

11. Shepherd 2016.

- Guido Menzio, a professor of economics from the University of Pennsylvania of Italian descent, was solving mathematical equations on his notepad while flying from Philadelphia to Syracuse in May 2016. He was reported to authorities by his seatmate, a woman who found his notes cryptic.[12] Not recognizing the script – and assuming the man to be of Middle Eastern origin – she took it to be either Arabic or a terrorist code.

- A University of California, Berkeley, student of Iraqi origin was removed from a Southwest Airlines flight in Los Angeles in April 2016 after another passenger became alarmed when she heard him speaking Arabic. The student, who was talking to his uncle, ended his conversation with "inshallah," which means "God willing." The passenger reported that she heard "potentially threatening comments."

- In March 2016, two Muslim women were escorted off a JetBlue flight from Boston to Los Angeles after a cabin crew member "didn't like the way [they] were staring back at her."[13]

Writing in an unusual script, speaking Arabic, staring – all can threaten a security-conscious public. There are other genres of misidentification as well, some with more tragic consequences. In 2016, Khalid Jabarra, the son of a Lebanese American family in Tulsa, Oklahoma, was killed by a neighbor who called the Jabarra family "filthy Arabs" and "Moose-lims" and told police that "they throw gay people off rooftops." The Jabarra family was Christian. A year later, on a Queens subway platform, a drunken bigot attacked an Orthodox Jewish mother and her adult daughter, whom he mistook for Muslims. The assailant, Dimitrious Zias, said, "Get out of my country, you dirty Muslim."[14] Not only, it seems, does the Muslim appear illegible, but the illegible also becomes Muslim.

And what is the Muslim response to the plight of opacity? Fleeing to legibility, they seek and wear uniforms.

Uniforms

Members of lower classes, and of subordinate racial and ethnic groups often find consolation, compensation, and security in uniforms. Uniforms hide, neutralize, and normalize different selves under generically legible cloth.

12. Rampell 2016.
13. Fox News 2016.
14. Parascandola 2017.

The task that citizenship performs invisibly and legally is reiterated visibly and locally by the uniform. It filters and normalizes Muslim bodies.

The summer of 2016 witnessed two symbolically rich cases of Muslim presence on the national stage: the example of Ibtihaj Muhammad, the first-ever *hijab*-wearing member of an American Olympic team; and that now-infamous confrontation between the Khan family and then-candidate Donald Trump. Wrapping oneself in America's sacred symbols to undo foreignness and fend off attacks is, of course, not a surprising strategy. So Ibtihaj Muhammad's fencing helmet (adorned, like her teammates', with a stars-and-stripes pattern across the face) perfectly and patriotically covers her *hijab*. A *Washington Post* profile published in the run-up to the Olympics began with the line, "When she fences, no one can tell that Ibtihaj Muhammad is wearing a headscarf."[15] It goes on to relate that the athlete chose her sport in part because she could compete without compromising her modest attire but that, like many *hijab*-wearing American women, in her everyday life, she often encounters demands that she remove her scarf. What Ibtihaj Muhammad performed at the Olympics – entwining the patriotic symbols of an athlete representing her country with the marks of a sometimes-maligned identity – is happening on a smaller scale in the everyday performances of many Muslim women, who devote considerable effort to combining the standard "look" of their professions with a recognizably Muslim self-presentation.

The presence and sacrifice of Muslims in the American military also becomes a crucial ground for proving the sincerity of their claims to membership in the nation.[16] Yet while his son Humayun Khan was protected by his military uniform and ultimate sacrifice, Khizr Khan felt it necessary to carry a copy of the Constitution in his pocket, like an amulet against Islamophobia. When Khan, in his public shaming of Trump, pulled out that pocket Constitution on the stage of the Democratic National Convention, he proved himself irreproachably American. Only by such conspicuous patriotism can Muslim bodies save themselves from illegibility and suspicion.

Khan's case is illustrative of two important points. First, of course, the deepening relationship between Muslims and American law finds its perfect symbolic expression in Khan's literally keeping the Constitution close to his heart at all times. Second, his presence at a political convention reminds us that, as Muslims are foregrounded in the public mind – either as bogeymen or as victims – they become grist for political polemic. It is fear that makes

15. Kaplan 2016.
16. Curtis 2016. See Edward Curtis's chapter in this volume, "Blood Sacrifice and the Myth of the Fallen Muslim Soldier in US Presidential Elections after 9/11."

Muslims subjects of citizenship. But that which is scapegoated becomes impossible not to acknowledge. This situation, in which Islam and Muslims become enmeshed in politics due to the widespread tendency to disparage them, both allows and forces Muslims to engage in acts of citizenship.

Muslim identity has become unavoidable in American public culture, and Muslims enter the American imagination at the extremes – as villains and heroes, terrorists and Gold Star parents. As Islam continues to be perceived as a threat on the world stage, American Muslims seek to flee from the opacity that draws their nation's wrath and take refuge in uniforms that offer clear assurances of familiarity and belonging. Thus, at the community level, we see a proliferation of Muslim soldiers, law enforcement officers, nurses, and firefighters stepping forward to represent Muslims.

Of course, one must note that not all efforts at finding refuge in the uniform are successful. There are moments when, for example, *hijab* cannot be part of a uniform, or situations in which it is, but its wearer continues to be harassed by non-Muslims unwilling to accept their Muslim peers in public service. The long, sad story of NYPD officer Bobby Hadid, who was marginalized and seen as suspicious soon after he began to question the methods employed by the NYPD in the surveillance of his own Muslim community, is but one example of a Muslim rebuffed in his attempt to "wear the uniform."[17]

The citizenship of Muslims in America depends on their making themselves ordinary, that is, extinguishing the negative charisma that attaches to them. This process is facilitated by national cultural filters like uniforms, flags, and other symbols of state whose legitimacy is beyond question. Islam may be becoming an inseparable part of the American nation, but for Muslims to claim their place as normal, individual Americans, they must first allay their fellow citizens' anxieties by passing through a phase of patriotic uniformity. Muslim edginess needs to be replaced with a patriotic smoothness.

Muslim Civility

Since the election of Donald Trump, American Muslims feel that they are facing a new, "authorized" Islamophobia – an environment in which hostile acts arising from popular anti-Muslim sentiment might go unpunished. As American Muslims struggle to preserve their basic civil liberties, generational change within the community and increasing cultural literacy make it possible for Muslims to emerge in public life as ordinary folks and to pursue different strategies for asserting their rights.

Muslims now recognize, more than ever before, that their survival as cit-

17. Aviv 2017.

izens depends on solidarity with other minorities and on embracing causes that are shared by the nation at large. An emblematic story in this respect is the striking Muslim response to a spate of desecrations of Jewish cemeteries and threats to Jewish community centers across the country, crimes which began in February 2017 and are still ongoing. In response to a particularly horrific instance of vandalism at a Jewish cemetery outside St. Louis, Muslim activists launched a crowdfunding appeal (justified with specific reference to Islamic ethical teachings), seeking $20,000 to repair the damage. Over the course of two weeks, the appeal generated more than $160,000 in donations; this was fortunate since desecrations continued, and the funds have also been used to repair cemeteries in Philadelphia and Colorado. These acts of charity on the part of the Muslim community of the internet garnered a great deal of favorable publicity nationwide and sparked interfaith meetings and pledges of mutual respect and assistance in the affected cities.[18]

This Muslim response to the desecration of Jewish cemeteries is indicative of a new stage in Muslim civic consciousness. In a time when the status of Muslims as equal citizens and equal humans is contested, gestures that reinforce neighborliness and shared interests are a means of turning back suspicion and seeding good will. A step beyond the donning of patriotic uniforms, American Muslims are beginning to seek ways of claiming their place in the civil discourse of citizenship.

American Muslim Patriotism

Looking back at the changes in immigrant Muslim attitudes toward America, one sees an interesting evolution. One way to trace this is to look at the titles of the annual convention held by ISNA, the Islamic Society of North America, whose annual gatherings – thought to be the largest convocation of American Muslims – attract upwards of 30,000 attendees. In the last two decades they have become increasingly domesticated and even partake of a Christian aesthetic.[19] Skeptical and confrontational convention titles like "Islam: Faith and Civilization" (2000) gave way first to ice-breaking rubrics like "Dialogue" (2004) then to completely at-home titles such as "Life, Liberty and the Pursuit of Happiness" (2009) and "Loving God, Loving Neighbor, Living in Harmony" (2011). This trend culminated in a direct embrace of foundational American phrases: "One Nation Under God: Striving for the Common Good" (2012) and "Envisioning a More Perfect Union: Building the Beloved Community" (2013).

18. For more on the interfaith response to the Philadelphia cemetery vandalism, see Itkowitz 2017.

19. Bilici 2012, 201.

The shift towards a tighter embrace of American identity, culture, and civil religion becomes crystallized in the second and third generations, where new ways of signaling patriotism emerge. Among them are a growing interest in the Founding Fathers' ideas about Islam and a new appreciation of the framers of the Constitution as heroes.[20] Khizr Khan, for example, in his books and speeches, points out that he lives practically in the shadow of Monticello, the home of one of his heroes, Thomas Jefferson.[21] Representative Keith Ellison of Minnesota famously borrowed the Qur'an owned by Jefferson to use in his swearing-in ceremony, and works like Spellberg's *Jefferson's Qur'an* give Muslims a sense of having been present at the nation's birth.[22] At the same time, unearthing Muslim slave narratives provides depth to Muslim belonging and satisfies the need for authentication.[23] Reclaiming African American figures like Muhammad Ali and Kareem Abdul-Jabbar within a framework of patriotism, as Amir Hussain does in his book, *Muslims and the Making of America*, is a way of reminding Muslims themselves and the rest of America that "there has never been an America without Muslims."[24] Another topos that reinforces the naturalness of Muslim presence in America is the tendency to equate *shari'ah* with the American Constitution. As an extension of this belief, one frequently comes across the idea that "America is more Islamic than Muslim countries." While Islamophobes passionately claim that Islam is "incompatible with the U.S. Constitution,"[25] some American Muslims argue with equal passion that, quite the contrary, the US Constitution is among the most Islamic of political documents, sharing the ultimate principles that constitute the foundations (*maqasid*) of *shari'ah*.[26]

Another example of the embrace of American identity in everyday Muslim life – one that may seem trivial but is actually quite revealing – involves the *hijab*. Both in real life and in artistic representations and media images, young Muslim American women are increasingly seen wearing American flag headscarves. The image came to prominence at the Women's March on Washington that followed the 2017 Inauguration. On the occasion of the march, the graphic artist Shepard Fairey made a series of three posters titled "We the People." One depicts a woman in stars-and-stripes *hijab* over the motto "We the People Are Greater Than Fear." Together, the image represents the intersection of several contested American themes: citizenship ("We the People"), gender (women's solidarity/empowerment), the

20. Shah 2017.
21. Khan 2017b.
22. Spellberg 2013.
23. Alryyes 2011; Diouf 2013; Alford 2007; Austin 1997.
24. Hussain 2017, 4.
25. Federer 2016.
26. Shah 2017; Humayun 2015.

flag (patriotism versus nativism). The result was an expression of feminist opposition to Donald Trump's politics (viewed as at once Islamophobic and anti-women), which at the same time normalized Muslim women as political actors. In this claim to citizenship and patriotism, Muslim women took part not only as objects of compassion but also as organizers and leaders (one of the four national co-chairs of the march, Linda Sarsour, is a Muslim activist). Suffice it to say that images of flag-*hijab* are reminiscent of the famous image of a black soldier saluting the French flag that appeared on the cover of *Paris Match* in June 23, 1953, and which Roland Barthes analyzed semiotically in his *Mythologies* (1972).

In the following sections, I focus on expressions of Muslim civility in the American context in the forms of "speech" and "action," two key concepts of political philosophy corresponding to equality and liberty, or the First Amendment and the Second.

Muslim Speech: First Amendment Muslims

I have already discussed the growing interest in reading the American Constitution through the lenses of Islam and vice versa. Here I want to pause for a moment on Khizr Khan's symbolically powerful act. It represents a different type of Muslim speech, where the addressee (another American) is not merely reminded of the equality of Muslims with non-Muslims but is chastised with reference to a higher principle (the American Constitution). With this and comparable "acts of citizenship,"[27] Muslims begin to exercise a form of civility that assumes responsibility for the well-being not only of themselves, but of others. This represents a shift from being an object of law to being a subject who shares in ownership of the law. This entails a parallel shift in horizon from self-preoccupied victimhood to other-aware universalism. Rather than begging rights from others, such a speaker participates in the distribution of those very rights.

Muslims typically have been limited to a particular type of speech. They either demand understanding from their compatriots or find themselves responding to those who blame all Muslims for the acts of terrorists who identify as Muslim. One may then ask: to what extent is Muslim speech free? This mode of speech is more like a response to an interrogation than true self-expression. The entry of Muslim subjects into public space is preceded by a discursive security clearance where they are forced to engage in a kind of speech they would not need or want, if left to themselves.

The Muslim subject is under pressure to speak in a way that does not permit him or her to be authentic. So interrogated, he or she turns into

27. Isin 2000.

an apologetic, needy, and grateful person who finds refuge in the law but is not the author of the law. Approached in this way, the law – no matter how progressive and democratic – can only "protect" the Muslim, it cannot grant him or her what is more valuable than mere protection: a share in sovereignty.

To not only speak and demand equality but also claim the higher moral ground against an interlocutor is, in a sense, the beginning of an agonistic civic consciousness. Instead of self-justification, to chastise the opponent with the universal values of the nation – not in the name of Islam or Muslims but in the name of American values and the Constitution: this is Muslims achieving "equality." It is not a protection granted from above by a caring social state but an equality earned by its bearer as an active citizen.

What about "liberty"? For Hannah Arendt, "human plurality, the basic condition of both action and speech, has the twofold character of equality and distinction."[28] This twofold character finds an articulation in Balibar's conceptualization of "equaliberty" which, in attempting to secure both equality and liberty, takes as a necessity the preservation of the potential for both *insurrection* and *constitution*.[29]

Muslim Sovereignty: Second Amendment Muslims

What is the basis of civility in a democratic society? Being civil is typically understood as being polite and peaceful. People concerned about civility often have in mind the everyday conduct of the self and speech acts. That is to say, challenges to and questions of civility are understood as falling within the domain of the First Amendment. Yet civility is not merely the absence of hate speech, it is intimately tied to violence. According to Balibar, civility is a politics of anti-violence, rather than a simple nonviolence: "A politics of civility is no more to be identified with nonviolence than with counterviolence that prevents and resists violence."[30] In short, civility requires an equitable distribution of the potential for violence.

For scholars like Balibar, Rancière, and Arendt, political participation and willful action are central to the notion of citizenship. Citizenship, for them, is characterized by the entitlement to public visibility. And in America, that visibility resides not simply in speech but also in the capacity for violence. For if the *polis* "is the space of appearance in the widest sense of the word,"[31] then citizenship ultimately is the right to occupy a

28. Arendt 1998, 175.
29. Balibar 2014, 8.
30. Balibar 2016, 148.
31. Arendt 1998, 198.

corner in the space of plurality where dissension, antinomy, or conflict are enacted and confronted. This form of citizenship, though built around the notion of the political, has very little to do with the state and a lot to do with citizens encountering other citizens. As Balibar observes, "Individuals who constitute the people confer basic rights upon one another mutually."[32] Citizenship thus is not membership in the homogeneity of the state but membership in the heterogeneity of the community.

Beneath its social-contract surface, citizenship reserves the absolute freedom of the state of nature. Some trace of the originary violence is preserved within the law and kept available for the citizens, in case either of self-defense or rebellion against tyranny. Many strands of the "sovereign citizen"[33] and militia movements lay claim to that original violence in their rejection of the later amendments to the Constitution and in their self-identification with the idea of "the three percent" – the percentage of Americans who supposedly participated in the Revolutionary War. By arrogating to themselves that constitutive violence, they declare their independence from the law.

Once seen as the "ethical horizon of politics"[34] where equality and liberty stand in dialogical tension, civility needs to be understood "not [as] a politics which suppresses all violence" but as one that "excludes extremes of violence so as to create a (public, private) space for politics."[35]

Turning back to American society, we may ask: what position does the Muslim subject occupy in the national economy of violence?

The Question of Muslim Violence

Not only are Muslims often on the receiving end of hate speech, verbal harassment, and everyday discrimination in the forms of bullying and crude gestures, they are sometimes physically attacked and even murdered. And this violence is unevenly distributed across genders: according to a 2017 poll conducted by the Institute for Social Policy and Understanding (ISPU), "Muslim women are more likely than Muslim men to report experiencing religious discrimination (68% vs 55%)." The same report notes that "Muslim women bear the brunt of discrimination" and do more work to counter it.[36] Part of this work may be seen in the increasing number of Muslim women enrolling in martial arts classes, reflected in the proliferation of media re-

---

32. Balibar 2014, 7.
33. FBI 2010.
34. Balibar 2002, 2.
35. Balibar 2002, 30.
36. Mogahed and Chouhoud 2017, 14.

ports like the *Washington Post*'s November 2017 piece, "'Hijab grab' defense: As reports of hate crimes spike postelection, Muslim women turn to self-defense."[37]

More and more Muslims feel that they can no longer take for granted their safety in American society. A newly emboldened violence directed at Muslims seems both to scare them deeply and to encourage the deepening of their claims of citizenship. This is reflected in surveys that present two seemingly contradictory facts: that Muslims are subject to the highest degree of discrimination in the country and that "Muslims [are] more satisfied with the U.S. than any religious group."[38]

Nearly a quarter of Americans (22%) either do not know or do not believe that American Muslims are granted the same constitutional protections as other citizens. Reporting the findings of the Constitution Day Civics Survey, conducted annually by the University of Pennsylvania's Annenberg Public Policy Center, a *Huffington Post* story notes that, "A scary number of Americans do not think Muslims or atheists have constitutional rights."[39] In other words, a significant number of Americans do not consider Muslims to be part of "We the People." The belief that Muslims do not have the protection of the Constitution is linked to Islamophobic propaganda that casts Islam as a violent political ideology rather than a religion. Seeing and presenting Islam as a totalitarian ideology produces two results: first, Muslims fall outside the fold of the nation and its protections; and second, violence against Muslims becomes not only legitimate but a patriotic obligation. At the same time, "Understanding Law Enforcement Intelligence Processes," a survey published in 2014 by the National Consortium for the Study of Terrorism and Responses to Terrorism (START) at the University of Maryland, ranked the threat from the "sovereign citizen movement" higher than the "Islamist extremist" threat.[40]

This brings us to an interesting intersection of Islam, violence, and American citizenship. Although most of the attention goes to the violence committed by Muslims, the overwhelming majority of acts of violence (domestic terrorism) in the United States are committed by right-wing citizens. A study of terrorism incidents between 2008 and 2016 reveals that white supremacist terrorist acts (115 incidents) far outnumber acts of Muslim domestic terrorism (63), even as there remains a persistent focus on "radical Islamic terrorism."[41] In another study, researchers found that "the news

37. Schmidt, 2016.
38. Abbasi 2017.
39. Blumberg 2017.
40. Carter et al. 2014.
41. Sampathkumar 2017.

media do not cover all terrorist attacks the same way. Rather, they give drastically more coverage to attacks by Muslims, particularly foreign-born Muslims – even though those are far less common than other kinds of terrorist attacks."[42] When does violence get labeled terrorism? The same study supports the idea that people are more likely to consider an attack to be terrorism when the perpetrator is Muslim.

It seems that the Muslim citizen is squeezed between, on the one hand, the external and externalizing phenomenon of terrorism and, on the other, the threat of Islamophobic violence. Where, in these conditions, does the path of Muslim civility lead? Accused of terrorism and threatened by guns, do the regular Muslim citizens of America perhaps see gun ownership and the assurances of the Second Amendment as an avenue of self-preservation?

Muslims with Guns: Terrorists or Patriots?

The notion of "Muslims with guns" does immediately strike one as dangerous. It is unsettling to think of a Muslim celebration of the Second Amendment. Far from patriotic, it sounds like a dangerous combination. Here we face an interesting dilemma, a conflict between two violences. Which equation is true: "Muslims plus guns equals 'terrorism'" or "Muslims plus guns equals 'patriotism'"?

The idea sounds dangerous, of course, only because the Muslim relationship to violence is conceived and imagined within the framework of terrorism. Meanwhile, terrorism perpetrated by non-Muslim American extremists is most often depicted simply as violence or crime and balanced against an accepted norm of "responsible gun ownership." Yet as Islam becomes more widespread across all sectors of American society – and the second and third generations of immigrant Muslim families become more confident in their embrace of American values – the identities of "Muslim American" and "responsible gun owner" are more likely to intersect.

As Hassan Shibly, a twenty-nine-year-old Muslim civil rights attorney who works for CAIR (the Council on American-Islamic Relations) in Tampa, Florida, told an interviewer in 2016,

> Unfortunately, and very reluctantly, this past year, especially with the dramatic increase in anti-Muslim hate crimes that's followed Donald Trump's rhetoric that demonizes the American Muslim community, I felt it necessary for my own safety and the safety of my loved ones to start carrying a weapon at all times when possible.

Among the recent hate crimes that convinced Shibly to carry a gun was a

42. Kearns et al. 2017.

horrifying voicemail left at the Islamic Center of St. Petersburg in December: a man identifying himself as Martin Schnitzler said he was "going to personally have a militia ... come down to ... firebomb [the mosque and] shoot whoever is there."[43]

"If white, Christian Americans can publicly embrace the Second Amendment," Shibly says, "it only makes sense that Muslim Americans, facing ever-increasing Islamophobia, should embrace it, too." This initially reluctant embrace of guns gradually turns into a matter of pride and patriotism. Making a virtue of necessity, Shibly goes on to say:

> I am a proud American citizen.... I have been raised in this country. Unfortunately, what we've often seen is sometimes American Muslims are actually shying away from both their First and Second Amendment protected activity. You find that some American Muslims are literally hiding their identity, changing their name because they are afraid if they express their First Amendment protected activity, if they express their faith or their political views, they will be targeted by the government, they will be targeted by hate crimes.... Basically, myself having a firearm here, keeping one in my office, is no different than any American business owner or leader or person, regardless of their race or religion, [who] may exercise their Second Amendment protected rights to carry arms. It is what we do as Americans. It's part of our culture and tradition, for better or for worse.[44]

Interestingly enough, there are de facto gun controls targeting Muslims. Multiple gun stores and shooting ranges have declared themselves "Muslim-free" and refuse to serve Muslim customers. As anti-Muslim bias rises across America, business owners who ban Muslims feel emboldened.[45] Muslims thus are not only targeted by white supremacists and various other Islamophobic groups, they are also excluded from equal access to the tools of legitimate violence.

Conclusion

The Muslim encounter with the American Constitution has both symbolic and practical dimensions. Muslims might have symbolically embraced various elements of the American Constitution, but there is a "learning" process that is at once need-based and survival-driven. Such practical learning and absorption of and into the environment (whether, with Giddens, one calls

43. Mathias 2016.
44. Mathias 2016.
45. Leon 2017.

it "practical consciousness" or with Bourdieu, "habitus") testifies to the emergence of a much deeper relationship between Muslims and American principles as canonized in foundational law. Thus, Muslim civility in America reaches a new level where it not only seeks equality but also asserts its liberty. If First Amendment Muslim culture is interested in freedom *from* limitations and is the indebted recipient of American sovereignty, Second Amendment Muslim culture reaches for the liberty to exercise that very sovereignty. Taken together, these two tracks of citizenship represent a striving for what Balibar calls "equaliberty."

American Muslims seeking to have both equality and liberty together are engaged in two complementary modes of citizenship: *citizenship from below* and *citizenship from above*. Citizenship from below is the condition of the subject citizen: the citizen as someone who is subject to the law. Citizenship from above is the condition of the sovereign citizen: the citizen as someone who is the author and owner of the law. Equality is never enough, nor liberty alone.

Muslims for a long time have spoken of their loyalty to America and to its juridical system on the basis of certain tenets of *shari'ah* that stipulate that Muslims must obey the law of the land wherever they live. Most of the now not-so-popular discussion about *fiqh al-aqalliyyat* (minority *fiqh*)[46] revolved primarily around this notion. We are now arguably at a juncture where both the intensification of Islamophobia and the maturation of American Muslim civic consciousness necessitate qualitative growth from an *ethics of minority* to an *ethics of majority*. The latter demands what I call Muslim civility, an attitude that is implicitly demanded by citizenship but that often makes its appearance only in the later stages of immigrant lives, as the newcomers begin to care about others in the society as they care about themselves (having come to the realization that they are one body). As citizens, they come to feel, they are shareholders in sovereignty, each citizen bearing a capacity for violence that makes him or her not only equal but free.

46. Al-Alwani 2003.

Works Cited

Abbasi, W. 2017. "Muslims Are More Satisfied With U.S. Than Any Religious Group, Poll Finds." *USA Today*, March 21, https://www.usatoday.com/story/news/nation-now/2017/03/21/muslims-more-satisfied-us-than-any-religious-group-poll-finds/99427254.

Al-Alwani, T. 2003. *Towards a Fiqh for Minorities: Some Basic Reflections.* London.

Alford, T. 2007. *Prince Among Slaves*. New York.

Ali, W., E. Clifton, M. Duss, L. Fang, S. Keyes, and F. Shakir. 2011. "Fear Inc.: The Roots of the Islamophobia Network in America." *Center for American Progress*, August 26. www.americanprogress.org/issues/2011/08/islamophobia.html.

Alryyes, A. 2011. *A Muslim American Slave: The Life of Omar Ibn Said*. Madison, WI.

Alsultany, E. 2012. *Arabs and Muslims in the Media: Race and Representation after 9/11*. New York.

Arendt, H. 1998 [1958]. *The Human Condition*. Chicago.

Austin, A. 1997. *African Muslims in Antebellum America: Transatlantic Stories and Spiritual Struggles*. New York.

Aviv, R. 2017. "The Trials of a Muslim Cop." *The New Yorker*, September 11. https://www.newyorker.com/magazine/2017/09/11/the-trials-of-a-muslim-cop.

Bail, C. 2015. *Terrified: How Anti-Muslim Fringe Organizations Became Mainstream*. Princeton, NJ.

Bakalian, A. and M. Bozorgmehr. 2009. *Backlash 9/11: Middle Eastern and Muslim Americans Respond*. Berkeley, CA.

Balibar, E. 2002. *Politics and the Other Scene*. London.

———. 2014. *Equaliberty: Political Essays*. Translated by J. Ingram. Durham, NC.

———. 2015a. *Violence and Civility: On the Limits of Political Philosophy*. Translated by G. Goshgarian. New York.

———. 2015b. *Citizenship*. Cambridge.

Barthes, R. 1972. *Mythologies*. Translated by A. Lavers. New York.

Bilici, M. 2012. *Finding Mecca in America: How Islam Is Becoming an American Religion*. Chicago.

Blumberg, A. 2017. "A Scary Number of Americans Don't Think Muslims or Atheists Have Constitutional Rights." *Huffington Post*, September 19. https://www.huffingtonpost.com/entry/muslims-atheists-first-amendment-rights-study_us_59c00848e4b0c4c31f81c10a.

Cainkar, L. 2009. *Homeland Insecurity: The Arab American and Muslim American Experience after 9/11*. New York.

Carter, D., S. Chermak, J. Carter, and J. Drew. 2014. "Understanding Law Enforcement Intelligence Processes." Report to the Office of University Programs, Science and Technology Directorate, U.S. Department of Homeland Security. College Park, MD: START. https://www.start.umd.edu/pubs/START_UnderstandingLawEnforcementIntelligenceProcesses_July2014.pdf.

Curtis IV, E. 2016. *Muslim Americans in the Military: Centuries of Service*. Bloomington.

Ernst, C., ed. 2013. *Islamophobia in America: The Anatomy of Intolerance.* New York.

Federal Bureau of Investigation (FBI). 2010. "Domestic Terrorism: Sovereign Citizen Movement." https://archives.fbi.gov/archives/news/stories/2010/april/sovereigncitizens_041310/domestic-terrorism-the-sovereign-citizen-movement.

Federer, B. 2016. "Is Islam Incompatible with U.S. Constitution?" *American Minute*, November 20. http://mobile.wnd.com/2016/11/is-islam-incompatible-with-u-s-constitution.

Fox News. 2016. "Two Muslim Women Removed From Jetblue Flight After 'Staring' at Flight Attendant." March 9. http://www.foxnews.com/travel/2016/03/09/two-muslim-women-removed-from-jetblue-flight-after-staring-at-flight-attendant.html.

Friedman, T. 2017. "If Only Stephen Paddock Were a Muslim." *New York Times*, October 3. https://www.nytimes.com/2017/10/03/opinion/stephen-paddock-las-vegas-terrorism.html.

Hammer, J. 2013. "Center Stage: Gendered Islamophobia and Muslim Women." In *Islamophobia in America: The Anatomy of Intolerance*, edited by C. Ernst, 107–144. New York.

Humayun, A. 2015. "Islam and the US Constitution." *UsIslam*. http://www.usislam.org/debate/IslamandtheUSConstitution.htm.

Hussain, A. 2017. *Muslims and the Making of America.* Waco, TX.

Isin, E. 2008. "Theorizing Acts of Citizenship." In *Acts of Citizenship*, edited by E. Isin and G. Nielsen, 15–43. London.

Itkowitz, C. 2017. "'Stand Together Against This Bigotry': Another Jewish Cemetery Vandalized and Again Muslims Reach Out to Help." *Washington Post*, February 27. https://www.washingtonpost.com/news/inspired-life/wp/2017/02/27/stand-together-against-this-bigotry-another-jewish-cemetery-vandalized-and-again-muslims-reach-out-to-help/?utm_term=.617d4f0b6f73.

Kaplan, S. 2016. "Meet Ibtihaj Muhammad, the History-Making Olympian Who Called Out SXSW for Telling Her to Remove Her Hijab." *Washington Post*, March 14. https://www.washingtonpost.com/news/morning-mix/wp/2016/03/14/meet-ibtihaj-muhammad-the-history-making-olympian-who-called-out-sxsw-for-telling-her-to-remove-her-hijab/?utm_term=.41a6bfd9f63f.

Kearns, E., A. Betus, and A. Lemieux. 2017. "Yes, the Media Do Underreport Some Terrorist Attacks. Just Not the Ones Most People Think Of." *Washington Post*, March 13. https://www.washingtonpost.com/news/monkey-cage/wp/2017/03/13/yes-the-media-do-underreport-some-

terrorist-attacks-just-not-the-ones-most-people-think-of/?utm_term=.
ce687d8842a8#comments.

Khan, G. 2016. "Trump Criticized My Silence. He Knows Nothing About True Sacrifice." *Washington Post*, July 31. https://www.washingtonpost.com/opinions/ghazala-khan-donald-trump-criticized-my-silence-he-knows-nothing-about-true-sacrifice/2016/07/31/c46e52ec-571c-11e6-831d-0324760ca856_story.html.

Khan, K. 2016. "Speech to the 2016 Democratic National Convention." *ABC News*, August 1. http://abcnews.go.com/Politics/full-text-khizr-khans-speech-2016-democratic-national/story?id=41043609.

———. 2017a. *An American Family: A Memoir of Hope and Sacrifice*. New York.

———. 2017b. *This Is Our Constitution: Discover America with a Gold Star Father*. New York.

Lean, N. 2012. *The Islamophobia Industry: How the Right Manufactures Fear of Muslims*. London.

Leon, H. 2017. "'Muslim-Free' Gun Stores Perfectly Exemplify Trump's America." *Vocativ*, April 26. http://www.vocativ.com/news/421031/muslim-free-gun-stores-trumps-america/index.html.

Mathias, C. 2016. "Why This Muslim American Civil Rights Attorney Decided To Buy A Handgun." *Huffington Post*, September 22. https://www.huffingtonpost.com/entry/muslim-gun-owner-hassan-shibly-islamophobia_us_57e2bfa4e4b08d73b82eefd2.

Mogahed, D. and Y. Chouhoud. 2017. "American Muslim Poll: 2017: Muslims at the Crossroads." *Institute for Social Policy and Understanding*. https://www.ispu.org/wp-content/uploads/2017/03/American-Muslim-Poll-2017-Report.pdf.

Parascandola, R. 2017. "Drunken Bigot Attacks Jewish Mom, Daughter He Mistook for Muslims at Queens Subway Station." *New York Daily News*, September 14. http://www.nydailynews.com/new-york/nyc-crime/bigot-attacks-jewish-mom-daughter-mistook-muslims-nyc-article-1.3495756.

Pew Research Center. 2017. "U.S. Muslims Concerned About Their Place in Society, but Continue to Believe in the American Dream: Findings from Pew Research Center's 2017 Survey of U.S. Muslims." July 26. http://www.pewforum.org/2017/07/26/findings-from-pew-research-centers-2017-survey-of-us-muslims.

Rampell, C. 2016. "Ivy League Economist Ethnically Profiled, Interrogated for Doing Math on American Airlines Flight." *Washington Post*, May 7. https://www.washingtonpost.com/news/rampage/wp/2016/05/07/ivy-league-economist-interrogated-for-doing-math-on-american-airlines-flight/?utm_term=.678d2f8216ab.

Sampathkumar, M. 2017. "Majority of Terrorists Who Have Attacked America Are Not Muslim, New Study Finds." *The Independent*, June 23. http://www.independent.co.uk/news/world/americas/us-politics/terrorism-right-wing-america-muslims-islam-white-supremacists-study-a7805831.html.

Samuels, R. 2017. "A Showdown over Sharia." *Washington Post*, September 22. http://www.washingtonpost.com/sf/national/2017/09/22/muslims-and-anti-sharia-activists-meet-armed-at-a-dairy-queen-to-talk-fears-about-americas-future.

Schmidt, S. 2016. "'Hijab Grab' Defense: As Reports of Hate Crimes Spike Postelection, Muslim Women Turn to Self-Defense." *Washington Post*, November 21. https://www.washingtonpost.com/news/morning-mix/wp/2016/11/21/hijab-grab-defense-as-reports-of-hate-crimes-spike-postelection-muslim-women-turn-to-self-defense/?utm_term=.a8938f96b1a3.

Shah, Z. A. 2017. "Founding Fathers of America and Islamic Thought." *Fiqh Council of North America*. http://www.fiqhcouncil.org/node/18.

Shepherd, K. 2016. "Township Saw a Zoning Issue. The Justice Dept. Saw Religious Discrimination." *New York Times*, August 7. https://www.nytimes.com/2016/08/08/us/politics/township-saw-a-zoning-issue-the-justice-dept-saw-religious-discrimination.html.

Spellberg, D. 2013. *Thomas Jefferson's Qur'an, Islam and the Founders*. New York.

Stone, A. 2011. "Muslim Scholars Issue Fatwa Declaring No Conflict Between Islamic Law And U.S. Constitution." *Huffington Post*, December 19. https://www.huffingtonpost.com/2011/10/19/muslim-scholars-fatwa_n_1020641.html.

Blood Sacrifice and the Myth of the Fallen Muslim Soldier in US Presidential Elections after 9/11

Edward E. Curtis IV

IN THE US PRESIDENTIAL ELECTIONS of 2008 and 2016, the blood sacrifice of two fallen soldiers named Khan became part of a new national myth, the myth of the fallen Muslim soldier.[1] In the election of 2008, it was re-tired general and former secretary of state Colin Powell who was the chief poet of such myth-making; in 2016, it was Democratic candidate Hillary Clinton. In using the label "myth" to interpret the meaning and function of stories about fallen Muslim American soldiers, I do not mean to argue that such narratives are in any way empirically false. Corporal Kareem Khan and Captain Humayun Khan, both of whom were killed in battle during the Iraq War, were real people. But narratives of their sacrifice were rendered mythic as they became part of public discourse about the meaning of communal belonging and national identity in the post-9/11 era. The blood of these US Muslim military members was transformed into a solemnity that could re-deem the nation.[2] Myths, as Bruce Lincoln argues, are a rare "class of stories that possess both credibility and authority." Like historical narratives, myths contain truthful claims; they are credible. But myths do more than simply recount what happened in the past; they also have social authority. They contain "*paradigmatic* truth," that is, a truth that sets forth a "model," even a "blueprint" not only for individuals but also for society. Myths have been essential to the social life of human beings: by making myths, people "evoke the sentiments out of which society is actively constructed."[3]

Muslims and Islam have always been a vital element of American society's mythmaking. Anti-Muslim or Islamophobic myths have played a noteworthy role in the making of US national identities since the coun-

---

1. While I am responsible for all content, a number of colleagues at Michigan State's spring 2017 conference and at IUPUI helped to make this chapter better. Special thanks to David Craig, Kelly Hayes, Jason Kelly, Missy Dehn Kubitschek, Peter Thuesen, Joseph Tucker Edmonds, and Rachel Wheeler.

2. Jonathan Z. Smith's *HarperCollins Dictionary of Religion* insists that the fundamental con-stitutive element of myth is the presence of superhuman beings. But the definition of myth, much like religion itself, remains highly contested, and I deploy multiple theories of myth in this chapter. See Smith 1995.

3. Lincoln 2014, 23.

try's founding.[4] Rooted strongly in apocalyptic Christian visions of Muslims and Islam as the anti-Christ, the myth of the superhuman Muslim "beast" first became a popular way of understanding real and imaginary Muslim adversaries in colonial New England. Americans have adapted this mythic anti-hero subsequently to respond to foreign policy challenges concerning the Ottoman Empire in pre-Civil War times, the US invasion of Mindanao in the Philippines, US support for Israel during the Arab-Israeli War of 1973, the Iranian hostage crisis in 1979–1980, the first Gulf War, and the post-9/11 war on terrorism. Throughout these moments, and at other times, the myth of the Muslim monster not only justified violence against Muslims abroad; it also worked to define American national identity at home – as in, "they" are violent, misogynistic, despotic, medieval, and untrustworthy, whereas "we" are peaceful, pro-woman, democratic, modern, and honest.[5]

But the myth of the fallen Muslim soldier after 9/11 challenged these anti-Muslim claims and sought to alter the symbolic role of Muslims in the making of US national identity. As Bruce Lincoln points out, myths can be used to sustain and support the political status quo or they can be used to contest it.[6] In the case of the fallen Muslim soldier, a different kind of story about Muslims in the United States was offered to displace the older myth of the Muslim beast. In this new liberal myth, Muslims would play the role of heroic patriot, and in exchange, the nation would owe them and all Muslims Americans social acceptance and an opportunity to become part of the multicultural melting pot.

The fact that the Khans were both Muslim immigrants was essential to the new myth. Even though African American Muslims had been defending the country since the War of 1812, if not the American Revolution, their symbolic utility to the myth of the fallen Muslim soldier was limited in the post-9/11 era.[7] In the twenty-first century, Islam's foreign-ness in US culture was represented mainly by Muslims who were perceived to be brown, Middle Eastern or South Asian. As some scholars have pointed out, Americans constructed Muslims as a race that embodied a foreign, threatening presence in the nation.[8] It was precisely because the Khans looked like "foreign" Muslims that US politicians such as Colin Powell and Hillary Clinton

---

4. For an extensive bibliography on anti-Muslim racism, see Abdul Khabeer et al.

5. Gottschalk and Greenberg 2008; Kidd 2013; Ernst 2013; and McAlister 2001.

6. Lincoln 2014, 24.

7. For a brief overview of US Muslim military history, see Curtis IV 2016.

8. One illustrative moment of this racialization in the 2008 presidential campaign was when a woman asked Republican candidate John McCain about his Democrat rival, Barack Obama, whom the woman called an Arab, which for her seemed to be synonymous with being Muslim. For more, see Rana 2007, and compare Selod 2014.

could employ their memories in myths of incorporation that echoed successful immigrant narratives. Conjuring images of these soldiers' graves and memories of their lives in order to renew the myth of a liberal, multicultural consensus, Democratic candidates and their supporters cast themselves as the most authentic practitioners of a faith in a religiously tolerant American nation.

This chapter argues, however, that in focusing on the incorporation of foreign Muslim blood into the nation, politicians such as Powell and Clinton offered a partial, ambiguous acceptance – one that both included and excluded Muslims from the American body politic. By emphasizing the importance of gaining Muslim American support in the war against terrorism, US politicians pointed to the very liminality of Muslim Americans. Muslim Americans were on the front lines, part "us" and "part them."[9] Somewhat suspect – valuable precisely because of their nearness to the enemy – Muslim American service members proved, by their blood sacrifice, that the US war on terrorism was just and right. Perhaps their symbolic sacrifices even sanctified US military intervention in the Muslim world, and thus unintentionally legitimated the wars that were an essential element of the cycle of anti-Muslim sentiment in the United States. Whether or not this was the case, I argue, the myth of the fallen Muslim soldier had limited effectiveness in national discourse as its authority was rejected by supporters of Donald Trump and Muslim activists alike. The chapter concludes by analyzing the limits of the myth's success as some Muslim American critics called out Hillary Clinton's campaign as stigmatizing and ultimately dehumanizing, while many Trump supporters disagreed with the underlying premise that Muslims could or should be incorporated into the nation.

Kareem Khan and the Election of 2008

On October 19, 2008, a little over a fortnight before the Nov. 4 election contested by Democrat Barack Obama and Republican John McCain, former Republican secretary of state and retired chairman of the Joint Chiefs General Colin Powell appeared on the NBC News Sunday morning program, *Meet the Press*, to endorse the Democrat. Powell outlined multiple reasons for his choice, many of which were driven by sober policy concerns and a sense of which person was better suited for the job. But there was also a "push factor" behind his choice. He had grown weary of anti-Muslim rhetoric in the Republican Party and the attempts to tarnish Obama as a Muslim. Powell pointed out that Obama was a Christian, but in perhaps the most dramat-

---

9. Kelly Hayes, personal correspondence, May 23, 2017.

ic moment of the interview, he asked rhetorically: "What if he is? Is there something wrong with being a Muslim in this country? The answer is, 'No, that's not America.' Is there something wrong with some seven-year-old Muslim American kid believing that he or she could be President?"

The reason for his dramatic declamation on this point was, he said, because of a powerful image. It was a photograph of Kareem Khan's mother at her son's gravestone in Arlington National Cemetery. Powell continued:

> And as the picture focused in, you could see the writing on the headstone. And it gave his awards--Purple Heart, Bronze Star-- showed that he died in Iraq, gave his date of birth, date of death. He was 20 years old. And then, at the very top of the headstone, it didn't have a Christian cross; it didn't have the Star of David; it had crescent and a star of the Islamic faith. And his name was Kareem Rashad Sultan Khan, and he was an American. He was born in New Jersey. He was 14 years old at the time of 9/11, and he waited until he can go serve his country, and he gave his life.[10]

This image of a mother at her son's grave spoke to former General Powell's deepest values as a patriot and his most fervent hopes for his nation.

As numerous scholars of religion and nationalism have argued, the willingness of citizens to sacrifice their own blood for the nation and for parents to sacrifice the blood of their children might be considered the ultimate act of religious piety in the modern world.[11] World War I poet Wilfred Owen called it the "old lie," and mocked it, but also recognized the power of this act of national devotion: "*Dulce et decorum est / Pro Patria Mori*," he wrote.[12] How sweet and fitting it is to die for one's country. Carolyn Marvin and David Ingle have asserted that the sacrifice of one's life, the shedding of one's blood, is "the holiest ritual of the nation-state."[13] There is no better example of this sentiment than the French national anthem, "La Marseillaise," which asks all citizens to take up arms, form battalions, and "let an impure blood soak our fields." "In the past Christians may have been willing to die for their faith," they opine, but in the modern world, the God of the nation-state has replaced the God of Christianity as the ultimate basis for communal formation and social agency. Agnieszka Soltysik Monnet riffs on this idea, stating that "while many people have abandoned religious beliefs and practices, it is almost impossible to have no nationality. Even people who have lost their

10. NBC News 2008.
11. See, for example, Cavanaugh 2009.
12. Owen 1921.
13. Marvin and Ingle 1996, 774.

citizenship one way or another usually consider themselves as 'belonging' to some nation in at least a spiritual and cultural sense."[14]

This is not to say that other forms of communal formation and social belonging have disappeared in the modern world. Transnational ties of confessional religion, ethnicity, politics, race, and global economic interests exist alongside the nation-state, sometimes even challenging its hegemony.[15] But these imagined affiliations are just as apt to accommodate, or in the case of capitalism, reify the nation-state as the most powerful institution of human community-making.[16] This is true even in the case of Islamist political formation, which is sometimes thought to be the most significant challenge to the nation-state in the contemporary world but more often than not supports and sustains nation building.[17] In the end, according to Monnet, "nationality is generally the first and most important way that social life on this planet is organized."[18]

In the election of 2008, America's most respected military man made the case on national television that the blood sacrifice of a Muslim American soldier for the nation was particularly meaningful in an era of anti-Muslim prejudice. His advocacy for the inclusion of Muslims in US nationalism echoed his own role in the military history of the United States.[19] As the first African American officer to become chairman of the Joints Chiefs of Staff, Powell signified the promise that America's military could embody, represent, and even heal a nation of many races and ethnicities. Analyzing Powell's role in the first Gulf War during 1990–1991, Melani McAlister argues that "Powell became ... the nation's premier citizen-soldier, the living embodiment of the institution in which the whole nation must recognize itself."[20] Liberals and conservatives alike lauded Powell's performance both during and after the war. Powell's willingness to lead this war was understood in ways similar to the military service of African Americans, Japanese Americans, Native Americans, and other non-white military service members in the past: it was seen as proof of America's multicultural promise and its essential fairness and goodness as a democratic state. Like other non-white service members before him, Powell embodied a multicultural vision of the United States that was tied inextricably to military intervention.

Thus Powell's eulogy of Kareem Khan echoed his own symbolic mean-

---

14. Monnet 2012, 8.

15. Appadurai 1996; Basch et al. 1994; and Hannerz 1996.

16. Mandaville 2004, 44.

17. For an introduction to Islamist democracies in Indonesia and Turkey and to Islamist national resistance movements in Palestine and Chechnya, see Ayoob 2007.

18. Monnet 2012, 8.

19. Um 2012.

20. McAlister 2001, 255.

ing to American nationalism. In praising Khan, Powell was doing more than including Muslims in a liberal and multicultural vision of the US nation-state, just as his own presence meant more than having a racially integrated military force. Powell was also justifying, indeed sanctifying wars in Muslim-majority lands as a part of the myth of American exceptionalism. Khan's outsider status as a Muslim – the fact that he was fighting as a Muslim against other Muslims – signified the religious importance of America's "mission" in the twentieth-first century. Powell made the point that it was Muslims who now renewed the myth of American exceptionalism, a myth that was rooted in the colonial founding of Massachusetts Bay Colony, where Puritans articulated the idea that they were chosen by God to occupy the land.[21]

Left unsaid in Powell's remarks, but essential to the making of Kareem Khan into a mythical figure, was the gendered nature of the image. One of the primary reasons why Powell noticed the photograph at all was the presence of Khan's mother, Elsheba Khan. She was the one who inspired the professional photographer, Platon, to take the photo in the first place. "One day I saw this lady," he remembered. "And every day she goes to her son's grave. She sits in front of her son's grave and reads to him." Platon asked if he might take her photograph, and "she took the book that she was reading and placed it at the base of the headstone, and got behind the stone and cuddled it as if she was embracing her son." [22] In the photograph, her eyes are closed. Her left arm is stretched out across the top of the gravestone. She rests her head on her left arm as she uses her right arm to hold onto her son's gravestone.

It was a reenactment, according to Ji-Young Um, of the Pietà, Michelangelo's sculpture in St. Peter's Basilica that depicts Mary, the mother of Jesus, embracing her dead son. "Like the Virgin Mary of the original pietà," Um argues, "she sacrificed her son without protest, calmly accepting her role in the larger narrative of collective national suffering and the redemptive figure (the son/soldier) who would die in the place of others so that they would be saved." Um points out that Elsheba Khan's ethnic and racial identity is perhaps understated in the black-and-white photograph but that Powell, the embodiment of multicultural liberalism, makes it clear that Khan and his family are part of the larger narrative of multicultural sacrifice for the nation.[23] It must also be said that her religious identity as a Muslim is ambiguous until Powell makes it legible. Elsheba Khan is clearly a maternal figure, and her serenity embodies the sacrifice of mother Mary. But unlike Mary and some Muslim American women, she does not wear a veil. This stereotyped

21. Miller 1956.
22. Video with Platon in Pitney 2016.
23. Um 2012.

material sign of Muslim femininity is absent, and it is Powell who makes it clear to his non-Muslim audience that she is mother of a Muslim son.

The setting, Arlington National Cemetery, was also important to Powell's interpretation of the photograph. His allusion to the presence of an Islamic star and crescent on Khan's gravestone and its implied nearness to the symbols of the Christian cross and Jewish Star of David established a solemn setting for his vision of a multicultural America. The crescent and the star proved that Muslims could be loyal to the United States, challenging the idea popular among some American voters that Muslims are inherently anti-American.

This is exactly what Kareem Khan had yearned for. Growing up in Manahawkin, New Jersey, so close to the fallen towers of 9/11, Khan had vowed to show the world that "not all Muslims were fanatics and that many, like him, were willing to lay down their lives for their country." This was no empty promise. As a high school freshman, he registered for Air Force Junior ROTC, or Reserve Officers' Training Corps, but he ended up enlisting in the US Army once he graduated from Southern Regional High School in 2005.[24]

For twenty-year-old Kareem Khan, military service was a way to prove that he belonged in and to America; it offered what Monnet calls "the promise of unassailable national credentials."[25] Ji-Young Um adds that such service "has an intimate connection to formal citizenship as well as to symbolic citizenship." As Um observes, military service often expedited pathways to citizenship after 9/11 as the US military sought to recruit native Arabic speakers and other linguists.[26] This connection between Muslim military service and US citizenship, both formal and informal, is one that dates to the Civil War. For foreign-born Muslims, World War I proved to be an important pathway to naturalized citizenship for hundreds, if not thousands of Muslims who might not have otherwise achieved it. In the 1920s, Arab American leaders, both Christians and Muslims, emphasized their service and their support of war bonds during World War I as proof of their contributions to the nation.[27]

As Kareem Khan knew, however, the ultimate proof of belonging to the nation is the willingness to die in battle – and in turn to kill others "for the sake of its self-preservation."[28] During his deployment in Iraq, his favorite movies were reported to be "Letters from Iwo Jima" and "Saving Private Ryan." Both of these films arguably depict the cruelties of war as redemptive

---

24. Mathur 2007.
25. Monnet 2012, 10.
26. Um 2012.
27. Curtis 2016.
28. Monnet 2012, 3.

or at the very least honorable, linking the fate of the nation – one Japanese, the other American – to the brotherhood that exists among military service personnel and their willingness to sacrifice to save a fellow soldier, sailor, or marine. Like those service members, Kareem Khan was stationed on the front lines. His job was to go house to house looking for insurgents. A member of the 1st Battalion, 23rd Infantry Regiment, 3rd Brigade, 2nd Infantry Division, also known as Stryker Brigade Combat Team, Khan sent emails to his family that expressed a deep commitment to the mission. On August 6, 2007, he was killed when a bomb exploded as he was attempting to clear a house in Baquba.[29]

Kareem Khan was an outsider who was symbolically incorporated into the American body politic as he was laid to rest in Arlington National Cemetery and memorialized by Colin Powell. But this was not the end of the story. The myth of the fallen Muslim American military member was no passing symbol in the post-9/11 era. Khan's memorialization as a fallen son mourned by his mother and a nation became a sign that was deployed again in the election of 2016. Oddly, the last name of the soldier was once again Khan. But this time around, the mythmaking was even more prominent on the national stage, and revealed not only the power of the myth but also its limitations to achieve national unity.

Captain Humayun Khan and the Election of 2016

On the final night of the Democratic National Convention in Philadelphia, Pennsylvania, Muslim American parents, Khizr and Ghazala Khan, took the stage at a dramatic moment. Attorney Khizr Khan would deliver the convention's closing argument for Hillary Clinton's campaign. The Khans were given a prime spot in the convention, appearing immediately before Chelsea Clinton, the candidate's daughter, introduced her mother as the party's official candidate for the presidency. As Khan faced thousands in the crowd and millions of viewers at home, an image of their fallen son, Army Captain Humayun Saqib Muazzam Khan (1976–2004) was shown on a large screen behind them. They both wore blue, the traditional color of the Democratic Party.

Khizr Khan's speech reiterated the myth of the fallen Muslim American military member and its symbolic centrality to American nationalism in the post-9/11 era. Introducing himself and Ghazala as "patriotic American Muslims with undivided loyalty to our country," he expressed his gratitude for the opportunities that the nation had provided to his three children. He also signaled his willingness to accept that his son had to die so that others might live. Humayun, he said, put aside his own dreams "the day he sacrificed his

29. Spoto and Woolley 2007.

life to save the lives of his fellow soldiers." Khan expressed his gratitude that Hillary Clinton had noticed his sacrifice: "Hillary Clinton was right," he said, "when she called my son 'the best of America.'" Clinton had made a point in earlier campaign speeches of holding up the willing sacrifice of twenty-seven year-old Humayun Khan, a Muslim American, as exemplary.[30]

Capt. Khan's death was indeed selfless. The soldiers under his command in the 1st Infantry 201st Forward Support Battalion were charged with guarding the gates of Forward Operating Base Warhorse in eastern Iraq. Over 1,000 Iraqis worked at the base as civilian employees. The beginning and end of their work shifts were dangerous since some Iraqi rebels would exploit these opportunities to attack the base with car bombs. Captain Khan's unit had mistakenly shot some Iraqi drivers whom they thought to be insurgents, and Khan was determined to reduce needless casualties while also protecting those under his command. He was willing to work even on his days off, including on June 8, 2004. That day, he saw a suspicious taxi making its ways through the serpentine barriers in front of the base entrance. He commanded his soldiers to back off and to get down. Khan signaled to the driver to stop. He approached the car. A bomb went off, killing him, two insurgents, and two Iraqi civilians. Posthumously awarded both a Bronze Star and Purple Heart, Khan was laid to rest in Arlington National Cemetery in a ceremony that included Islamic funeral prayers.[31]

As he interpreted his son's death for a national audience in 2016, Khizr Khan evoked the sacred ground in which his son's body had been laid to rest. He accused Donald Trump of profaning a holy place, asking rhetorically, "Have you ever been to Arlington Cemetery?" If he had, said Khan, he would have seen "the graves of brave patriots who died defending the United States of America. You will see all faiths, genders, and ethnicities." This discussion of Arlington is another indication of the mythmaking involved in memorializing the war dead, as it appeals to the sacred power of the nation's most sacred cemetery. Military cemeteries evidence the power of blood sacrifice to save the nation, as Abraham Lincoln argued when he dedicated the cemetery at Gettysburg: "we have come to dedicate a portion of this field as a final resting place for those who here gave their lives that this nation might live." As Monnet points out, Lincoln "articulated one of the most enigmatic paradoxes of national identity: namely, that it is strengthened by the lives that are lost in its name." For the nation, it was a "new birth."[32] Khan's

30. K. Khan 2016.
31. The account above is based on Ryan 2016 and Pitard 2016.
32. Monnet 2012, 3–4.

evocation of his son's final resting place both renewed the power of this myth and attempted to use it as a political weapon.

Trump violated the national faith in another way, according to Khan. If Donald Trump were successful in banning Muslims from immigrating to the country, Khan said, the nation would be deprived of those willing to sacrifice for it. Trump's prejudice rested on his own ignorance of or blatant disregard of the nation's holy text, the Constitution. Khan scolded Trump for his ignorance: "Let me ask you," he said, "have you ever read the US Constitution? I will gladly lend you my copy." Naming Trump as an American who had shirked the duty of blood sacrifice for the nation, he told Trump that "you have sacrificed nothing and no one." And he concluded by asking fellow Americans, immigrants, and Muslims "to honor the sacrifice of my son" by voting for Hillary Clinton.[33]

Rather than addressing any of the substantive issues raised by Khizr Khan's speech, Donald Trump insulted Ghazala Khan, who had not spoken at the convention:

> "If you look at his wife," Trump told George Stephanopoulos of ABC News, "she was standing there. She had nothing to say. She probably—maybe she wasn't allowed to say. You tell me. But plenty of people have written that. She was extremely quiet. And it looked like she had nothing to say.[34]

In other words, according to Trump, Ghazala Khan was another oppressed Muslim woman whose husband had denied her the chance to speak.

In response, Hillary Clinton's campaign accused Trump of dishonoring a Gold Star family, and even some Republicans criticized Trump for his lack of respect. One of them was retired Major General Dana J. H. Pitard, Captain Khan's senior officer. "My family has been Republican ever since my maternal grandparents migrated from Jim Crow South Carolina to Philadelphia in the late 1920s," he stated. But party shouldn't matter when it comes to respecting the Khan family's sacrifice. "I join all those who stand in support of the Khan family. This family is our family, and any attack on this wonderful American Gold Star family is an attack on all patriotic and loyal Americans who have sacrificed to make our country great." For General Pitard, the Khans were off limits. "Any politically or racially motivated attack on the Khans is despicable and un-American."[35]

33. K. Khan 2016.
34. ABC News 2016.
35. Pitard 2016.

Ghazala Khan herself also spoke out to reject Trump's insult. In a *Washington Post* op-ed she explained why she decided not to speak at the convention:

> Every day I feel the pain of his loss. It has been 12 years, but you know hearts of pain can never heal as long as we live. Just talking about it is hard for me all the time. Every day, whenever I pray, I have to pray for him, and I cry. The place that emptied will always be empty. I cannot walk into a room with pictures of Humayun. For all these years, I haven't been able to clean the closet where his things are—I had to ask my daughter-in-law to do it. Walking onto the convention stage, with a huge picture of my son behind me, I could hardly control myself. What mother could? Donald Trump has children whom he loves. Does he really need to wonder why I did not speak?[36]

Just as Platon's photograph presented Elsheba Khan as a maternal figure who mourned her son by silently embracing his tombstone, Ghazala Khan discussed her own mourning in maternal terms. Because of her motherly grief, Mrs. Khan said, she was unable to speak at the convention. Instead, she offered a silent witness, standing next to her husband, testifying to her devotion.

Strangely perhaps, Donald Trump also remained silent about the incident after his initial response. Such silence can be interpreted in a variety of ways. For one, some members of the military and veterans, including Republicans, found Trump's comments to be at the least distasteful. But it is also tempting to conclude that, for Trump, there was nothing more to say because he found the symbolic blood sacrifice of Muslim service members to be meaningless. It did not gel with his myth of America. Trump's vision of making American great again did not include the multicultural liberal consensus that Clinton was reiterating. He did not seek to include Muslims in the body politic; his policy of a ban on Muslim immigration sought to keep them out.

Though Trump remained silent about Humayun Khan during the fall, some partisans developed a more robust critique of the use of this fallen Muslim soldier as part of Clinton's campaign. One was *Drudge Report* staffer and *Breitbart News* contributor Charles Hurt, who claimed that Hillary Clinton's campaign had tricked Khizr Khan. Her "campaign was all too eager to take advantage of him and his family," he wrote. Hurt acknowledged that Khizr Khan was a "fine American and the father of a true American patriot." But Khan shared some of the blame for "allowing his dead son to be used

36. G. Khan 2016.

for the most hideous of purposes and dragged through the gutter of nasty and dishonest partisan politics." This was a telling line, as Hurt attempted to wrest the use of Humayun Khan's sacred memory from the Clinton campaign by claiming that it was Clinton's politicization of Khan's story that had profaned his service. "For just about every American alive, Capt. Khan is an inspiring and unifying figure," he wrote, alluding once again to the power of blood sacrifice to unite the nation. "To Hillary Clinton, he is a tool to be used to divide people."[37] In aiming to describe Khizr Khan as Clinton's pawn, Hurt dismissed the agency and free will of Khan and adopted a patronizing attitude toward the Khan family.

While such criticism spoke only to Trump's partisans, Hurt opened up another line of attack that was more likely to score points with anti-war voters, including those who had voted for Senator Bernie Sanders in the Democratic Party primaries. "Perhaps a better testimony from Khizr Khan," Hurt proclaimed, "would have been for him to talk about how Hillary Clinton was in the US Senate when she voted to invade Iraq." Hurt rightly pointed to Hillary Clinton's vote for the Iraq war in 2003 as perhaps the most important vote of her political career. It made her vulnerable in the 2008 campaign for the US presidency, and her main rival, then-Senator Barack Obama, received support from many Democrats in part precisely because he had been against what eventually became an unpopular war. "It was her vote," wrote Hurt, "that sent Capt. Khan to his death."

However hyperbolic, Hurt's rhetoric identified what was the most important aspect of Hillary Clinton's inclusion of Humayun Khan in the myth of the American blood sacrifice. The nation *had* sent Khan to his death. But the Khan family demanded no apology. Instead, they sought public recognition of the sacrifice so that Muslims could be included in the body politic. Khan's death was sad, but for Hillary Clinton, it was not a tragedy. It sustained the national faith. In fact, as US secretary of state under President Obama, she continued to advocate for American leadership, a euphemism for American exceptionalism and US military intervention. She was one of the architects of the violent overthrow of Libyan dictator Muʻamar Qaddafi, and Clinton urged Obama to intervene more forcefully in the Syrian civil war to aid the rebels who were fighting both Bashar al-Assad and Daʻish, or the Islamic State. The fact that she was a female secretary of state added even more political significance to her advocacy of aggressive military interventions as she performed a feminist valorization of the military.[38]

In articulating this position, Clinton echoed support for the liberal

37. Hurt 2016.
38. For context, see further Khalid 2015.

religious consensus that had its roots in the Cold War. Starting with Republican President and former Allied Commander Dwight D. Eisenhower, US presidents have linked the country's religious freedom for all to the willingness of religious minorities to sacrifice their children in the nation's wars. Eisenhower and his vice-president, Richard M. Nixon, saw belief in God as central to the ideological struggle against Communism and its spread in the developing world. During this era, the words "under God" were added to the Pledge of Allegiance, and "In God we Trust" was adopted as the national motto. Drawing upon the central myth of American exceptionalism that began with Massachusetts Bay Colony, Eisenhower claimed that the whole system of American government "makes no sense unless it is founded on a deeply held religious belief, and I don't care what that is."[39] Rejecting the Christian confessionalism of Puritans and twentieth-century Christian fundamentalist doctrines, Eisenhower's Cold War ideology included Jews and Muslims and all others of "sincere religious belief" in his vision of America as freedom's defender. This is why Eisenhower attended the opening of the Islamic Center of Washington, DC, in 1957. "It is fitting that we re-dedicate ourselves to the peaceful progress of all men under one God," said Eisenhower during the visit. "I should like to assure you, my Islamic [Muslim] friends," the President said, "that under the American Constitution, under American tradition, and in American hearts, this Center, this place of worship is just as welcome as could be a similar edifice of any other religion."[40]

Beginning with the first Gulf War in 1991, US Presidents attempted to assure both domestic and foreign Muslim populations that US wars in Muslim lands were not religious crusades. President George W. Bush renewed that commitment by reenacting the Eisenhower visit to the Islamic Center in Washington, DC, on September 17, 2001. As Muslims were physically attacked and harassed in the wake of 9/11, Bush sought to restate the bargain that Eisenhower had struck. He drew a sharp line between terrorists and authentic Muslims, and he called on non-Muslims to recognize the contributions of Muslims to the United States: "America counts millions of Muslims amongst our citizens, and Muslims make an incredibly valuable contribution to our country," Bush said. "Muslims are doctors, lawyers, law professors, members of the military, entrepreneurs, shopkeepers, moms and dads. And they need to be treated with respect."[41]

39. Springs 2012, 39.

40. IIP Digital, "Eisenhower's 1957 Speech at Islamic Center of Washington," June 28, 1957, http://iipdigital.usembassy.gov/st/english/texttrans/2007/06/20070626154822lnkais0.6946985.html#axzz4IcvFMoOf.

41. "U.S. Presidential Visits to Domestic Mosques."

As many scholars have documented, however, there was a wide gulf between this rhetoric of inclusion and the ways in which Bush and then Obama administrative policies targeted Muslims as potential terrorists. Policies that stigmatized Muslims without any evidence of wrongdoing ranged from massive counter-intelligence operations and the "Countering Violent Extremism" program to proxy denaturalization, the National Security Entry-Exit Registration System, the detention facility at Guantanamo Bay, Cuba, and drone strikes.[42] Hillary Clinton was a champion of most of these policies, as Muslim Americans themselves were aware. Her strong opposition to the BDS movement (to boycott, divest from, and sanction Israel for its violations of Palestinian human rights) also alienated some Muslim voters. But in the end Donald Trump's explicit anti-Muslim prejudices made most Muslim Americans feel as if they had little choice: according to one exit poll, 74% of them voted for Clinton while 13% voted for Trump.[43]

As the 2016 campaign transitioned from the summer convention to the fall debates, an increasing number of Muslim American critics called out Hillary Clinton for seeing Muslims only in light of their value to national security. In all three debates Clinton framed Muslim Americans as "our eyes and ears on our front lines," leading writer Ismat Sarah Mangla to declare that "her framing of Muslims solely in terms of national security has an insidious effect in continuing to stigmatize them as something less than fully American." In the third debate, Clinton and Trump were asked about physical attacks on Muslims and other hate crimes. Trump responded by cautioning against political correctness in dealing with terrorism, which rearticulated his essential vision of the Muslim as terrorist, while Clinton once again said that Muslim Americans were on the front lines of fighting the war on terror. Activist Linda Sarsour tweeted that she was "tired of hearing how Muslims [a]r[e] only on front lines of fighting terrorism. What about front lines on immigrant rights, #BlackLivesMatter?" Writer Hussein Rashid was even more pointed: "@Hillary Clinton makes Muslims conditional citizens in America, It's standard GOP line. It would be nice to not be your toys." One of the funniest responses came from *St. Louis Post Dispatch* columnist Aisha Sultan: "It's weird how politicians keep telling me I'm on the front line of fighting terrorism when I'm just trying to get through a sugar detox."[44]

This sarcasm and the more sober criticisms exposed the limits of Hillary Clinton's mythmaking. But Clinton continued to put the Khans' story at the center of her campaign. In the final three weeks before the election, the campaign ran an emotional minute-long ad in seven battleground states

42. Cainkar 2009; Aaronson 2014; Malek 2011; and Human Rights Watch 2014.
43. Council on American-Islamic Relations 2016.
44. Mangla 2016.

that featured Khizr Khan. In the ad, Khan tells the story of his son's sacrifice. He looks wistfully at pictures of his son in uniform. He tells the audience that his son was a Muslim American. The ad then shows Donald Trump on the stump, and Khizr Khan says that he has a question for Mr. Trump. With tears in his eyes, he asks, "Would my son have a place in your America?"[45]

Competing Myths of US Political Belonging

After Trump's surprise victory in November and his two subsequent attempts to prevent Muslim immigrants and refugees from entering the nation via executive orders, it became clear that the mythic Humayun Khan would not have a place in Trump's America. As powerful as the myth of the fallen Muslim American soldier was for Americans who shared tears with Khan's father, the older myth of the Muslim beast, the unassimilable foreigner, would not be replaced in narratives of US communal formation. Keeping Muslims out of the nation both through mythmaking and policymaking remained at the center of US political life.

Scholars of religion and violence have offered several theories for why the myth of blood sacrifice fails to work, especially how it fails to unify a country.[46] In the case of Humayun Khan and Kareem Khan, and all those Muslims who have served in the US military since the Revolutionary War, attempts to make myth around the fallen Muslim soldier have gained in popularity since 9/11, but have not been successful vehicles for the establishment of an authoritative multicultural liberal consensus touted by Colin Powell and Hillary Clinton. Because the country is at war in Muslim lands, and because half the country believes it is at war with Islamic religion, this myth, as appealing as it may be, is not powerful enough to overshadow the myth of the Muslim beast.[47] Moreover, even as the liberal myth of incorporation seeks to uplift the sacrifice of Muslim Americans for the nation, it simultaneously casts Muslims as useful to the nation precisely because they come from and are intimately connected to the nation's foreign enemies. The domestication of these particular Muslim bodies – the "good" Muslims – ultimately flaunts the values of American lives over the lives of Muslim "others."

Perhaps the only way to put an end to the myths of Muslim monsters and partial incorporation alike is to end the war on terror or completely reimagine it as a different kind of policy challenge. Without some radical

---

45. "No Regrets, Trump Vows as Clinton Ad Targets His Criticism of Muslim-American Family" 2016.

46. Monnet 2012, 10–13.

47. Lopez 2016.

reshaping of this defining characteristic of US foreign policy in the twenty-first century, Muslims are likely to continue to serve, often against their own wishes, as the symbols in, and on, and through which the nation is contested and created. Since the nation remains a primary form of community-formation in the contemporary world, sacrificing one's blood in battle for one's country will likely continue to be narrated in mythic ways.

Such mythologizing is not itself immoral. The questions in the case of the myth of the fallen Muslim soldier are: What policies does such myth-making inspire and justify? Who benefits and who suffers? In the twenty-first century, the victims of direct US military invasion and covert military operations often happen to be Muslim. They suffer as a result of the national commitment to a preponderance of global power and the nation's assumption that terrorism is an existential threat to its empire.[48] The US empire may have reached its limits, but the approximately 800 US military bases outside the United States along with its other military assets insure the country's superior military power.[49] Some resistance, including asymmetrical attacks from foreign Muslims who are affected by US military power, is likely. If Americans cannot find less violent means to deal with this resistance, the cycle of anti-Muslim racism is unlikely to end. For some, the detention, surveillance, torture, and mass killing of Muslim bodies is a necessary price paid for American empire. For other Americans, the political and economic and moral costs of global dominance are too high. In either case, the deaths of US Muslim military members can have limited symbolic utility as the nation remains divided over the question of who can – and must – be sacrificed for its unity.

48. For the origins of this policy, see Leffler 1992.
49. For a critique of contemporary U.S. military power, see, for example, Vine 2015.

Works Cited

Aaronson, T. 2014. *The Terror Factory: Inside the FBI's Manufactured War on Terrorism*. New York.

ABC News. 2016. Transcript of *This Week*, July 31. http://abcnews.go.com/Politics/week-transcript-donald-trump-vice-president-joe-biden/story?id=41020870.

Abdul Khabeer, S., A. Ali, E. Alsultany, S. Daulatzai, L. Deeb, C. Fadda, Z. Grewal, J. Hammer, N. Naber, and J. Rana. N.d. "Islamophobia is Racism." #IslamophobiaIsRacism Syllabus. https://islamophobiaisracism.wordpress.com.

Appadurai, A. 1996. *Modernity at Large: Cultural Dimensions of Globalization.* Minneapolis.

Ayoob, M. 2007. *The Many Faces of Political Islam: Religion and Politics in the Muslim World.* Ann Arbor.

Basch, L., N. G. Schiller, and C. S. Blanc. 1994. *Nations Unbound: Transnational Projects, Postcolonial Predicaments and Deterritorialized Nation-States.* Amsterdam.

Cainkar, L. A. 2009. *Homeland Insecurity: The Arab American and Muslim American Experience after 9/11.* New York.

Cavanaugh, W. T. 2009. *The Myth of Religious Violence: Secular Ideology and the Roots of Modern Conflict.* New York.

Council on American-Islamic Relations. 2016. "CAIR Releases Results of Presidential Election Exit Poll," November 22. https://www.cair.com/press-center/press-releases/13909-for-the-record-cair-releases-results-of-presidential-election-exit-poll.html.

Curtis IV, E. 2016. *Muslim Americans in the Military: Centuries of Service.* Bloomington.

Ernst, C., ed. 2013. *Islamophobia in America: The Anatomy of Intolerance.* New York.

Gottschalk, P. and G. Greenberg. 2008. *Islamophobia: Making the Muslims the Enemy.* Lanham, MD.

Hannerz, U. 1996. *Transnational Connections: Culture, People, Places.* London.

Human Rights Watch. 2014. "Illusions of Justice: Human Rights Abuses in US Terrorism Prosecutions." http://www.law.columbia.edu/sites/default/files/microsites/human-rights-institute/files/final_report_-_illusion_of_justice.pdf.

Hurt, C. 2016. "Khizr Khan Was Tricked Into Smearing Donald Trump." *The Hill,* July 31. http://thehill.com/blogs/pundits-blog/presidential-campaign/289932-khizer-khan-was-tricked-into-smearing-donald-trump.

Khalid, M. 2015. "Feminist Perspectives on Militarism and War." In *The Oxford Handbook of Transnational Feminist Movements*, edited by R. Baksh and W. Harcourts, 632–650. New York.

Khan, G. 2016. "Trump Criticized My Silence. He Knows Nothing About Me." *Washington Post,* July 31. https://www.washingtonpost.com/opinions/ghazala-khan-donald-trump-criticized-my-silence-he-knows-nothing-about-true-sacrifice/2016/07/31/c46e52ec-571c-11e6-831d-0324760ca856_story.html?utm_term=.75c560621304.

Khan, K. 2016. "Speech to the 2016 Democratic National Convention." ABC News, August 1. http://abcnews.go.com/Politics/full-text-khizr-khans-speech-2016-democratic-national/story?id=41043609.

Kidd, T. S. 2013. *American Christians and Islam: Evangelical Culture and Muslims from the Colonial Period to the Age of Terrorism.* Princeton, NJ.

Leffler, M. P. 1992. *A Preponderance of Power: National Security, the Truman Administration, and the Cold War.* Stanford.

Lincoln, B. 2014. *Discourse and the Construction of Society: Comparative Studies of Myth, Ritual, and Classification.* 2nd ed. New York.

Lopez, G. 2016. "Polls Show Many—Even Most—Trump Supporters Deeply Hostile to Muslims and Nonwhites." *Vox*, September 12. http://www.vox.com/2016/9/12/12882796/trump-supporters-racist-deplorables.

Malek, A. 2011. *Patriot Acts: Narratives of Post-9/11 Injustice.* San Francisco.

Mandaville, P. 2004. *Transnational Muslim Politics: Reimagining the Umma.* London.

Mangla, I. S. 2016. "Hillary Clinton Has an Unfortunate Way of Talking about American Muslims," October 20. https://qz.com/814438/presidential-debate-hillary-clinton-contributes-to-anti-muslim-bias-in-the-way-she-talks-about-american-muslims.

Marvin, C. and D. W. Ingle. 1996. "Blood Sacrifice and the Nation: Revisiting Civil Religion." *Journal of the American Academy of Religion* 64.4:767–780.

Mathur, S. L. 2007. "Blast Kills Jersey Shore GI." *South Jersey Courier Post*, August 10. Reproduced in "Kareem Rashad Sultan Khan," Arlington National Cemetery Website. http://www.arlingtoncemetery.net/krkhan.htm.

McAlister, M. 2001. *Epic Encounters: Culture, Media, and U.S. Interests in the Middle East, 1945–2000.* Berkeley.

Miller, P. 1956. *Errand into the Wilderness.* Cambridge, MA.

Monnet, A. S. 2012. "War and National Renewal: Civil Religion and Blood Sacrifice in American Culture." *European Journal of American Studies* 7.2:1–17.

NBC News. 2008. *Meet the Press*, October 19. http://www.nbcnews.com/id/27266223/#.V7tAnWUUgkc.

"No Regrets, Trump Vows as Clinton Ad Targets His Criticism of Muslim-American Family." 2016. *Chicago Tribune*, October 21. http://www.chicagotribune.com/news/nationworld/politics/ct-trump-clinton-campaign-20161021-story.html.

Owen, W. 1921 (online: n.d.). "Dulce et Decorum Est." *Poetry Foundation.* https://www.poetryfoundation.org/poems/46560/dulce-et-decorum-est.

Pitard, D. J. J. 2016. "I Was Capt. Khan's Commander in Iraq." *Washington Post*, August 3. https://www.washingtonpost.com/opinions/i-was-capt-khans-commander-in-iraq-the-khan-family-is-our-family/2016/08/03/9a4c0e4e-598f-11e6–9aee-8075993d73a2_story.html?postshare=6761470256574118&tid=ss_tw&utm_term=.7bcb67329e00.

Pitney, N. 2016. "Why Colin Powell's Emotional Obama Endorsement Is Going Viral Again." *Huffington Post*, August 5. http://www.huffingtonpost.com/entry/colin-powell-khan-photograph_us_57a3aebce4b021fd98781442.

Rana, J. 2007. "The Story of Islamophobia." *Souls* 9.2:148–161.

Ryan, M. 2016. "Capt. Humayun Khan, Whose Grieving Parents Have Been Criticized by Trump, Was 'An Officer's Soldier.'" *Washington Post*, August 2. https://www.washingtonpost.com/news/checkpoint/wp/2016/08/02/slain-army-captain-at-center-of-political-storm-was-a-soldiers-officer.

Selod, S. 2014. "Citizenship Denied: The Racialization of Muslim American Men and Women Post-9/11." *Critical Sociology* 41.1:77–95.

Smith, J. Z. 1995. "Myth." In *HarperCollins Dictionary of Religion*, edited by J. Z. Smith, 749–751. New York.

Spoto, M. and W. Woolley. 2007. "Ocean GI Is State's 80th Casualty." *New Jersey Star Ledger*, August 10. Reproduced in nj.com. http://blog.nj.com/njwardead/2007/08/army_spc_kareem_r_khan_august.html.

Springs, J. 2012. "Civil Religion." In *Religion and Culture: Contemporary Practices and Perspectives*, edited by R. Hecht and V. Biondo III, 29–46. Minneapolis.

Um, J. 2012. "Citizen and Terrorist, Citizen as Terrorist." *Postmodern Culture* 22.3, May. https://muse.jhu.edu/article/503686https://muse.jhu.edu/article/503686.

"U.S. Presidential Visits to Domestic Mosques." N.d. White House Historical Association. https://www.whitehousehistory.org/press-room/press-fact-sheets/u-s-presidential-visits-to-domestic-mosques.

Vine, D. 2015. *Base Nation: How U.S. Military Bases Abroad Harm America and the World*. New York.

Part Two

Anti-Muslim Politics

Muslim Presence: Anti-Muslim Politics in the United States and the Rise of Muslim American Culture

Salah D. Hassan

IN THE YEARS since September 11, public hostility toward Muslims in the United States appears to have increased in direct relation to increased public displays of Muslimness. Or perhaps the inverse is the case: expressions of Muslimness have become more public in the face of an unbridled vilification of Muslims and Islam. Confident displays of Muslimness – for instance, in the ever-rising number of new mosques, or the many women who wear *hijab*, or the mainstreaming of *halal* foods – are affirmations of an American Islam that has historic roots and has now manifest its presence despite the still very small numbers of Muslims residing in the United States. But it would be a mistake to interpret as cultural acceptance these and other public displays of Muslimness, which are also targets of anti-Muslim organizations. The anti-Muslim politics of organizations such as Jihad Watch, the American Freedom Defense Initiative, and the Center for Security Policy circulate widely, shaping the prevailing national discourse on Muslims, conditioning public opinion, and influencing US domestic and foreign policies.

This chapter identifies anti-Muslim politics as a core component of contemporary US national culture, which is beset by the irreconcilable tension between the founding principle of religious and cultural pluralism and a widespread and historic antipathy towards Muslims and Islam. On the one hand, some Americans, among them Muslim Americans, seek to create a space for Islam within the national body politic by disassociating the religion and its practitioners from regional Islamist movements, such as al-Qaeda or Islamic State; from this perspective, suicide bombings and other forms of violence are the acts of "bad Muslims," who are described as aberrations and anti-Islamic. On the other hand, a powerful network of quasi-corporate entities has formulated and diffused a virulent anti-Muslim politics, which define Islam as the greatest existential threat to American society. Contemporary anti-Muslim politics advance the idea that Islam is engaged in a global jihad and has declared war on the United States. The implication is obvious: Islam is the enemy of the United States and all Muslims are suspect. I am interested in providing a modest outline of the map of anti-

Muslim politics, which gained renewed traction with the election of Obama in 2008, whose identity became the subject of conspiracy theories, declaring that the first black president was a crypto-Muslim.[1] And when Donald Trump entered the White House, anti-Muslims became a controversial feature of the administration when the newly elected president attempted to pass the infamous Muslim Ban executive order.

In many respects, anti-Muslim politics in the twenty-first century are not new; rather it is grounded in the continuation, reassertion, and intensification of a discourse that was already well established by the US media, "experts" and policy makers in the 1970s. As Edward Said argued initially in a 1980 *Nation* article titled "Islam through Western Eyes" (and more substantially in his 1981 book *Covering Islam*),

> [f]ar from attempting to refine, or even dissent from, the gross image
> of Islam as a threat, the intellectual and policy community in the
> United States has considerably enforced and concentrated the [media]
> image ... "Islam" means the end of civilization as "we" know it. Islam
> is anti-human, antidemocratic, anti-Semitic, antirational.

Said's analysis focused on a consistently crude representation of Islam, which provided simplistic explanations for complicated US foreign policy issues. He explained that the 1979 Iranian Revolution, the 1979 Soviet occupation of Afghanistan, and the 1978 Camp David Accords between Israel and Egypt were translated into a reductive "cleavage separating good Moslems from bad." Framed by US Cold War strategic interests, the "good Moslems" of that era, like Egypt's Anwar Sadat, Pakistan's General Zia ul-Haq, and the Afghan Mujahedeen, were anti-Communist, embraced Western values, and served US foreign policy in the Middle East, while "bad Moslems" – Said mentions Iran's Ayatollah Khomeini, Libya's Colonel Mu'amar Qaddafi, the Saudi oil minister Sheik Ahmad Zaki Yamani, and Palestinian terrorists – are "portrayed as backward fanatics."[2]

Despite the collapse of the Soviet Union and George H. W. Bush's 1991 declaration of a post-cold war "New World Order," one can trace a virtually unbroken line of anti-Muslim politics from the 1970s to early 2000s. Mahmood Mamdani argues in his 2002 *American Anthropologist* essay "Good Muslim, Bad Muslim" that the association of Islam with terrorism is a defining trope of twenty-first century US "culture talk," which turns "religious experience into a political category."[3] Mamdani's 2004 book *Good Muslim,*

1. Bailey 2015.
2. Said 1980.
3. Mamdani 2002, 766.

Bad Muslim[4] elaborates further his assertions that contemporary culture talk presents Islam as essentially impervious to democracy and anti-modern.[5]

Edward Said in the early 1980s and Mahmood Mamdani twenty years later exposed how cultural claims about Islam and Muslims have served to underwrite and justify US foreign policy in the Middle East. Even as conditions in the region change, the structuring of anti-Muslim politics in terms of good Muslim/bad Muslim continues to provide a policy rationale in the present. This last point was illustrated on January 27, 2017, only a week after Donald Trump's inauguration as president, when he followed up his anti-Muslim campaign rhetoric by signing an executive order entitled "Protecting the Nation from Foreign Terrorist Entry into the United States." The executive order, which came to be known as "the Muslim travel ban" because it sought to bar citizens from seven Muslim-majority countries – i.e. "bad Muslims" – from entering the United States, provoked protests and was initially almost blocked by US Federal Court judges in the Ninth and Fourth Circuits. While the public protests were a response of anti-Trump activists, who saw the anti-Muslim executive order as an opportunity to expose the intolerant character of the new administration, the decisions of the courts represented the reaffirmation of liberal rights in the face of an authoritarianism that violated the First Amendment. The initial public and legal opposition to the executive order must be interpreted as a minor challenge to Trump's authority rather than as a definitive defeat of anti-Muslim politics in the United States, which persist in various forms. After all, In June 2017, the US Supreme Court agreed to hear the government's case in defense of the revised executive order targeting Muslim travelers to the US. In any case, the very idea that the administration would impose a "Muslim travel ban" underscores the centrality of anti-Muslims politics in the contemporary United States.

In contrast with Trump's anti-Muslim and xenophobic executive order, the 2017 Academy Awards sought to correct its history of racial exclusions and celebrated in unprecedented fashion the creative successes of Muslims. An Iranian film, *The Salesman* directed by Asghar Farhadi, won the Oscar in the category of Best Foreign Language Film. Farhadi did not attend the award ceremony, declaring his solidarity with Muslim immigrants in his

4. The titles of Mamdani's essay and book are a paraphrase of a line in Said's 1980 *Nation* article.

5. Mamdani 2004, 11. Mamdani also notes in the introduction to the book that Islamist political violence, notably the al-Qaeda attack on the World Trade Center and the Pentagon, needs to be understood "first and foremost as the unfinished business of the Cold War," (13) and in doing so suggests powerful connections across the historic dividing line of September 11, 2001.

acceptance speech, which Anousheh Ansari delivered on his behalf: "My absence is out of respect for the people in my country and those of the other six nations whom have been disrespected by the inhumane law that bans entry of immigrants to the U.S."[6] But possibly more culturally significant, if less politically oppositional, was Mahershala Ali's Oscar in the category of Best Actor in a Supporting Role for his performance in *Moonlight*. Ali is the first Muslim actor to receive an Academy Award and was greeted with enthusiastic cheering and applause as he took the stage. However, even in the context of an Academy Awards show seeking to undo a long history of racism, the othering of a Muslim American black actor became a revealing side story when host Jimmy Kimmel joked about the unique name Mahershala. The name may be easily misidentified as Muslim when attached to an actor whose last name is Ali, even though it is derived from the biblical name Maher-shalal-hash-baz, which appears in Isaiah 7 of the Hebrew Bible. Kimmel's playful mocking of Mahershala Ali did not appear to offend the actor, who avoided criticism of Trump's anti-Muslim and anti-immigrant politics in his acceptance speech, unlike the host of the award show and Farhadi and other actors who took the stage, using the public occasion to denounce Trump's racist policies.

The Oscar's recognition of Asghar Farhadi's film and Mahershala Ali's acting are two recent examples of the increased Muslim presence in the US public sphere. And during the last decade, numerous other Muslim actors, stand-up comedians, musicians, filmmakers, artists, and writers have established national reputations and attracted unprecedented media attention, defying anti-Muslim politics.[7] Without diminishing the accomplishments of Muslim artists, the celebration of the artistic achievements of individual Muslims symbolically confirms the pluralistic values of the United States without undermining anti-Muslim politics that perpetuate a culture of suspicion about ordinary Muslims, many of whom are subject to surveillance, physical assaults, verbal harassment, and ridicule.

One of the fundamental themes of the current anti-Muslim politics is the claim that the culture of Muslims and/or Arabs, often collapsed into the same undifferentiated racial formation, is necessarily antithetical to Americanness. A June 2014 Zogby poll of American attitudes toward Muslims and Arabs found that between 2010 and 2014,

6. Oscar 2017 Winner Speech.

7. Consider, for example, John Burnett's National Public Radio report "In Hollywood, The Actor Who Gives The Call To Prayer," Steven Levingston's *Washington Post* article "Ayad Akhtar: On Muslim identity, and life in America," and Katrease Stafford's *Detroit Free Press* article "U-M Arabic poetry translator wins 'genius' grant."

there has been continued erosion in the favorable ratings given to both communities, posing a threat to the rights of Arab Americans and American Muslims. Favorable attitudes have continued to decline – from 43% in 2010 to 32% in 2014 for Arabs; and from 35% in 2010 to 27% in 2014 for Muslims.

The poll also shows that a "growing percentage of Americans say that they lack confidence in the ability of individuals from either community [Arab or Muslim] to perform their duties as Americans should they be appointed to an important government position" and that a "significant number of Americans (42%) support the use of profiling by law enforcement against Arab Americans and American Muslims."[8] The language and results of the poll indicate a correlation between the generalized antipathy ("erosion of favorable rating") toward Muslims and Arabs and a widespread willingness to limit or violate their civil rights.

Since 2011, Pamela Geller's American Freedom Defense Initiative ads on public transportation in New York City, San Francisco, and other cities around the United States have been among the most controversial anti-Muslim provocations. One of Geller's first bus ads stridently calls on Americans to oppose Islam: "In any war between the civilized man and the savage, support the civilized man. Defend America. Defeat Jihad."[9] Here Jihad operates synecdochally, a part standing in for the whole of Islam, which is by allusion defined as savagery. Echoing in the twenty-first century a central trope of nineteenth-century imperial discourse, Geller's ad bluntly equates Islam with uncontrollable violence ("savagery"). In the current context, anti-Muslim politics have taken on a particularly virulent tone that positions Muslims as an ideological wedge issue; Geller's ads and other public insults to Islam inflame hostility toward Muslims, whose assertions of their religious, cultural, or political values in US public life become the targets of anti-Muslim actions, as exemplified by the odd spectacle of Reverend Terry Jones's burning of a Quran. From the perspective of Muslims in the United States, Geller's ads are a form of hate-speech: the words are an act of violence directed at the group (that is, Muslims or anybody mistaken for a Muslim) and aim to intimidate its members, to make them feel unwelcome, to undermine their sense of belonging.

Anti-Muslim politics operate as a cover for domestic political alignments that can be viewed as the extreme right-wing edge of existing US foreign policy, as is evident in the configuration and alignment of anti-Muslim orga-

8. "American Attitudes Toward Arabs and Muslims" 2014.
9. For a news report on the ad controversy, see Mackey 2012.

nizations led by ideologically conservative writers and media personalities, such as Frank Gaffney at the Center for Security Policy, Robert Spencer at Jihad Watch, and Brigitte Gabriel at ACT! for America. These organizations have elaborated the position that Muslims are not merely a foreign-policy concern but constitute the major contemporary threat to US national security. Claiming expertise in security, Islamic terrorism, and Middle East foreign affairs, they promote policies restricting the freedoms of Muslims in the US, arguing that draconian measures are justifiable and necessary to prevent a Muslim takeover of the United States ("stealth *jihad*"). Quoting an interview with Frank Gaffney conducted at the offices of the Center for Security Policy, Jonathan Kay explains the scope of this American anti-Muslim conspiratorial culture: "Gaffney then ticked off a long list of [Obama] foreign-policy decisions he disagreed with, and cited them as evidence for what he's previously called an 'obvious and worrying pattern of official US submission to Islam and the theo-political-legal program the latter's [i.e Islam's] authorities call sharia.'"[10]

Organizations like Gaffney's Center for Security Policy, working in cohort with Jihad Watch, ACT! for America, and others, all of which are identified by the Southern Poverty Law Center as part of the "Anti-Muslim Inner Circle,"[11] recklessly spread misinformation about Islamic religious beliefs at the center of which are conspiracies about a Muslim takeover of the United States. Largely ideological and incoherent, these groups at times appeal to liberal principles of free speech, human rights and freedom of religion, and at the same time are aligned with neoconservative political forces, with linkages to anti-Muslim zealots in the Republican party, represented by politicians such as Peter King and Michele Bachmann, and right-wing Christians headed by the likes of Pat Robertson and Jerry Falwell Jr., the president of Liberty University, not to mention the more dubious figure of Reverend Terry Jones. Anti-Muslim organizations also are ardent defenders of Israel, which is positioned as a frontline state in the battle against Islamic terrorism, for example by the David Horowitz Freedom Center. I return below in more detail to the Horowitz Freedom Center and the linkage between anti-Muslim politics and attacks on Palestine solidarity advocacy.

These groups reduce the complexities of regional politics – whether in connection with Iraq, Iran, or Israel, or with al-Qaeda, the Muslim Brotherhood, or Hamas – to a singular view of political Islam, which produces an ideologically effective, if intellectually erroneous, conflation of Muslim and Arab, Iran and Hamas, Saddam Hussein and Osama bin Laden. At the center

10. Kay 2012.
11. See Steinback 2011.

of the discourse is the rather blunt assertion that Islam – often associated with a variety of Middle Eastern political figures – is inherently a religion of terror, aspiring to global domination. While the names have changed, the tropes of anti-Muslim politics today are the same as those elaborated in the 1970s and 1980s.

Since the Arab Spring of 2011, the political landscape has become even more complex, as the initial hopes for democratic reforms gave way to growing instability and ruinous civil wars in which Islamist political movements have emerged as one of the forces of opposition to US hegemony in the region. The fall of regimes in some countries has witnessed the rise to power of Islamic political parties, notably in Egypt with the election and then the overthrow of the Muslim Brotherhood. The civil war in Syria and constant crisis in Iraq contributed to the rise of the Islamic State (IS) and an exceedingly complex war across the borders of both countries in 2014. These historically significant events across the Arab region, from North Africa to the Persian Gulf, had little impact on the anti-Muslim discourse in the United States, which has merely incorporated Islamic State and the Muslim Brotherhood into its exaggerated rhetoric: "Every jihadist act in America ('terrorism') in recent memory can be linked to a Muslim Brotherhood organization which radicalized, prepared, or supported jihadis."[12] The rise of the Islamic State in Iraq and Syria and its particularly violent seizure of Mosul and the surrounding area in the summer of 2014 provided yet another opportunity to equate Islam with an inherent atavistic violence that poses a threat to the United States. While these anti-Muslim positions echo the negative image of Islam in the context of the Cold War, the political discourse has been re-scripted for the post-September 11 era.

A central feature of the anti-Muslim politics is the model inspired by Israel's bellicose approach to Hamas in the Gaza Strip. In an editorial titled "Netanyahu's ISIS Moral Clarity," published by the David Horowitz's Freedom Center, Joseph Klein writes,

> Whatever name they go by, whether it is ISIS, Hamas, al-Qaeda, Boko Haram, al-Shabab, Hezbollah, Islamic Jihad or the Islamic Republic of Iran that supports some of these groups and others, they all represent an indivisible threat to global peace, security and individual liberties. They are, in short, part of a common enemy.[13]

---

12. Thin Blue Line Project 2013. The Thin Blue Line Project is part of Gabriel's Act! For America and claims to provide training and education in counter-terrorism that is "designed by law enforcement for law enforcement."

13. Klein 2014.

In the interest of representing a global threat, Klein effaces the many contextual and tactical differences between the groups, differences that are especially evident in the contrasts between Hamas and Boko Haram, or al-Shabab and Hezbollah. But perhaps more important is the invocation of Netanyahu's policies toward the Palestinians as a model for US foreign policy. By invoking Israel's response to Hamas in Gaza, Klein collapses the Palestinian national struggle into the broader war against Muslim militant movements.

This rhetorical move is connected to the Horowitz Center's attack on Palestinian human rights advocates, especially those calling for boycott, divestment, and sanctions (BDS) against Israel, as is illustrated in the Center's glossy poster and social media campaign targeting pro-BDS students and faculty. The carefully crafted posters seek to delegitimate Palestine solidarity in general and BDS in particular by linking them simultaneously to anti-Semitism and to Islamic militancy. By connecting BDS to Hamas and more broadly to terrorism, the Horowitz Center mobilizes American hostility toward Palestinians and defense of Israel. The Horowitz Center poster campaign exposes the central place of anti-Muslim politics in the present moment to consolidating the United States-Israel special relationship and rolling back the successes of BDS, especially at a time when more and more Americans have expressed reservations about the America's unconditional support of Israel.[14]

Similarly, during the election campaign, Trump deployed anti-Muslim politics as a wedge issue, playing on the public fear and hostility toward Muslims. And as is transparently obvious, his anti-Muslim and anti-Arab and anti-Iranian executive order, like his anti-immigrant policies aimed at the further militarization of the US-Mexico border, are oriented toward externalizing domestic problems, such as public awareness of the growing income gap, police violence against people of color, and the defunding of public schools, or justifying misguided public policies, such as tax cuts for the wealthy and increased military spending. Simultaneously indulging the xenophobia of many Americans and inciting hatred of "foreigners," some of Trump's most high-profile policies take aim at Muslims and Mexicans, easy targets whose difference unsettles Anglo-Christian definitions of the United States.

With some noteworthy exceptions, mainstream news reporting on the Middle East and Muslims in the United States provides a less extreme ver-

14. See, for example, the Brookings Report on the 2016 poll of "American Attitudes on the Israeli-Palestinian Conflict": https://www.brookings.edu/research/american-attitudes-on-the-israeli-palestinian-conflict.

sion of anti-Muslim politics but has a far greater capacity to influence US public opinion.[15] Even if it is difficult to assess precisely the role of the media in shaping public opinion,[16] representations of Islam and the Arab World have tended to reinforce the association of Arab Muslims with violence and terror, as is evident in the daily stream of war reporting about the Arab Middle East, which is only occasionally balanced by human interest stories about Muslims in the United States that often counter anti-Muslim bigotry and challenge normative Muslim American cultures. Muslims who make it into the news are either violent or somehow defy American expectations of what it means to be Muslim.[17]

Under such conditions, the visible presence of Muslims and Arabs, in public life and in the media, has generated a range of responses from sympathetic portrayals in the contemporary US mediascape to violence against Muslims and attacks on Mosques to anti-Islamophobia political awareness initiatives. For example, in response to the growing hostility toward Muslims in the United States, the American Civil Liberties Union launched the *Protecting the Religious Freedom of Muslims* project. The ACLU project suggests that a significant threat to US political life does not come from Muslim Americans but rather from the anti-Muslim assault, which undermines the ostensible foundations of US political culture: "Religious freedom is one of America's most fundamental liberties, and a central principle upon which our nation was founded." The online overview of *Protecting the Religious Freedom of Muslims* explains the motivation behind the project, which documents hundreds of cases of rights violations:

> Muslim communities in the U.S. have faced a disturbing wave
> of bigotry and outright hostility. From religiously motivated
> discrimination and attacks on existing and proposed Islamic
> centers to vicious rhetoric from presidential candidates, Muslims in
> America are being unfairly targeted simply for exercising their basic
> constitutional right to religious liberty.[18]

The advocacy efforts of the ACLU and other rights organizations on behalf of Muslims – sometimes in collaboration with the Council on American-Islamic

15. Gerges 82–83.

16. For an interesting attempt to understanding the important role of the media in forming public opinion on foreign policy, see M. Baum and P. Potter 2008.

17. See, for example, the *New York Times* articles by Sarah Khan, "A Muslim American's Homecoming: Cowboys, Country Music, Chapatis" (September 26, 2017), and Erik P. Piepenburg, "Pakistani-American from California Blazes a Gay Leather and Fetish Trail" (May 31, 2017).

18. Protecting the Religious Freedom of Muslims.

Relations (CAIR), American-Arab Anti-Discrimination Committee (ADC), Arab American Institute, and Muslim Public Affairs Council (MPAC) – are echoed in critiques of anti-Muslim politics published by alternative media sources such as *HuffPost* (formerly the *Huffington Post*), the *Daily Beast*, and *Counterpunch*. Working from distinct political positions but with a shared commitment to exposing anti-Muslim politics and securing a space for Muslims within US public life, this loose alignment of groups constitutes a counter-trend to the anti-Muslim organizations, but each has its own political motivations and constituencies. For instance, while the ACLU takes up a wide variety of issues, from religious freedom to reproductive rights, MPAC's mission is specifically focused on establishing "a vibrant Muslim American community that will enrich American society through promoting the Islamic values of mercy, justice, peace, human dignity, freedom, and equality for all."[19]

MPAC advocates Muslim American involvement in US public life through a strategy of Americanization, which connects Muslim religious difference with liberal democratic ideals and a US nationalist ethos. Nowhere is this more evident than in MPAC's *Safe Spaces Initiative: Tools for Developing Healthy Communities*, which makes available to leaders of mosques and Islamic centers

> a toolkit to address any signs of violent extremism. The strategies include a focus on awareness and dialogue in the broader community environment so that individuals on the fringe never find a receptive community or have any chance to go down a violent path. We all have a shared stake in keeping our nation and our communities safe from any threats.[20]

Even though MPAC's approach is distinct from law enforcement, and the *Safe Spaces Initiative* opposes the usage of terms like Islamic extremism or *jihadism*, the toolkit is motivated in the first place by a presumed presence "on the fringe" of "violent extremism" within mosque communities.

MPAC's focus on mosques is not analogous to the FBI's so-called "mosque outreach program" nor is it akin to the notorious NYPD mosque surveillance operations,[21] but the initiative is premised on the idea that American mosques are sites of extremist recruitment or organizing. But there is little significant evidence to support this assertion; conversely, there are numer-

19. "Our Vision."
20. Safe Spaces Initiative 3.
21. See, for example, Apuzzo and Goldman 2013.

ous documented cases in which mosques are in fact the targets of anti-Muslim hate crimes.[22] Existing mosques have been vandalized and the construction of new mosques has catalyzed malicious anti-Muslim protests. Katherine Pratt Ewing sees the controversies surrounding new mosque construction as "actually a sign Muslims are creating a permanent place for themselves in many areas of the United States."[23] In effect, mosques are among the most visible forms of public Islam in the United States and constitute historically the single most significant indicator of an enduring Muslim presence in the United States that will continue to grow in spite of a virulent anti-Muslim politics.

Rather than retreat from public view or totally assimilate to an acculturated secularism, many Muslim Americans have responded through cultural projects that stage an oppositional Muslimness that performs a critique of racial and religious hatred and is also aligned with anti-poverty, anti-sexist, and anti-homophobic movements. Linda Sarsour's central role in organizing the Women's March in January 2017 and her remarkable speech are perhaps among the most important recent examples of Muslims taking the stage. But over the last ten years or more, performances by many Muslim Americans, such as the Hijabi Monologuists, the hip hop artist Omar Offendum, the music of the Taqwacore band The Kominas, and Mipsterz (Muslim Sister Hipsters), have participated in an important movement of self-defining and reaffirming Muslimness against the backdrop of public hostility outlined above. But the forms of Muslimness that have taken shape in these cultural projects also challenge normative understandings of Islam defined by Muslim religious authorities and resist ethnically specific modes of belonging modeled on homogenous national communities. The Muslim American artists and cultural projects mentioned above are part of a growing trend of self-fashioning that is not contained within the limits of ethnic identity, religious doctrine, or bigotry. These creative performances redefine the very notion of Muslimness by contributing to contemporary counter-cultural movements set against anti-Muslim politics as well as the socio-cultural limitations imposed by established mosque-going communities.

22. See the ACLU's map and data of Nationwide Anti-Mosque Activity, https://www.aclu.org/maps/map-nationwide-anti-mosque-activity.
23. Ewing.

Works Cited

Alsultany, E. 2013. "Arabs and Muslims in the Media after 9/11: Representational Strategies for a 'Postrace' Era." *American Quarterly* 65.1:161–169.

"American Attitudes Toward Arabs and Muslims." 2014. Arab American Institute (July 29, 2014). http://www.aaiusa.org/american-attitudes-toward-arabs-and-muslims-2014.

Apuzzo, M. and A. Goldman. 2013. *Enemies Within: Inside the NYPD's Secret Spying Unit and bin Laden's Final Plot Against America.* New York.

Bailey, S. 2015. "A Startling Number of Americans Still Believe Obama is a Muslim." *Washington Post*, September 14. https://www.washingtonpost.com/news/acts-of-faith/wp/2015/09/14/a-startling-number-of-americans-still-believe-president-obama-is-a-muslim/?utm_term=.95c4b90565f4.

Baum, M. and P. Potter. 2008. "The Relationships Between Mass Media, Public Opinion, and Foreign Policy: Toward a Theoretical Synthesis." *Annual Review of Political Science* 11:39–65.

Burnett, J. 2013. "In Hollywood, The Actor Who Gives The Call To Prayer." NPR, July 24. http://www.npr.org/2013/07/24/203661722/in-hollywood-the-actor-who-gives-the-call-to-prayer.

Ewing, K. N.d. "Putting Mosque Controversies in Perspective." The Legacy of 9/11. A Russell Sage Foundation Forum. https://www.russellsage.org/research/9-11-forum/katherine-ewing.

Farhadi, A. "Oscar 2017 Winner Speech delivered by Anousheh Ansari." http://oscar.go.com/news/winners/asghar-farhadi-oscar-2017-winner-speech-delivered-by-anousheh-ansari.

Gerges, F. A. 2003. "Islam and Muslims in the Mind of America." *Annals of the American Academy of Political and Social Science* 588 (July):73–89.

Gewen, B. 2008. "Muslim Rebel Sisters: At Odds With Islam and Each Other." *New York Times,* April 27. http://www.nytimes.com/2008/04/27/weekinreview/27gewen.html.

"Islamophobia: Understanding Anti-Muslim Sentiment in the West." Gallup 2014. http://www.gallup.com/poll/157082/islamophobia-understanding-anti-muslim-sentiment-west.aspx?version=print.

Kay, J. 2012. "Bachmann, Gaffney, and the GOP's Anti-Muslim Culture of Conspiracy." *Daily Beast,* July 23. http://www.thedailybeast.com/articles/2012/07/23/bachmann-gaffney-and-the-gop-s-anti-muslim-culture-of-conspiracy.html.

Khan, S. 2017. "A Muslim American's Homecoming: Cowboys, Country Music, Chapatis." *New York Times*, September 26.

Klein, J. 2014. "Netanyahu's Moral Clarity." David Horowtiz Freedom Center, September 18. http://www.horowitzfreedomcenter.org/joseph_klein_netanyahu_s_isis_moral_clarity.

Levingston, S. 2014. "Ayad Akhtar: On Muslim identity, and life in America." *Washington Post*, July 19. http://www.washingtonpost.com/entertainment/ayad-akhtar-on-muslim-identity-and-life-in-america/2014/07/17/29496290–05e6–11e4-bbf1-cc51275e7f8f_story.html.

Mackey, R. 2012. "Anti-Islam Ads Remixed in San Francisco and New York." *The Lede: New York Times News Blog*, August 21. http://thelede.blogs.nytimes.com/2012/08/21/anti-islam-ads-remixed-in-san-francisco-and-new-york/?_php=true&_type=blogs&_r=0.

Mamdani, M. 2002. "Good Muslim, Bad Muslim: A Political Perspective on Culture and Terrorism." *American Anthropologist* 104.3:766–775.

———. 2004. *Good Muslim, Bad Muslim*. New York.

Mosk, M. 2008. "An Attack That Came Out of the Ether." *Washington Post*, June 28. http://www.washingtonpost.com/wpdyn/content/article/2008/06/27/AR2008062703781.html?hpid=topnews.

Nance, S. 2009. *How the Arabian Nights Inspired the American Dream, 1790–1935*. Chapel Hill.

"Our Vision." MPAC 2013 Annual Report. https://www.mpac.org/annual-report/mission_vision.php.

Piepenburg, E. 2017. "Pakistani-American From California Blazes a Gay Leather and Fetish Trail." *New York Times*, May 31. https://www.nytimes.com/2017/05/31/style/ali-mushtaq-international-mr-leather-fetish-gay.html.

"Protecting the Religious Freedom of Muslims." N.d. American Civil Liberties Union. https://www.aclu.org/issues/national-security/discriminatory-profiling/protecting-religious-freedom-muslims.

"Safe Spaces Initiative: Executive Summary." N.d. MPAC. http://www.mpac.org/assets/docs/publications/MPAC-Safe-Spaces-summary.pdf.

Said, E. 1980. "Islam Through Western Eyes." *The Nation*, April 26. www.thenation.com/article/islam-through-western-eyes.

———. 1997. *Covering Islam*. Revised edition. New York.

Serwer, A. 2011. "Pamela Geller: Beware 'Stealth Halal' Turkeys This Thanksgiving." *Mother Jones*, November 21. http://www.motherjones.com/mojo/2011/11/pamela-geller-beware-stealth-halal-thanksgiving-turkeys.

Spellberg, D. 2013. *Thomas Jefferson's Qur'an: Islam and the Founding Fathers*. New York.

———. 2006. "Could a Muslim Be President? An Eighteenth-Century Constitutional Debate." *Eighteenth-Century Studies* 39.4:485–506.

Stafford, K. 2014. "U-M Arabic poetry translator wins 'genius' grant." *Detroit Free Press*, September 17. http://www.freep.com/story/news/local/ michigan/2014/09/17/um-macarthur-fellow/15752847.

Steinback, R. 2011. "The Anti-Muslim Inner Circle." Southern Poverty Law Center, June 17. http://www.splcenter.org/get-informed/intelligence-report/browse-all-issues/2011/summer/the-anti-muslim-inner-circle.

Thin Blue Line Project. 2013. Act! For America Education. http://thinbluelineproject.org.

Williams, R. and G. Vashi. 2007. "*Hijab* and American Muslim Women: Creating the Space for Autonomous Selves." *Sociology of Religion* 68.3:269–287.

Real Time with Bill Maher and the Good Muslims of Liberal Multiculturalism[1]

Evelyn Alsultany

ON OCTOBER 3, 2014, THE PANEL on the HBO show *Real Time with Bill Maher* included *New York Times* bestselling author and key figure in the New Atheism movement Sam Harris, actor/filmmaker Ben Affleck, Pulitzer Prize-winning journalist Nicholas Kristof, and former chairperson of the Republican National Committee Michael Steele.[2] During the panel's discussion, both Bill Maher and Sam Harris asserted that Islam fundamentally clashes with liberal principles, yet liberals in the United States fail to point this out because of their commitment to political correctness. The only solution to this problem, Maher and Harris argued, was for the West to throw support behind "nominal Muslims" – Muslims in name only, not in practice – in the hopes of effecting reform. The other panelists challenged these comments and the whole episode soon went viral, prompting yet another cycle of op-eds[3] and news coverage[4] in which Islam's diversity or lack thereof was debated.

This paper seeks to unpack the implications of Bill Maher and Sam Harris's arguments, paying particular attention to the limits of liberal multiculturalism they reveal and the reductive and contradictory categories of Muslims they construct. Maher and Harris present liberalism as promoting individual rights, equality, and pluralism – principles, they insist, that are opposed by Islam and hence Muslims. To simply write-off Maher and Harris's comments as Islamophobic or blanket generalizations, however, misses the nuance and complexity that makes such statements repugnant, yes, but also resilient. In the first part of the paper, rather than argue that it is Maher and Harris who are being illiberal, I point out how their arguments are, in fact, entirely consistent with Western liberalism, its checkered history, and internal contradictions. Next, I discuss the various categories of "good Muslims" produced within liberal discourse since 9/11 – namely, the patriotic Muslim, the moderate Muslim, and the native informant – and compare

---

1. I would like to thank Belquis Elhadi and Areeba Jibril for research assistance and Kim Greenwell and Mohammad Khalil for feedback on this essay.
2. Maher 2014, "Episode 331."
3. Kristof 2014; Spencer 2014; Aslan 2014; Kilpartick 2014.
4. "Reza Aslan: Bill Maher 'not very sophisticated'" 2014.

these with the different types of Muslims that emerged during the course of the panel discussion – from Maher and Harris's "nominal Muslims" to Steele and Kristof's "heroic Muslims" and Affleck's "sandwich-eating Muslims." Before proceeding though, I will provide a more detailed summary of the episode of *Real Time* in question.

The Debate on *Real Time with Bill Maher*

The discussion relevant to this essay lasted approximately ten minutes. Maher begins the discussion as follows:

> Liberals need to stand up for liberal principles ... like freedom of
> speech, freedom to practice any religion you want without fear of
> violence, freedom to leave a religion, equality for women, equality for
> minorities including homosexuals. These are liberal principles that
> liberals applaud for, but then when you say in the Muslim world, this
> is what's lacking, then they get upset.

Sam Harris chimes in, agreeing and stating that liberals have "failed on the topic of theocracy" because they do not want to criticize the failure of liberal principles within the Muslim world. Any criticism of Islam, he argues, gets conflated with criticism of the people and unproductively labeled as Islamophobia. Ben Affleck, clearly offended by their line of thinking, asks if they are questioning whether Islamophobia is a real thing. Bill Maher replies, "Well, it's not a real thing when we do it." The audience laughs at this seemingly facetious response, but a serious Maher repeats, "It really isn't." Harris acknowledges that some people are bigoted against Muslims but argues that he and Maher are simply making the point that bad ideas should be subject to criticism – and that "Islam at this moment is the mother lode of bad ideas."

The discussion becomes heated as Affleck describes their argument as racist and offensive. Nicholas Kristof points out that the image Maher and Harris are painting is "hugely incomplete"; that ISIS might fit that profile, but not those Muslims who fight for liberal principles like Muhammad Ali and Malala Yousafzai. Affleck interjects, "Or how about the over a billion people who aren't fanatical, who don't punch women, who just want to go to school, have some sandwiches, pray five times a day and don't do any of the things that you're saying?" Michael Steele agrees with Kristof and states that voices challenging extremists do not get heard or receive the same platform as extremists. He cites the example of clerics in Australia, Europe, and the United States who have risked their lives to take a stance against ISIS, but have not received media coverage. Maher retorts that it is not about a platform, but that Muslims are too scared to speak out because they will be killed "if you say the wrong thing, draw the wrong picture, or write the wrong book."

Throughout the discussion, both Maher and Harris insist that while only a minority of Muslims are violent extremists, the majority hold extremist views that are in opposition to liberal principles. Maher cites a Pew poll showing that 90% of Egyptians believe that death is appropriate for those who leave the religion. When Affleck challenges Harris to provide a solution, however, Harris seems to contradict this point by saying, "There are hundreds of millions of Muslims who are nominal Muslims, who don't take the faith seriously, who don't want to kill apostates, who are horrified by ISIS, and we need to defend these people, prop them up, and let them reform their faith." Nonetheless, both Harris and Maher end by reaffirming that extremists are not a minority; as Maher puts it, "In the Muslim world, it [extremism] is mainstream belief."

The Limits of Liberalism

The debate on *Real Time with Bill Maher* reveals that the level of conversation about Islam in the United States is less than rudimentary and in urgent need of remediation. Despite having researched and written extensively about stereotypical representations of Islam and Muslims in post-9/11 America, I found myself speechless as I watched the discussion unfold. Under what conditions can accurate statements be made about 1.6 billion people? While Maher and Harris's views seem to blend into one voice on the show, their approaches are actually distinct from one another. Maher tends to present the world's Muslims as being essentially the same: against liberal principles like freedom of speech and freedom of religion and against equal rights for women and LGBTQ people. In contrast, Harris (both on the show and in his writings) conceptualizes Muslims in concentric circles with "jihadists," like ISIS and al-Qaeda, at the core followed by Islamists who are politically motivated but not violent. He says that these two circles comprise 20% of Muslims, and he adds that 20% is a conservative estimate. The next concentric circle comprises Muslims who support violent jihad in some way but would not be personally involved. The next circle he describes in his 2015 book with Maajid Nawaz, *Islam and the Future of Tolerance*, as follows:

> Finally, one hopes, there is a much larger circle of so-called moderate Muslims, whether they would label themselves that way or not, who want to live by more modern values. Although they may not be quite secular, they don't think that groups like [ISIS] represent their faith.

Perhaps there are also millions of truly secular Muslims who just
don't have a voice.[5]

Those who are violent or support violence are at the center of Islam while
those who are not oriented toward violence are farther away; all ultimately
exist within a spectrum of one's closeness to or distance from violence. On
the show, Harris says, in agreement with Maher's larger argument, that Muslims who are not jihadists nonetheless hold problematic views on human
rights, women's rights, and gay rights, and "keep women and homosexuals
immiserated in these cultures." Thus he concludes, "we have to empower
the true reformers in the Muslim world to change it and lying about the
link between doctrine and behavior is not going to do that."[6] In other words,
Muslim moderates are problematic because they believe in the doctrine
while secular Muslims (that is, nominal Muslims) are the true hope because
they presumably are not religious.

In his 2004 book, *The End of Faith: Religion, Terror, and the Future of Reason*, Harris argues that there are problems inherent to all faiths and that
religious moderates get in the way of understanding those problems. Such
moderates, he states,

> are themselves the bearers of terrible dogma: they imagine that the
> path to peace will be paved once each of us has learned to respect the
> unjustified beliefs of others.... [T]he very ideal of religious tolerance –
> born of the notion that every human being should be free to believe
> whatever he wants about God – is one of the principle forces driving
> us toward the abyss.[7]

While Harris is critical of all religious moderates, he reserves his harshest
criticisms for Muslim moderates. It is this perspective that he was promoting on *Real Time with Bill Maher* and is the reason Maher, who identifies as
an atheist, invites Harris on his show: to bolster and add credibility to his
own position that all religious Muslims pose a danger to liberalism and that
nominal Muslims are needed to reform Islam.

On the one hand, there was nothing surprising about the discussion.[8] As
is common in conversations about Islam in the United States, Islam figured
throughout the discussion as a foreign religion but not a domestic or historic part of the United States (aside from Nicholas Kristof's passing reference
to Muhammad Ali). All too familiar, too, were the invocations of women's

5. Harris and Nawaz 2015, 16–17.
6. Maher 2014, "Episode 331."
7. Harris 2004, 15.
8. See Salaita 2008; and Alsultany 2012.

rights and LGBT rights as the purported litmus tests of Western liberalism – invocations that, as usual, elided any opposition to or ambivalence regarding such rights within the United States.[9] In addition, Islam is discussed as if there are no debates or internal disagreements, as if Western interference – in this case propping up nominal Muslims – is necessary to bring about social change within Islam.[10] These are common themes that several scholars and civil rights groups have identified in news media and dominant discourses that produce and justify anti-Muslim racism. For example, in their examination of op-eds published in *The Wall Street Journal*, Suad Joseph and Benjamin D'Harlingue find that Islam is portrayed as incompatible with modernity and as linked to fanaticism and terrorism.[11] Similarly, Deepa Kumar points to Western representations of Islam in the media as a monolithic, uniquely sexist, and an inherently violent religion.[12]

On the other hand, it was the consistent reoccurrence of this approach to Islam on *Real Time with Bill Maher* – a show (and host) generally considered "progressive," if not explicitly left-leaning – that struck many as surprising, thus fueling the episode's "viral" popularity. For many on the political left, Islamophobia is understood as something based in hatred and ignorance and perpetrated solely by those on the political right. Frequently cited examples include laws like the PATRIOT Act, the emergence of an "Islamophobia industry,"[13] and hate crimes against Muslims and mosques. Among right-wing commentators, the very notion of Islamophobia is often derided as a politically correct way to shut down legitimate criticism of Islam, disabling rational efforts to confront real problems like terrorism. What was so notable about Maher's arguments was their resonance with this logic and their identical denial of any kind of bias or racism.

When it comes to Muslims, however, it is not unusual to find ideological convergence between the political left and right. Steven Salaita has written extensively on how the left promotes anti-Muslim racism, revealing that such ideologies are not unique to the right.[14] Arun Kundnani identifies

9. For example, despite a major shift in public opinion regarding LGBT rights in the last two decades, a Gallup Poll shows that 40% of Americans still oppose gay marriage. See McCarthy 2016.

10. Many organizations have been created by Muslims to promote inclusion and rights for all, such as Muslims for Progressive Values, Feminist Islamic Trouble Makers of North America, The Al-Fatiha Foundation, the Inclusive Mosque Initiative, and others. On the long history of reform debates within Islam, see Grewal 2013.

11. Joseph and D'Harlingue 2012, 132–164.

12. Kumar 2012.

13. On the Islamophobia industry, see Lean 2012; Bail 2015; Sheehi 2011; and Council on American-Islamic Relations 2013.

14. Salaita 2008.

a "liberal form of anti-Muslim racism" that uses the language of "values" rather than race or ethnicity. Like Maher, its proponents rationalize it as "no more than criticism of an alien belief system – hostility to religious beliefs rather than to a racial group – and therefore entirely distinct from racism."[15] But as Kundani points out, such arguments merely use religious belonging as a proxy for racial difference, thus producing a form of anti-Muslim racism entirely consistent with liberal principles.[16] Indeed, I would argue that it is liberal principles – or at least a particular vision of liberal principles – that unites such anti-Muslim racist arguments on both sides of the political spectrum.

To be sure, not all criticisms of Islam fall into the category of anti-Muslim racism. However, what makes Maher a promoter of this form of racism is his essentialist approach to Islam and Muslims. Harris, meanwhile, contributes to anti-Muslim racism through his simplistic understanding of terrorism and religious extremism. In *The End of Faith*, he states that 9/11 happened because the Muslim men involved believed that they would go to paradise for doing so. Echoing Bernard Lewis's seminal text, "The Roots of Muslim Rage," Harris writes that we can understand terrorism not through the optics of grievances with Western imperialism, but through understanding Muslims as fearing Western contamination and being wrought with feelings of humiliation because the West has surpassed them as a great empire. He states that bin Laden's grievances with US support of Israel and US troops in Saudi Arabia are religious in nature, not political, that they derive from scripture.[17] Ultimately he is claiming that the key to understanding terrorism is understanding Islam. This is a very dangerous and misleading approach that dismisses the complex factors that contribute to terroristic ideologies, from Western foreign policies to failed Arab governance and social and economic factors that produce social alienation.[18]

Mohammad Khalil takes on Harris's arguments about Islam and Islamic scripture, pointing out the many flaws in his assessments: that he is unfamiliar with modern Muslim scholarly arguments against the practice of

15. Kundnani 2012, 155, 160.

16. I am part of a cohort of scholars who deliberately locate Islamophobia as a form of racism and prefer to use the term "anti-Muslim racism" over "Islamophobia" to move away from understanding this phenomenon as an individual problem or fear and towards understanding it as a systemic problem resulting from a confluence of factors, such as the history of white supremacy and nativist movements in the United States, the history of reductive representations of Muslim in the US media, the impact of domestic and foreign policies on Muslims, and other factors that result in the racialization of religion. For more on the racialization of Islam, see Bayoumi 2006; Rana 2007; Naber 2008; and Meer 2013.

17. Harris, 2004, 30.

18. See Mamdani 2004; and Esposito and Mogahed 2007.

aggressive jihad, that he overlooks the many Muslim leaders and scholars who condemn terrorism, that he ignores that many Muslims in the West are active and proud citizens, that he pays no attention to the fact that countless religious Muslims have lived peacefully with people of all faiths. Khalil writes, "All things considered, most Muslim theologians would likely balk at [Harris's] claim that the non-Muslims who died on 9/11 were all simply 'fuel for the eternal fires of God's justice.'"[19] While Harris's approach to Muslims might seem more nuanced than Maher's, he nonetheless echoes and bolsters Maher's argument about the fundamental incompatibility between Muslims and liberal society.

Falguni Sheth provides a useful definition of liberalism as "a political philosophy that identifies the rational individual as the primary political unit in society."[20] Central to this political approach is the freedom individuals to govern their affairs, limited interference from the state, a commitment to the rule of law and pluralism through tolerating cultural, ethnic, religious, and other kinds of "difference."[21] As a result of its aims to be culturally diverse and tolerant, this political philosophy is promoted as unique, especially in contrast to other political orders that are deemed illiberal and thus barbaric.[22] Both political liberals and conservatives embrace liberalism as a political philosophy, though they disagree on the role of the government in solving social problems.

What I want to highlight here is liberalism's reliance upon and reinforcement of monolithic oppositional binaries – freedom/non-freedom, modern/barbaric, tolerance/intolerance, and so on. Of course, such binaries are not new to liberalism, Eurocentrism, nationalism, and other hierarchical ideologies, and numerous scholars have shown liberalism's historical role in legitimating imperial and colonial projects. Lisa Lowe argues that "liberal philosophy, culture, economics, and government have been commensurate with, and deeply implicated in, colonialism, slavery, capitalism, and empire."[23] And Sheth writes that "[t]he British and American empires promoted the ideal vision of liberalism at the same time that they were engaged in extremely destructive and violent expansionism.... In fact, a great deal of insight can be gained by understanding how the ideal vision of liberalism and empire were working hand-in-hand."[24] Therefore it is not the exception, but the rule in liberalism that humanity would be denied

19. Khalil 2018, 101.
20. Sheth 2009, 14.
21. Sheth 2009, 88.
22. Brown 2008, 151.
23. Lowe 2015, 2.
24. Sheth 2009, 14–15.

to some, whether based on race, religion, or in the this case, the racialization of religion. Given that liberalism has been implicated in slavery and colonialism, and continues to be implicated in interventionist policies, it is not inconsistent for it to exclude Muslims today. Furthermore, the position of religious Muslims as incompatible with liberal principles is not unique. Catholics, Jews, Mormons, atheists and other religious minorities have been historically excluded from US conceptions of Americanness despite a commitment to liberalism as an ideal political system.[25] Liberalism should be understood as rooted in a paradox of inclusion and exclusion, equality and inequality. Thus, Maher and Harris's argument that dehumanizes observant Muslims exemplifies this paradox, in which exclusion is consistent within liberalism, not exceptional to it.

Indeed, Joseph Massad argues that Islam has been central to the formation of liberalism as an ideology and political identity in the same way that Edward Said describes Orientalism[26] as central to the formation of European identity in the nineteenth century, in that Islam became the Other through which Western liberalism would define itself. Massad points out how Western liberalism has constructed Islam as its Other – opposed to "freedom, liberty, equality, the rights-bearing individual, democratic citizenship, women's rights, sexual rights, freedom of belief, secularism, rationality, etc., in short as a pathology."[27]

The racialized assumptions of liberalism are thus built into the terms of "liberal" debate itself, regardless of whether or not one identifies as being on the political left or right. Most remarkably, liberal values can be used to justify their own suspension. Consider Maher's invocation of the common argument in liberal multicultural societies that there ought to be a limit to liberalism's tolerance – that is, liberalism cannot and should not tolerate intolerance.[28] By painting Islam and thus all religious Muslims as intolerant, Maher rationalizes their derogation as reasonable criticism of "bad ideas." It is precisely his self-identified commitment to liberal values that enables Maher, I argue, to insist that he is not being racist and that it is not Islamophobia "when we do it." Maher touts statistics to justify the dehumanization of Muslims and to exempt himself from being a promoter of anti-Muslim racism similar to how racial scientists have used "facts" throughout history to justify racism and inequality.[29] The tautology of the argument immunizes

25. See Marzouki, 2017; Spellberg 2013, "Afterword"; GhaneaBassiri 2010; and Nussbaum 2012.

26. Said 1978.

27. Massad 2015, 3.

28. See Brown 2006.

29. See Roberts 2011.

the liberal subject (read: Maher) from critique, while stripping its target (read: Muslims) of reason and thus humanity. For if Muslims were capable of reasoning, they would embrace liberal principles; but because religious Muslims reject liberal principles *by definition*, they cannot be capable of reasoning and therefore are not deserving of respect or human dignity.[30]

Maher does not mention that the same Pew poll he cites that finds that 90% of Egyptians agree that death is the appropriate response to those that leave Islam also finds that the majority of Muslims favor religious freedom for people of other faiths, favor democracy over authoritarian rule, and see no inherent tension between being religiously devout and living in a modern society.[31] This complex portrait depicted in the Pew poll is overlooked. Furthermore, a 2017 Pew poll showed that Muslims in the United States have become more accepting of homosexuality; that 52% say homosexuality should be accepted by society and 33% say it should be discouraged.[32] Among the other findings were that 64% said that there is more than one way to interpret Islamic teachings, 69% said that working toward social justice is part of the faith, and 75% said that targeting civilians can never be justified for a religious or political cause. These findings are a direct challenge to Maher and Harris's claim that Muslims are incompatible with liberal values. Given the essentialized portrait of Islam commonly promoted in US media and political discourses, it is no surprise that the poll also revealed that half of American Muslims have experienced at least one form of religious discrimination in the last year.

In the following section, I shift from exploring liberalism's limits to its internal contradictions – specifically, as manifested in the various types of "good Muslims" imagined and allowed for within liberal multiculturalism. These categories are contradictions because just as liberalism is premised on the rejection of Islam, so too does it offer Muslims the possibility of inclusion. But as I will argue, the terms of inclusion are, themselves, contradictory.

The Good Muslims of Liberal Multiculturalism

As I have written about elsewhere, when liberalism intersects with the US security state post-9/11, certain kinds of acceptable "good Muslims" emerge: the patriotic Muslim, the moderate Muslim, and the native informant.[33] I will review these categories as a way to contextualize the related, yet dis-

---

30. See Nussbaum 2012.
31. Pew Research Center 2013, 9–10.
32. Pew Research Center 2017.
33. Alsultany 2012.

tinct types of Muslims invoked on this episode of *Real Time with Bill Maher* – specifically, Maher and Harris's "nominal Muslim," Kristof and Steel's "heroic Muslim," and Affleck's "sandwich-eating Muslim."

Shortly after September 11, 2001, Mahmood Mamdani highlighted a distinction made by President George W. Bush in his post-9/11 speeches between "good" and "bad" Muslims.[34] In the immediate aftermath of 9/11, the default assumption was that all Muslims were "bad" (potential terrorists) unless they proved their allegiance to the United States and its War on Terror. To this day, recognition as a "good" Muslim can be sought in various ways: through placing a high value on community service in order to prove moderation,[35] through making claims that Islam is compatible with American values,[36] through Muslims making their religion conform to American civil religions,[37] through modifying the expression of one's Muslim identity, to name a few.[38] The patriotic Muslim is one of the most popular pathways. Muslims eager to differentiate themselves from terrorists can prominently display US flags,[39] publicly affirm their commitment to the United States and its values, and even enlist in the military with the possibility of performing the highest form of service, namely, dying for one's country. Post-9/11 saw an uptick in the number of patriotic Arab and Muslim American characters on TV[40] but, more recently, the nation found its most famous patriotic Muslim in real life at the 2016 Democratic National Convention. Khizr and Ghazala Khan's son, Humayan, was killed in Iraq in 2004 while serving in the US military. In his nationally televised speech, Khizr Khan received national attention for challenging Donald Trump's proposed Muslim ban, rhetorically asking the then presidential candidate, "Have you even read the United States constitution?"[41] Having made the ultimate patriotic sacrifice of their own son, the Khans publicly demonstrated their understanding of and commitment to the Constitution and, thus, its liberal principles. As Khizr Khan proclaimed himself, he and his wife are "patriotic American Muslims with undivided loyalty to our country." Humayan Khan's sacrifice became a political symbol of what it means to be an American and for the Clinton campaign in particular, Khizr Khan became symbolic of the "good Muslim" who can also be an American.[42]

34. Mamdani 2004, 15.
35. Corbett 2017.
36. Alsultany 2007, 593–622.
37. Bilici 2012, 201.
38. Beydoun 2017.
39. Grewal 2003, 535–561.
40. Alsultany 2012.
41. Owen 2016.
42. Curtis 2016, 6.

Another promised pathway to inclusion is as a moderate Muslim. This category is embedded within and given meaning through national security frameworks. The moderate Muslim is the counterpoint to the extremist or terrorist Muslim. At one point, this figure was exemplified by Imam Faisal Abdul Rauf, a longtime Sufi religious leader in New York City who conducted trainings about Islam for the FBI after 9/11. Much of his life's work has focused on improving relations between Muslims and the West. Abdul Rauf was considered a moderate Muslim leader partly because he is a Sufi imam and Sufism came to be positioned in public discourse as the "good" kind of Islam following 9/11.[43] He was also considered to be moderate because he argued that the United States is a country founded upon "Abrahamic ethics" and thus that American liberal democracy and the free market system actually embody Islamic principles.[44] Ultimately, Abdul Rauf's status as a moderate Muslim was tainted by controversy, when his interfaith program, the Cordoba Initiative, received backlash for its proposal to erect a mosque in lower Manhattan, two blocks away from Ground Zero, one of the sites of the 9/11 terrorist attacks. Abdul Rauf's case shows that the moderate Muslim is a fragile category. Crucially, the moderate Muslim must publicly seek to reject or resolve the purported conflict between Islam and liberal values by continually disavowing extremism and demonstrating their "moderate-ness," a performance as ill-defined and ambiguous as it is required. According to the good/bad Muslim paradigm, all Muslims are bad until proven otherwise. What is important to note is that even when proven otherwise, one's moderate status can be easily revoked.

Another kind of "good Muslim," native informants can sometimes come in the form of the patriotic Muslim or moderate Muslim, but more often they have left Islam entirely. Native informants are often used to validate monolithic claims about Islam – that is, that it is uniquely sexist, homophobic, violent, intolerant, and unreasonable – and even to justify US intervention in Muslim countries.[45] The native informant is a critic of Islam, often someone who has left Islam as the result of brutal experiences and who uses their own experience to stand in for the entire religion. As Krista Melanie Riley points out, this method of gaining acceptance often requires native informants who are threatened by other Muslims. As such, these "good Muslims" gain credibility as courageous, while also affirming beliefs about "bad Muslims."[46] Not surprisingly, native informants are often

43. For more on Sufism as moderate Islam, see Aidi 2014; Corbett 2017; and Marzouki 2017.

44. Corbett 2017, 20–21.

45. See Abu-Lughod 2015; Maira 2009; Bayoumi 2010; and Alsultany 2013a.

46. Riley 2009, 65–66.

featured prominently by US media, including *Real Time with Bill Maher*. In particular, Maher has invited Muslim women (and less often, men) native informants on the show to support his message that Islam is especially oppressive of women and basically incompatible with liberalism.[47] To be fair, some of these guests try to avoid monolithic portraits of Islam, even while discussing a larger "Muslim problem," but their attempted distinctions, for example, between Islamism and Islam do not seem to register with Maher nor, one suspects, with his audience.

Most importantly, though each of these "good Muslims" seems to offer the possibility of belonging and acceptance, they are not guarantees and their status is always at risk of being revoked. Patriotic Muslims can still have their loyalty called into question. As Edward Curtis in this volume shows, even when patriotic Muslims in the military give the ultimate blood sacrifice, they are still not fully incorporated into the US national imaginary. Similarly, moderate Muslims must not only endure but also participate in endless discussions about how they are against extremism and terrorism, as commentators like Maher, Harris, and others insist that moderates exist on a spectrum of beliefs that are dangerous to liberalism.[48] Furthermore, the continual positioning of both moderate Muslims and native informants as useful for national security actually has the effect of stigmatizing them as less than American.[49] Lauding them, for example, as "our eyes and ears on the front lines" as Hillary Clinton did in 2016, ensures that even "good" Muslim Americans are indelibly linked with terrorism in the popular imagination. Muslims, it seems, cannot be imagined as having any other relation to the US state.

The Contradictions of Liberal Multiculturalism

If the patriotic, moderate, and native informant Muslim categories were generated in the immediate aftermath of 9/11, what kind of new possibilities for acceptance exist today? Though the October 3, 2014, episode of *Real Time with Bill Maher* became a viral sensation given its seeming revelation of anti-Muslim racism "even" on a show with a progressive reputation,[50] what made it most interesting was not the repetition of old stereotypes, but the

47. For example, see Irshad Manji in (2011) Season 9, Episode 13; Maajid Nawaz (2013) Season 11, Episode 31; Ayaan Hirsi Ali (2015) Season 13, Episode 17; Asra Nomani (2015) Season 13, Episode 34; and Raheel Raza (2016) Season 14, Episode 7. Rula Jebreal is one of the few Muslim guests on the show who challenges Maher on his approach to Muslims; see (2014) Season 12, Episode 32.

48. For example, see Kilpatrick 2016.

49. Mangla 2016.

50. Maher's problematic views on Muslims are not new. See Alsultany 2012, chapter 4.

articulation of three new varieties of "good Muslims": the nominal Muslim, the heroic Muslim, and the sandwich-eating Muslim. Though clearly related to their predecessors, the nominal and heroic Muslim categories offer new insights into the contradictions of liberal inclusion, while, Ben Affleck's sandwich-eating Muslim opens a space for Muslim Americans in the popular imagination predicated on their common humanity, rather than their difference.

As stated above, in defining the nominal Muslim, Harris says that the hundreds of millions of Muslims who are not religious should be supported and encouraged to reform Islam. Harris assumes that the prevailing interpretations of Islam are threatening and thus that the entire religion needs reform. Who should lead this reform movement? Nominal Muslims – those who are Muslim in name only but not in practice; someone who was raised Muslim but for whom Islam is insignificant in their lives. Maher's native informant guests, like Ayaan Hirsi Ali, who is now an atheist, would fit this role.

Here we see the continuation of an age-old colonial strategy of using particular groups of "natives" to assimilate others. It assumes that Muslims have no capacity for agency unless it is activated and directed by the West. In addition, Muslims who are not religious or who have left Islam are embraced or propped up as those who should reform the religion. Where is the line between the nominal Muslim and other kinds of "good Muslims," such as the moderate Muslim? It seems to me that the nominal Muslim is not the same as the moderate Muslim. The moderate Muslim can still be Muslim but knows to keep their religion private (and to cooperate with the government in counterterrorism endeavors). The nominal Muslim, however, is either no longer a practicing Muslim or has left the religion entirely. In other words, this version of the "good Muslim" is no longer Muslim; they are cultural Muslims, as opposed to religious Muslims.[51]

To be fair, Harris did modify his position marginally when Fareed Zakaria interviewed him on his CNN show about his *Real Time* comments. Harris said, "I slightly misspoke there. I didn't mean nominal followers in the sense that only Muslim atheists could reform the faith. What I meant is followers who don't take these specific dangerous beliefs very seriously and want to interpret jihad as an inter-spiritual struggle as opposed to holy war."[52] Thus, Harris imagines one level of his concentric circles participating in reforming the faith that involves both moderate and nominal Muslims. Yet notwithstanding its diverse interpretations, he considers "the doctrine

51. For more on how the "good Muslim" is no longer Muslim, see Alsultany 2016.
52. Fareed Zakaria GPS 2014.

of Islam" dangerous and moderate Muslims particularly problematic. As a result, nominal Muslims play a special role because they no longer believe in the faith.

According to Maher and Harris, Muslims writ large represent a crisis in liberalism and the solution to the crisis lies in those who are Muslim in name, but not in practice. Kundnani states that

> there is a pessimism as to the possibility of resolving this supposed crisis of Muslim identity and liberal values through conventional democratic processes of representation and negotiation between different [European] citizens; rather, the crisis is defined as marking an exception to the normal functioning of politics.[53]

In other words, liberal multiculturalism cannot resolve the "Muslim problem" on its own through inclusion and accommodation. A different strategy is required. Thus we see an embrace of a common colonial strategy of propping up certain "natives" to remake them in the likeness/to the liking of their colonizer, and in this case the Muslim who can be included in liberal multiculturalism is no longer a practicing Muslim.

Yet the nominal Muslim is a category wrought with contradictions. Maher and Harris contradict their own insistence that nominal Muslims are a tiny minority. At times these potential reformers consist of "hundreds of millions of Muslims," whom the West should prop up to "let them reform" their faith; these would not be a small minority. Yet at other times, it seems that Maher and Harris suggest that practically *all* Muslims-majority societies, and by default practically *all* Muslims are extremist by arguing that Muslims will be killed for speaking out and by citing the Pew poll showing that 90% of Egyptians believe that people should be killed for leaving Islam. We could think of the nominal Muslim as the "impossible Muslim" because it is an oxymoron according to this category's own logic. How can nominal Muslims be the most promising in reforming Islam if there are hundreds of millions of them on the one hand and only a brave few who must risk their lives on the other?

Unlike the moderate Muslim, nominal Muslims "don't even take the faith seriously," but unlike native informants, they're also not seen as having left it entirely. Nominal Muslims are essentially not Muslims, but they can still be referred to and activated *as* Muslims by a West seeking to reform Islam from within. This crucially leaves agency not with the Muslims, but with those who know how to prop them up to serve Western interests. In contrast, the native informant seems to have some amount of agency in

---

53. Kundnani 2012, 158.

their choice to critique Islam or even leave it and join the chorus of mono-lithic understandings of Islam.

The internal contradictions of the "nominal Muslim" category and its impossibility reveal that Maher and Harris don't even *really* believe in the possibility of reform. They offer this possibility of propping up nominal Muslims as a seeming concession that Islam could be reformed – but their whole premise for how to do it is so contradictory and impractical (relying on such a tiny/non-existent minority) that it suggests that Islam is hopeless and cannot be reformed. If the nominal Muslim who is a cultural Muslim, not a religious Muslim, is the answer, then according to this logic, Muslims are acceptable in liberal multiculturalism as long as they are not religious.

Maher and Harris position themselves as courageous for speaking out despite the norms of political correctness. They also position nominal Muslims as courageous for risking their lives to speak out against Islam. Maher regularly commends his Muslim native informant guests for their courage, for standing up to Islam. While it is certainly courageous for people like Ayaan Hirsi Ali to face opposition and even death threats, the use of the lan-guage of courage and bravery serves to co-opt courage, to morally position the perspective that Islam and liberalism are incompatible as the more cou-rageous one in speaking out against injustice. This is a common tactic used by those in the Islamophobia industry in promoting anti-Muslim racism, to present individuals and their arguments as courageous, instead of racist.[54]

Courage also plays a central role in Kristof and Steele's disagreement with the portrait of Islam promoted by Maher and Harris. They do not see Islam as incompatible with liberalism, and to make their point, they list courageous Muslims who fight for humanity and speak out against injus-tice. According to Kristof and Steele, there are Muslim heroes who present a more diverse portrait of Islam. These are Muslims who have been victimized – like Malala Yousafzai – and who have fought for their rights and for the rights of others – like Muhammad Ali. Kristof (on the show and then in his op-ed that elaborated on his position in the show) gives the examples of Mo-hammad Ali Dadkhah in Iran, who has been in prison for years for defending Christians, and Rashid Rehman, who was killed in Pakistan for defending people accused of apostasy. What is important here is that Kristof and Steele are challenging Maher's depiction of Muslims as having no agency unless activated by the West. They are showing that Muslims do have agency and do fight for liberal principles and risk their lives doing it. It is an important challenge, but it also reinscribes the notion that to be Muslim is essentially

---

54. Salah Hassan's essay in this volume shows how leaders in the Islamophobia industry portray themselves as courageous.

to be a victim unless one has the courage to be a hero. Most of the examples of heroic Muslims are outside the United States, thus once again marking Islam as a foreign religion. The things heroic Muslims have done are truly extraordinary in the sense that they are not ordinary everyday actions. Most of them end up dead, seriously injured, or in prison, making them a kind of martyr. Thus a doomed form of heroism is possible for a small number of people. This narrative reinforces the notion that only a small minority of Muslims are "good," in this case as heroes.

And then we have Ben Affleck's challenge to Maher and Harris, which oddly ends up being the most astute criticism in this debate. I say oddly because the film *Argo*, which Affleck produced and in which he stars, is an exercise in monolithic portraits of Islam; it portrays Iranian Muslims as threatening, irrational, and incapable of individual rational thought.[55] Affleck says, "how about the over a billion people who aren't fanatical, who don't punch women, who just want to go to school, have some sandwiches, pray five times a day and don't do any of those things?" He importantly criticizes Maher and Harris for painting a monolithic image of Islam as fanatical and unreasonable and challenges it through the "ordinary Muslim" who wants to eat sandwiches. He is asking, what about Muslims who are just people living their lives – who are not heroes, or nominal, or patriotic, or defectors? In the political climate in which we live, where remediation is needed in conversations about Islam, such a banal statement becomes a significant intervention into this debate. In other words, "sandwiches" is not radical in itself, especially coming from someone who promoted anti-Muslim racism in the film *Argo*. But given the context in which Muslims come in pre-determined categories that deny their humanity, "sandwiches" becomes an important intervention in this conversation.

Given that Maher and Harris's nominal Muslim is wrought with internal contradictions and ultimately implies that this category comprises a small minority, and that Steele and Kristof suggest that a small minority of Muslims risk their lives to be heroes, Affleck's invocation of "over a billion people" is significant. Affleck does not vilify or exalt Muslims. His reference to Muslims who want to eat sandwiches is banal and that is what makes it an important intervention. Martha Nussbaum writes,

> it is a gross failure to cling to a conception of Muslims as all alike
> and all threatening to U.S. security. In short, people thinking about
> American Muslims often fail, imaginatively ... they accept a stock

55. Alsultany 2013b, 104–107.

image that is framed in part by irrational fear ... and they use that image to think about public choices rather than actually looking at the people who are in front of them, people who are tremendously varied and individual, pursuing a wide range of human purposes.[56]

Maher clings to a conception of Muslims as all alike with their illiberal views while Harris's concentric circles conceptualizes all Muslims in relation to their proximity to violence, thus placing Muslims in a position of having to defend their humanity. Affleck, in contrast, defends Muslims' humanity by simply insisting that they are like anyone else.

In conclusion, I am seeking to expand our understanding of how liberal logics produce restrictive categories of what constitutes a "good Muslim" and to show that the left and right are drawing from the same unquestioned logics. I have considered the various kinds of "good Muslims" that liberal discourses have promoted since 9/11/01 in order to highlight the limited ways in which Muslims can be imagined and thus the limits of liberal multiculturalism. On the one hand, Maher assumes that liberalism is the ideal political ideology because it promotes individual rights, equality, and pluralism and that religious Muslims are illiberal and thus do not belong in Western liberal democracies. On the other hand, the history of liberalism has been linked to colonialism, empire building, slavery, and exclusion despite promoting notions about individual rights, equality, and pluralism. Thus the exclusion of Muslims from liberal multicultural society, unless they exemplify certain categories of the "good Muslim," is actually consistent with, as opposed to exceptional within, liberalism.[57] The new categories of Muslims suggests that liberalism does evolve to a certain extent, yet that it remains wrought with contradictions in promoting freedom and diversity, while also justifying the exclusion and dehumanization of certain people. The new category that promises inclusion at the moment, the nominal Muslim, is predicated on not being a religious believer. Maher's commitment to liberal values enables him to exclude religious Muslims while arguing for inclusive ideals. It is assumed in this logic that to be pro-liberal principles as a Muslim is only possible if Islam is religiously insignificant or irrelevant to one's life. Otherwise, the Muslim who eats sandwiches must pass a slew of litmus tests in advocating for women's rights, LGBT rights, and free speech (litmus tests to which other Americans are not subjected) or be designated a lesser human who deserves to be dehumanized.

56. Nussbaum 2012, 236.
57. See Lowe 2015; and Sheth 2009.

Works Cited

Abu-Lughod, L. 2015. *Do Muslim Women Need Saving?* Cambridge, MA.

Aidi, H. 2014. *Rebel Music: Race, Empire and the New Muslim Youth Culture.* New York.

Alsultany, E. 2007. "Selling American Diversity and Muslim American Identity Through Non-Profit Advertising Post-9/11." *American Quarterly* 59:593–622.

———. 2012. *Arabs and Muslims in the Media: Race and Representation after 9/11.* New York.

———. 2013a. "Arabs and Muslims in the Media after 9/11: Representational Strategies for a 'Post-race' Era." *American Quarterly* 65:161–169.

———. 2013b. "Argo Tries But Fails to Diffuse Stereotypes." *The Islamic Monthly* 29:104–107.

———. 2016. "The Cultural Politics of Islam in U.S. Reality Television." *Communication, Culture and Critique* 9:595–613.

Aslan, R. 2014. "Bill Maher Isn't the Only One Who Misunderstands Religion." *New York Times*, October 8. https://www.nytimes.com/2014/10/09/opinion/bill-maher-isnt-the-only-one-who-misunderstands-religion.html?action=click&contentCollection=Opinion&module=RelatedCoverage&region=EndOfArticle&pgtype=article.

Bail, C. 2015. *Terrified: How Anti-Muslim Fringe Organizations Became Mainstream.* Princeton.

Bayoumi, M. 2006. "Racing Religion." *CR: The New Centennial Review* 6:267–293.

———. 2010. "The God That Failed: The Neo-Orientalism of Today's Muslim Commentators." In *Islamophobia/Islamophilia: Beyond the Politics of Enemy and Friend*, edited by A. Shryock, 79–93. Bloomington.

Beydoun, K. 2017. "Acting Muslim." *Harvard Civil Rights-Civil Liberties Law Review* 53.

Bilici, M. 2012. *Finding Mecca in America: How Islam is Becoming an American Religion.* Chicago.

Brown, W. 2008. *Regulating Aversion: Tolerance in the Age of Identity and Empire.* Princeton.

Corbett, R. 2017. *Making Moderate Islam: Sufism, Service, and the 'Ground Zero Mosque' Controversy.* Stanford.

Council on American-Islamic Relations. 2013. "Legislating Fear: Islamophobia and its Impact in the United States." CAIR. https://www.cair.com/images/islamophobia/Legislating-Fear.pdf.

Curtis, E. 2016. *Muslim Americans in the Military: Centuries of Service.* Bloomington.

Esposito, J. and D. Mogahed. 2007. *Who Speaks for Islam?: What a Billion Muslims Really Think.* New York.

GhaneaBassiri, K. 2010. *A History of Islam in America: From the New World to the New World Order.* Cambridge, MA.

Grewal, I. 2003. "Transnational America: Race, Gender, and Citizenship after 9/11." *Social Identities* 9:535–561. DOI: 10.1080/1350463032000174669.

Grewal, Z. 2013. *Islam Is a Foreign Country: American Muslims and the Global Crisis of Authority.* New York.

Harris, S. 2004. *The End of Faith: Religion, Terror, and the Future of Reason.* New York.

Harris S. and M. Nawaz. 2015. *Islam and the Future of Tolerance: A Dialogue.* Cambridge, MA.

Joseph, S., and B. D'Harlingue. 2012. "The Wall Street Journal's Muslims." *Islamophobia Studies Journal* 1:132–164.

Khalil, M. 2018. *Jihad, Radicalism, and the New Atheism.* New York.

Kilpatrick, W. 2014. "The Myth of Islam's Diversity." *Crisis Magazine*, November 11. http://www.crisismagazine.com/2014/myth-islams-diversity.

Kilpatrick, W. 2016. "The Moderate Muslim Majority Myth." *Frontpage Magazine,* October 17. http://www.frontpagemag.com/fpm/264492/moderate-muslim-majority-myth-william-kilpatrick.

Kristof, N. 2014. "The Diversity of Islam." *New York Times*, October 8. https://www.nytimes.com/2014/10/09/opinion/nicholas-kristof-the-diversity-of-islam.html?_r=0.

Kumar, D. 2012. *Islamophobia and the Politics of Empire.* Chicago.

Kundnani, A. 2012. "Multiculturalism and Its Discontents: Left, Right and Liberal." *European Journal of Cultural Studies* 15:155–166.

Lean, N. 2012. *The Islamophobia Industry: How the Right Manufactures Fear of Muslims.* New York.

Lewis, B. 1990. "The Roots of Muslim Rage." *The Atlantic Monthly* 226.3 (September):47–60.

Lowe, L. 2015. *The Intimacies of Four Continents.* Durham, NC.

Maher, B. 2011. "Season 9, Episode 13." *Real Time with Bill Maher.* Directed by Paul Casey. HBO. Hollywood, CA, April 15.

———. 2013. "Season 11, Episode 31." *Real Time with Bill Maher.* Directed by Paul Casey. HBO. Hollywood, CA, October 25.

———. 2014. "Season 12, Episode 29." *Real Time with Bill Maher.* Directed by Paul Casey. HBO. Hollywood, CA, October 3.

———. 2014. "Season 12, Episode 32." *Real Time with Bill Maher.* Directed by Paul Casey. HBO. Hollywood, CA, October 31.

———. 2015. "Season 13, Episode 17." *Real Time with Bill Maher.* Directed by Paul Casey. HBO. Hollywood, CA, May 15.

———. 2015. "Season 13, Episode 34." *Real Time with Bill Maher*. Directed by Paul Casey. HBO. Hollywood, CA, November 13.

———. 2016. "Season 14, Episode 7." *Real Time with Bill Maher*. Directed by Paul Casey. HBO. Hollywood, CA, March 4.

Maira, S. 2009. "'Good' and 'Bad' Muslim Citizens: Feminists, Terrorists, and U.S. Orientalisms." *Feminist Studies* 35:631–656.

Mamdani, M. 2004. *Good Muslim, Bad Muslim: America, the Cold War, and the Roots of Terror*. New York.

Mangla, I. 2016. "Hillary Clinton Has an Unfortunate Way of Talking about American Muslims." *Quartz*, October 20. https://qz.com/814438/presidential-debate-hillary-clinton-contributes-to-anti-muslim-bias-in-the-way-she-talks-about-american-muslims.

Marzouki, N. 2017. *Islam: An American Religion*. New York.

Massad, J. 2015. *Islam in Liberalism*. Chicago.

McCarthy, J. 2016. "Americans' Support for Gay Marriage Remains High, at 61%." *Gallup*, May 19. http://www.gallup.com/poll/191645/americans-support-gay-marriage-remains-high.aspx.

Meer, N. 2013. "Racialization and Religion: Race, Culture and Difference in the Study of Anti-Semitism and Islamophobia." In *Racialization and Religion: Race, Culture and Difference in the Study of Antisemitism and Islamophobia,* edited by N. Meer, 1–14. London.

Naber, N. 2008. "'Look, Mohammed the Terrorist Is Coming!': Cultural Racism, Nation-Based Racism and the Intersectionality of Oppressions after 9/11." In *Race and Arab Americans Before and After 9/11*, edited by N. Naber and A. Jamal, 276–304. Syracuse.

Nussbaum, M. 2012. *The New Religious Intolerance: Overcoming the Politics of Fear in an Anxious Age*. Cambridge, MA.

Owen, P. 2016. "Fallen Muslim American soldier's father scolds Trump: 'have you even read the constitution?'" *The Guardian*, July 29. https://www.theguardian.com/us-news/2016/jul/29/khizr-khan-democratic-convention-constitution-trump.

Pew Research Center's Forum on Religion and Public Life. 2013. "The World's Muslims: Religion, Politics, and Society." The Pew Research Center (April 30). Washington, DC. http://www.pewforum.org/files/2013/04/worlds-muslims-religion-politics-society-full-report.pdf.

———. 2017. "U.S. Muslims Concerned About Their Place in Society, but Continue to Believe in the American Dream: Findings from Pew Research Center's 2017 survey of U.S. Muslims." The Pew Research Center (July 26). Washington, DC. http://www.pewforum.org/2017/07/26/findings-from-pew-research-centers-2017-survey-of-us-muslims.

Rana, J. 2007. "The Story of Islamophobia." *Souls: A Critical Journal of Black Politics, Culture, and Society* 9:148–161.

Riley, K. M. 2009. "How to Accumulate National Capital: The Case of the 'good' Muslim." *Global Media Journal* 2:65–66.

Roberts, D. 2011. *Fatal Invention: How Science, Politics, and Big Business Re-create Race in the Twenty-First Century.* New York.

"Reza Aslan: Bill Maher 'not very sophisticated.'" 2014. YouTube video, 5:37, from an interview by CNN on September 29, 2014. Posted by CNN (September 29). https://www.youtube.com/watch?v=2pjxPR36qFU.

Said, E. 1978. *Orientalism.* New York.

Salaita, S. 2008. *The Uncultured Wars.* New York.

Sheehi, S. 2011. *Islamophobia: The Ideological Campaign Against Muslims.* Atlanta.

Sheth, F. 2009. *Toward a Political Philosophy of Race.* Albany, NY.

Spellberg, D. 2013. "Afterword." *Thomas Jefferson's Qur'an: Islam and the Founders.* New York.

Spencer, R. 2014. "The Diversity of Islam?" *Frontpage Magazine*, October 12. http://www.frontpagemag.com/fpm/242867/diversity-islam-robert-spencer.

Zakaria, F. 2014. ""Sam Harris on GPS 'Islam has been spread by the sword.'" *Fareed Zakaria GPS.* CNN, November 2. http://cnnpressroom.blogs.cnn.com/2014/11/02/sam-harris-on-gps-islam-has-been-spread-by-the-sword.

Muslim Women, Anti-Muslim Hostility, and the State in the Age of Terror

Juliane Hammer

THAT MUSLIM WOMEN ARE oppressed, both by Islam and Muslim men, seems to be taken for granted in mainstream US politics and media landscapes. This assumption has led to many an argument about just how they could be saved from one or both of these sources of oppression. We have here a case of what post-colonial theorist Gayatri Spivak has famously described as "a case of 'White men saving brown women from brown men,'"[1] with the caveat that white women, here American feminists, have willingly and enthusiastically participated in the construction of this ideology together with white men. It is also worth noting that not all Muslim women or men are "brown."

More concerning is the fact that the project of saving Muslim women, of liberating them from their oppression by their religion and the men in their societies and communities, needs to be denounced as problematic in the first place. The project of saving someone who has been designated as a victim of oppression entails, always, a need to deny the victim's agency and it creates a hierarchical power structure in which the savior does not need to interrogate their privileged access to such power or the potential for misreading their own implicatedness in the oppressive structures they are ostensibly saving the victim from. It is akin to claiming that benevolent patriarchy, or benevolent colonialism, or even benevolent slavery can be used as tools to combat the worst excesses of patriarchy, colonialism, or slavery, by the very people and institutions that perpetuate these systems in the first place.

And yet, we still ask the question whether Muslim women need saving. When Lila Abu-Lughod made it the title of first an article and then a book, it became a provocation as much as a poignant question. In 2002, she argued that,

> rather than seeking to "save" others (with the superiority it implies
> and the violences it would entail) we might better think in terms
> of (1) working with them in situations that we recognize as always

---

1. Spivak 1988.

subject to historical transformation and (2) considering our own larger responsibilities to address the forms of global injustice that are powerful shapers of the worlds in which they find themselves.[2]

In her book, she expands her critique by calling out the political use of the Muslim woman as a tool for military intervention in Muslim majority societies.[3] Abu-Lughod's considerations as to whether Muslim women need saving (her answer is no, but it is complicated) focus on oppressed and victimized Muslim women abroad and on the ways in which they are utilized for foreign policy debates and decisions here in the United States.

In my own work on Muslim women's activism in the United States, Abu-Lughod's question has served as a signpost for the complex ways in which Muslim women are both subjects and objects in public discourse and politics.[4] All such activism, for gender justice in Muslim communities, against domestic violence, for the right to lead prayers, and for many other – often intersectional causes – takes place under the continuous gaze of the surrounding society and with assumptions made about the oppression of Muslim women. It is confined by a binary in which they can only be oppressed or not oppressed, and in which their supposed oppression is blamed on their religion and on Muslim men, and not on political and economic structures, on the aftershock of colonialism, the pervasiveness of patriarchy, or global economic inequalities.

Since 2011, I have repeatedly waded through the mucky depths of Islamophobic media materials that focused on Muslim women. In two previous articles, I argued that there was a paradox at the center of the enduring fascination of the Islamophobia industry with Muslim women: that (predominantly white) feminist producers of anti-Muslim discourse argued both for the need to save oppressed Muslim women from their religion while also making the same (especially visibly) Muslim women the targets of anti-Muslim harassment and hate crimes by casting Islam as foreign to the United States and Muslims as inherently dangerous.[5] At that time, Muslim women had clearly been targets of anti-Muslim discrimination in many forms for years, with a steep increase since 9/11.

In this chapter, I want to focus on significant shifts in the parameters of gendered anti-Muslim discourse. We, scholars, readers, advocates, need to see these shifts in a longer historical trajectory and we need to recognize the specific historical moment in which this analysis takes place. The

2. Abu-Lughod 2002, 783.
3. Abu-Lughod 2013.
4. See Hammer 2012.
5. Hammer 2013a; Hammer 2013b.

latter is especially important because the purpose of this analysis is to provide tools for advocacy against such anti-Muslim discourses and actions, and those tools will need to change with the shifting parameters laid out in these pages.

"Islamophobia," Racism, and Feminism

The term Islamophobia, while widely used, should not be taken for granted. I find it problematic for several reasons, most importantly that a phobia implies an individualized as well as medical condition rather than capturing the systemic and constructed nature of a set of phenomena typically associated with Islamophobia. This reduction to a personal dislike or fear, rather than acknowledging the production of Islamophobic discourse releases the producers of such discourses from responsibility, and severely limits the possibility of fighting it (rather than treating it in pseudo-medical terms). It is now also so widely applied as to risk losing meaning altogether: hate crimes against Muslims, pronouncements by media and politicians about Islam, racist discrimination and attacks, hate speech, and myriad forms of rhetorical and practical othering are all captured within it. While there is of course discursive power in a singular term and the potential for unified political activism, this lumping together risks misreading the causes for these various phenomena and with it the attribution of political agency and responsibility. It is for all these reasons that I have been searching for a better term, which I found it in the most widely used German term for the same phenomena: "Islamfeindlichkeit." *Feindlichkeit* is hostility or enmity and to me this term in translation, as anti-Muslim hostility, while no longer a single word, captures far better the nature of the phenomena under scrutiny, and I am using it in place of Islamophobia (including in the title of this chapter).[6]

The most significant erasure in casting anti-Muslim hostility as an individualized fear of Islam and Muslims is that of racism as the central tenet of many of the phenomena listed above. For a recent public syllabus, which I helped put together, our group of scholars decided after much deliberation to make an even bolder statement: Islamophobia *Is* Racism, which we made the title and hashtag of the syllabus.[7] In *Islamophobia and Racism in America*, Erik Love argues that "Islamophobia is a complex phenomenon," involving religion, gender, class, and sexuality, in addition to race, which makes it pos-

6. I am grateful to Zaid Adhami, Cemil Aydin, I. Augustus Durham, Amal Eqeiq, Anastasia Karklina, Caleb Lazaro Moreno, Jessica Namakkal, Saadia Yacoob, and Imani Wadud for pushing me to find a better term.

7. https://islamophobiaisracism.wordpress.com, by Su'ad Abdul Khabeer, Arshad Ali, Evelyn Alsultany, Sohail Daulatzai, Lara Deeb, Carol Fadda, Zareena Grewal, Juliane Hammer, Nadine Naber, and Junaid Rana.

sible to overlook the centrality of not only race but also racism to many Islamophobic hate crimes and policies.[8] The racialization of Muslims as non-white and thus foreign bodies in the social fabric of the United States, whose otherness is variously linked to skin color, culture, and/or religion, has been demonstrated in a growing body of scholarship which has influenced my own work. Kimberlé Crenshaw's proposition of intersectionality was never solely the consideration of gender, race, class, and other factors as influential for power differentials in society. Rather, her analysis of structural, political, and representational intersections between race and gender carried forward the need to recognize and criticize racism and sexism as systemic and interconnected issues in need of change.[9]

In my consideration of the gendered dimensions of anti-Muslim hostility at the nexus of racism and religious othering, various claims to feminism need to be considered. In fact, as will become clear below, Muslim women's claims to being feminists, to making political demands from within feminism, and also to criticize (mostly white) feminists for their active participation in Islamophobic production play an important role in the arena of gendered anti-Muslim hostility. European and later American feminist thinkers and activists played an important role in the construction of oppressed Muslim women as a cornerstone of colonial ideology and later imperialist and military intervention. As Saba Mahmood and others have shown, these feminists continue to be important agents in anti-Muslim discursive production because they represent female and feminist authenticity.[10] In their support for military intervention, in Afghanistan and Iraq, such feminists cast Muslim women as victims of Muslim men, Muslim societies, and Islam, who are in need of saving, naturally by American and/or European intervention. There is no recognition though of the myriad ways in which Muslim women are victimized, harassed, discriminated against, threatened and killed in, and by the American society they are part of. It is this victimization of Muslim women that demonstrates the power of anti-Muslim hostility as a political discourse turned into acts of violence and that especially targets women who wear a headscarf because they are most easily recognizable as Muslim women.[11]

---

8. Love 2017, 18.
9. Crenshaw 1993.
10. Mahmood and Hirschkind 2002; Mahmood 2008.
11. There are quantitative studies of the discrimination and harassment American Muslims experience as well as organizations that track hate crimes. I opt here for the creation of a qualitative picture instead. It is important to note that a single incident has ripple effects in Muslim communities that reverberate as increased fear and threat of violence beyond the families of those attacked.

Muslim Women as Victims[12]

Our Three Winners

On the night of February 10, 2015, I received a frantic text message from a friend, telling me that three Muslims had been murdered in Chapel Hill. Earlier that day, Craig Stephen Hicks, a white man in his forties, had shot three residents of the apartment complex he lived in with his wife. Deah Barakat, 23, his wife, Yusor Abu-Salha, 21, and her sister, Razan Abu-Salha, 19, had been shot in the head at the entrance to their apartment. Barakat was a dentistry student at UNC Chapel Hill, where I teach; his wife of less than two months had graduated from NC State University and was planning to start dentistry school later that year. Her sister Razan was a student at NC State University. The public debate and representations of the murders were dominated by designations of the incident as the outcome of a parking dispute on the one hand and clear recognition of the events as a hate crime and tangible outcome of Islamophobic as well as racist sentiment. The three victims had been active members of their Muslim community and mosque; they were active humanitarians involved in many projects, including Habitat for Humanity, and, raised by families that were of Syrian-Palestinian and Jordanian-Palestinian backgrounds respectively, they had been model American Muslim citizens.

The local Muslim community was reeling in pain and shock at the loss of three young people who had their lives ahead of them. The families tried to make sense of their violent deaths through celebrating their achievements in the short time they had on earth, designating them "Our Three Winners."[13] Suzanne Barakat, Deah's older sister, became a media spokesperson on behalf of victims of Islamophobic violence,[14] and his brother, Farris, continued his work through the Lighthouse Project, a center for youth and community engagement in Chapel Hill.[15]

Yusor and Deah had been married for less than two months when they were murdered. Deah had lived in their apartment by himself until their wedding and did not report any issues with Hicks, a neighbor, until Yusor moved in. Yusor wore a headscarf and so did her sister Razan who, together with other friends and family members, came to visit the young couple. It

---

12. In what follows, I will be retelling the stories of several incidents in the recent past. The information is easily found online, so I will refrain from linking to specific news stories for every detail and claim.

13. http://ourthreewinners.org.

14. See Suzanne Barakat's TED talk, "Islamophobia killed my brother; let's end the hate," https://www.ted.com/talks/suzanne_barakat_islamophobia_killed_my_brother_let_s_end_the_hate; October 2016.

15. https://projectlight.house.

is impossible to ignore the signs of an anti-Muslim hate crime despite attempts by media, local leadership, and law enforcement to cast doubt on the motivations of the killer by casting him as a gun-loving atheist who was frustrated by the lack of parking in the compound.[16] In other words, a lone white man who may or may not have been mentally unstable. At the time I write this, in July 2017, Hicks is still awaiting trial and sentencing.

Defending the Victim

On May 26, 2017, a 17-year old Muslim girl wearing a headscarf and her 16-year old African American friend were riding a light rail train in Portland, Oregon, when they were approached by Jeremy Joseph Christian, who verbally harassed her by shouting anti-Muslim as well as racist slurs at her and her friend. Other passengers on the train intervened and tried to shield the girls from the attacker. Three men in particular, Ricky John Best, 53, Taliesin Myrddin Namkai-Meche, 23, and Micah David-Cole Fletcher, 21, formed a barrier in front of the girls and attempted to de-escalate the situation. Christian then attacked the three men with a knife. Best and Namkai-Meche died of their injuries and Cole-Fletcher required hospitalization for a knife wound to his neck but survived. The original victims of the attack fled the train and only the friend of the Muslim girl came forward several days later.

The three men were hailed as heroes and their deaths were mourned by their communities and families as well as politicians, law enforcement, and rights organizations. The attacker, Jeremy Christian, was identified as a previous violent offender with right-wing views and neo-nazi ties and tendencies. In one court hearing as well as after his arrest, he repeated his racist, anti-Muslim, and xenophobic statements. His family and friends claimed that he had become unstable and would have required mental health support.

The murders of Best and Namkai-Meche on that train were Islamophobic hate crimes as well. They demonstrated not only the vulnerability of visibly Muslim women and girls but also the threat of violence against those who stand to defend them. While the defenders were rightfully hailed as representatives of true civic values and the best of America, they paid with their lives for their willingness to protect a Muslim girl under threat.

Murder in Ramadan

On June 18, 2017, Nabra Hassanen, a 17-year old Muslim girl of Sudanese-American background was abducted, sexually assaulted, and then killed in

16. Katz 2015.

Fairfax in Northern Virginia. At 4am, she had been out with a group of Muslim friends for *sahur*, the traditional meal before the commencing of daytime fasting in Ramadan, and on their way back to the mosque. The suspect in her murder, Darwin Martinez Torres, identified as an un-documented immigrant from El Salvador, was arrested the next day. Nabra also wore a headscarf and was an active member of her Muslim community, the ADAMS Center, and would have started her junior year of high school in fall 2017.

While law enforcement and investigators argued that the assault and murder were not a hate crime and did not investigate it as such, Nabra's father, family, and community have maintained that the assault was motivated by anti-Muslim hatred and by racism. The community has struggled to make sense of the tragic incident and of the increased fear and threat that American Muslims have had to recognize as central to their lives over the past decade.

These are three incidents, events in which people lost their lives by violent means, and they are only the tip of an iceberg of physical assaults, verbal intimidation, and many other facets and forms of discrimination leveled specifically against Muslim women.[17] They could be reduced to the singular responsibility of their perpetrators, and in each case both media representations and treatment by law enforcement and the legal system suggest that their acts have effectively been reduced to individual culpability. What is erased in the process is the pervasive climate of anti-Muslim hatred and racism, which makes such individualized attacks not only possible but inevitable. When Yusor and Razan Abu-Salha were killed, where was the outrage from white feminist pundits who were otherwise so eager to save Muslim women? Who would protect Muslim women from harassment and assault after the deaths of Ricky Best and Taliesin Myrddin Namkai-Meche in Portland, realizing that it might cost them their lives?

Instead of an organized effort to save Muslim women and girls from Islamophobic attacks, the Islamophobia industry[18] continues to focus its efforts on the casting of Muslim men as inherently dangerous and potential terrorists. In 2013, I argued that the oppressed, terrified, and silenced Muslim woman was the other side of the same coin of representation: Muslim men as violent and Islam the religion that enables such violence to then

---

17. See, for example, Perry 2014.

18. Reports such as Fear Inc. have described the production of Islamophobic discourse as a multi-million dollar industry financed by right-wing organizations and networks that also support pro-Israel lobbying and white supremacy projects in American politics and media. See Ali et al. 2011.

be inflicted on both Muslim women and non-Muslims. This discursive construction is then used to cast Islam as alien to American liberal values and Muslim countries as in need of military intervention.[19] However, the playbook of anti-Muslim discourse has evolved such that Muslim women themselves, in more varied and complex ways, have become threats.

Muslim Women as Threats

I have never been comfortable with the language of immigration waves. Similarly, the story of Muslims in the United States has often been told as one of consecutive waves of Muslim immigrants or an influx of them in certain periods. Aside from the problematic erasure of African Muslim slaves who were forcefully and violently brought to the Americas rather than immigrating, this narrative likens migrating groups of people to the potential violence of nature. A wave can be a tsunami; it can flood the lands and wreak destruction. Migrants, with their cultural, ethnic, and linguistic diversity can similarly be cast to threaten the supposed homogeneity of a country and overwhelm its society with their difference.

The United States has a troubled relationship with its own settler colonialist history and the ways in which later groups of immigrants were perceived as new to a country that did not belong to the original settlers in the first place but belonged even less to their later counterparts. It was constructed as a nation of white Protestant Christians with the right to colonize and populate the land and all those who, like Native Americans, African American descendants of slaves, East Asian immigrants, and many other people of color, and of other religions, needed to be defined as foreign and in need of assimilation.[20] From early twentieth-century immigration policies and regulations that favored Northern Europeans and thus whites as immigrants to the racist rules of the National Origins Act and the Asian Exclusion Act to the 2017 Muslim Ban, the US government has defined the limits of inclusion by means of categories that make some immigrants much more welcome than others.

19. The Islamophobia industry is deeply embedded in the US political system rather than being a media production venture only. Agency and power differentials matter for understanding the ways in which Islamophobic discourse is deployed for both domestic and foreign-policy purposes and decisions. Right-wing media outlets and media pundits are not easily distinguished from journalism and reporting in the era of fake news and alternative outlets. There is at the very least a triangle of actors, media consumers (a.k.a. the public), media producers, and policy makers, who all interact with each other.

20. The irony is of course that assimilation into whiteness was promised to some but never possible. Conversion to (Protestant) Christianity held greater promise but could not yield inclusion and acceptance as it always intersected with racial exclusion.

For American Muslims, 63 percent of whom were born outside the United States, their essential foreignness is cast in terms of cultural and religious difference as well as racial non-whiteness. Muslim women play a significant role in these constructions because they are perceived as (re)producing Muslim bodies that increase the number of Muslims in the country. It is only a short step from there to representing Muslim women as the foundation of a fifth column that grows in size with every Muslim baby that is born.

Threatening Babies

In one stunning example of such discriminatory logic, Texas Congressman Louie Gohmert, in 2010, took to the floor of the House to argue that Muslims were involved in a plot that would bring women to the United States to birth what would later be dubbed "terror babies." He reportedly said:

> It appeared they would have young women who became pregnant [and] would get them into the United States to have a baby. They wouldn't even have to pay anything for the baby, ... And then they would return back where they could be raised and coddled as future terrorists. And then one day, 20, 30 years down the road, they can be sent in to help destroy our way of life."[21]

No evidence of Gohmert's claims was ever presented. However, they represent one version of the deep-seated distrust and dislike of the presence of Muslims in American society. In addition, Gohmert's remarks link Muslims in the United States and the children born to them to the discussion of "anchor babies" as brought into the conversation by South Carolina Republican Senator Lindsey Graham, also in summer 2010. Graham alleged that illegal immigrants were abusing the Fourteenth Amendment by entering the United States to birth United States citizens.[22]

In March 2017, Iowa congressional representative and prominent Republican, Steve King, tweeted: "We can't restore our civilization with somebody else's babies." In response to outrage and criticism he then doubled down and explained in a CNN interview that "You cannot rebuild your civilization with somebody else's babies. You've got to keep your birth rate up, and that you need to teach your children your values." He explained: "In doing so, you can grow your population, you can strengthen your culture, and you can strengthen your way of life." He reiterated his concern about the decline of American culture and that he is "a champion for Western civilization," fur-

21. Hu 2010.
22. NPR 2010.

ther elaborating that different people "contribute differently to our culture and civilization."[23]

King's remarks are easily linked to both the Trump administration's promises to control and limit immigration and the specific provisions of what came to be called the "Muslim Ban." Western civilization as well as American culture have long been stand-ins for white and Christian values in the parlance of conservative and right-wing discourse. Both deem people of color and people of other religions to be outside of such Western and/or American culture and make it impossible for Muslims to be read as anything other than foreign and a threat to such cultural homogeneity. Note also King's emphasis on "re-building" this Western civilization, which implies that it is not only threatened (by brown and black bodies and by other religions) but that damage has already been inflicted on it which needs repairing.

Megan Goodwin has developed a powerful theoretical tool for analyzing the construction of religious and racial others as sexually deviant and a threat to American women. Her notion of "contraceptive nationalism"[24] helps make sense of both pulp nonfiction like Betty Mahmoody's book, *Not Without My Daughter* and broader narratives of the sexual threat that Muslim men pose to American society:

> Hostage narratives like *Not Without My Daughter* – or *Argo*, or *Reading Lolita in Tehran* – are prophylactic, protecting the American body politic from invasion by presumably contaminating outside forces. In *Daughter*, Islam presents a racialized sexual peril embodied by Iranian Muslim men, who attempt to compromise a white Protestant woman's freedoms. Betty Mahmoody instantiates contraceptive nationalism in her vehement rejection of Muslim masculinity as irredeemably un-American, and exculpates her own exogamous transgressions through her grueling and treacherous bid for liberation. *Daughter* is thus not only a tale of captivity, but one of atonement. Betty Mahmoody narrates her repentance of exogamy and is redeemed through her embodied resistance and ultimate triumph over the sexual peril of Islam.[25]

23. Schleifer 2017.

24. "This discourse emerges in the wake of second-wave US feminist activism toward gender equality during 1970s.... Contraceptive nationalism discredits and contains religious and sexual difference by characterizing religious outsiders as sexual predators. This discourse participates in the negotiation and regulation of public morality; it is an ostensibly secular discourse that is deeply (if sometimes unconsciously) inflected by conservative Christian sexual ethics." Goodwin 2016, 768.

25. Goodwin 2016, 769.

From the sexual peril that Muslim men pose to American women (a woman can obviously never be both Muslim and American) it is but a short logical step to keeping Muslims out of the United States altogether.

Banning Muslims

On January 27, 2017, the president of the United States, Donald Trump, issued Executive Order #13769, which suspended the US Refugee Admissions Program for 120 days, the entry of Syrian refugees indefinitely, and barred individuals, both immigrants and non-immigrants from seven countries (Iran, Iraq, Libya, Somalia, Sudan, Syrian, and Yemen), from entering the United States for an initial period of ninety days while also imposing additional screening procedures. Crucially, all seven of the countries on the list were Muslim majority nations. The "Muslim Ban" was immediately challenged in several courts and effectively suspended by court orders.

On March 6, 2017, the administration then produced an amended document, Executive Order #13780, which removed Iraq from the list of countries and lifted exclusionary measures from some individuals, including green card holders from the countries listed.[26] It responds to allegations that the original executive order targeted Muslims and provides some explanations for why individuals from the now six countries listed are an especially high security risk to the United States. This Muslim Ban 2.0 was also challenged in court and at least partially suspended until June 26, 2017, when the Supreme Court overruled earlier legal challenges and decided to hear full arguments later in the year. Earlier massive protests, especially at international airports, were drowned in legal details and debates that made it difficult for organizers to rally the broad support they enjoyed in January.

The text of the original executive order contains this statement linking immigration restrictions for Muslims back to the task of protecting Muslim women:

> In order to protect Americans, the United States must ensure that those admitted to this country do not bear hostile attitudes toward it and its founding principles. The United States cannot, and should not, admit those who do not support the Constitution, or those who would place violent ideologies over American law. In addition, the United States should not admit those who engage in acts of bigotry or hatred (*including "honor" killings, other forms of violence against women, or the persecution of those who practice religions different*

---

26. Executive Office of the President 2017b.

from their own) or those who would oppress Americans of any race, gender, or sexual orientation.[27]

I have good reason to discuss the Muslim Ban here: while the statement above on honor killings and violence against women seems to single out Muslim women as victims, the executive orders themselves do not contain any provisions for protecting Muslim women (or children) by allowing them to enter the country. Quite the opposite, the ban on immigrants, refugees, and visitors applies indiscriminately to people of all genders, thus extending the embodied threat of Muslim immigrants to women as well as men. The (supposed) concern for oppressed and threatened Muslim women has been replaced by mapping the inherent violence and danger of Islam onto their bodies as much as onto those of Muslim men. This perhaps newly fabricated fear of Muslim women, not only as biological producers of more Muslims, has found one further expression in the representation of women as accomplices in men's terrorist attacks on American soil.

Muslim Women Terrorists

On December 2, 2015, fourteen people were killed and twenty-two others were seriously injured in a mass shooting at the Inland Regional Center in San Bernadino, California. The shooting was carried out by Syed Rizwan Farook and his wife, Tashfeen Malik, who lived in Redlands, and targeted the Christmas party of the San Bernardino County Department of Public Health, where Farook worked. Both Farook and Malik were shot and killed in a shootout with police later that day. Farook was a US-born citizen of Pakistani descent and Malik, born in Pakistan, held a green card.

Much has been written about the couple's motivations for the attack, with the FBI investigation concluding that both had been radicalized by propaganda from radical Islamist groups. However, no direct connection to any such group in the form of instructions and their participation in radical networks has been discovered. They had traveled abroad, including to Saudi Arabia, and police found large amounts of weapons, ammunition, and bomb-making equipment in their home after their deaths.

Tashfeen Malik is notable as the first Muslim woman on American soil to have actively participated in a violent attack herself. In media descriptions of her, I was struck by the struggle with apparent contradictions: how could a woman who was described by neighbors and acquaintances as quiet, a housewife, a new mother (she reportedly left her six-month old

27. Executive Office of the President 2017a.

daughter with her mother-in-law on the morning of the attack) also be a terrorist? The fact that she wore *niqab* was mentioned repeatedly as a sign of her gradual radicalization and some reports suggested that she may have been the instigator of the attack and a radicalizing influence on her husband of two years. The reports of her petite stature created an image of a physically unimposing, covered figure, who would wield a heavy gun with as much strength as her husband and kill as many victims in the attack. Malik presented as a contradiction to gendered representations of Muslim women as oppressed and without agency, thus effectively contributing to a new image of Muslim women as an embodied, violent threat to other Americans.

On June 12, 2016, Omar Mateen, 29, walked into the Pulse nightclub in Orlando, Florida and opened fire on the LGBTQ patrons present. In an attack that turned into a hostage situation and a standoff with law enforcement, Mateen killed forty-nine people and wounded fifty-eight others. The club was hosting a Latin night and the majority of the victims were Latinx as well as members of the LGBTQ community. Many claims were made about Mateen's motivations, including that he had frequented the club and struggled with his own sexuality and that he was not only inspired by the Islamic State group but had received direct assistance from them as well. He was described as disgruntled by his financial situation and confused about his religious and cultural values.

Mateen had been married to his first wife from 2009 to 2011 and she reported after the attack that he had been mentally unstable and physically abusive to her. Early news reports also claimed that his second wife, Noor Salman, had been a victim of domestic violence. However, in January 2017, she was arrested and charged with aiding and abetting a terrorist act as well as with obstruction of justice. Salman presented a very different profile of a Muslim woman. She did not wear a headscarf and scarcely appeared in early reporting on the attack, even though her husband's claimed struggles with his sexuality as well as domestic abuse suggested that she was primarily a victim as well. Little has been disclosed about how and why she might have supported the attack or at least knew about his plans and did not report or prevent it. However, her arrest and prosecution point to a development in which Muslim women are held responsible for not resisting their violent husbands and/or reporting them to law enforcement.

Both Malik and Salman point towards the emergence of new representations of Muslim women: the Muslim woman terrorist who is herself a threat to America and the Muslim woman supporter of terrorism who fails to turn her husband in. Both paint a picture of Muslim women exercising the wrong kind of agency; they are not coerced into these acts but they do not resist them either. They also, by including both women with and without headscarves, create a representation whereby *any* Muslim woman can be a suspect. Malik can also be said to hide her dangerousness behind her *niqab*, which when read as a tool of women's oppression would suggest that she does not have agency. Muslim women then join Muslim men as inherently suspicious as well as inherently prone to violence or at least violent ideology.

Dangerous Muslim Women Activists

Should the remedy for Muslim women's oppression not be that they become activists on their own behalf and exercise their liberal and individualized agency to be full human beings? Muslim women's agency, it seems, can only be actualized in a specific feminist framework that defines freedom of choice, individuality, and self-determination as the hallmarks of Eurocentric modernity. Like colonial feminists of the nineteenth century, who helped justify colonial domination with reports about the oppression of women in Muslim societies while they themselves did not even have the right to vote, feminist supporters and producers of Islamophobic discourse today can only accept and support Muslim women's activism when it supports these ideals *and* when they are willing to denounce their religion altogether. Nominal Muslimness may be acceptable if the representative activist is willing to question and criticize every aspect of their religion and promote Islam's need for a reformation.

Saba Mahmood, Moustafa Bayoumi, and Lila Abu-Lughod have all written extensively about the important role certain Muslims play in the production of anti-Muslim discourse. Such activists act as "native informers" and provide legitimacy to representations of Islam by offering personal confirmation and sharing terrible experiences of discrimination and oppression that both confirm negative ideas about Islam and Muslim men and justify various forms of intervention. One example of the complicated nature of this contested activist landscape is the documentary film, *Honor Diaries*, released in early 2014, which follows a group of mostly Muslim women activists who are brought together from their various activist projects to discuss their experiences as Muslim women and the abuses of women they are fighting against. The film chronicles female genital cutting, forced marriage, and child marriage practices in various countries and communities and generates outrage at the oppression and violation (mostly) Muslim women experience. Subtitled "culture is no excuse for abuse," it aims to enrage the viewer enough to support intervention in countries that allow or support these abuses of women and children. The film was produced by the Clarion Project, a major producer of Islamophobic materials, and received praise at film festivals and on college campuses.[28]

It was also identified as anti-Muslim propaganda material, as in the review of progressive Jewish blogger Richard Silverstein:

> There may be genuine, sincere feminists involved with this film. There may even be some legitimacy to the issues offered. But under the auspices of an Islam-hating outfit like Clarion, whatever good might've been possible in this project has been completely undermined. The participants have either been used without their awareness, believing they were doing good; or they've participated out of sharing the values of ... Clarion.[29]

However, Muslim women activists have limited agency when they dare to frame their advocacy projects and goals outside of the fold of "saving Muslim women" in that specific way. The past years have seen numerous instances of concerted (social) media attacks on those activists who do not work within Islamophobic networks and/or dare to define their political agendas in opposition to the "saving" movement. The most prominent example of the latter is Linda Sarsour.

Linda Sarsour

Sarsour, born in 1980 in Brooklyn, New York, is a Palestinian-American political activist and grassroots organizer. She is a former leader of the Arab American Association and was one of the organizers of the 2017 Women's March on Washington. Sarsour proudly represents her political goals as systemically connected and a fight against injustice: she supports Palestinian liberation and self-determination, self-identifies as a feminist activist, and supports the Black Lives Matter movement. She has a large social media presence (on Facebook and Twitter) and a large following of supporters and fellow activists. Sarsour, who wears a headscarf, has repeatedly framed her activism as inspired by her Islamic religion and is critical of those in her own Muslim community who want to limit women's participation and leadership in Muslim communal practice, knowledge production, and activism. With her increased national fame have come invitations for public speaking, including the commencement speech at City University of New York (CUNY) in June 2017.

28. http://www.honordiaries.com.
29. Silverstein 2014.

What interests me here is the barrage of rhetorical attacks on Sarsour and the consistent drawing of boundaries around who can define feminism, patriotism, and justice as American values and universal values. A few specific examples will illustrate this broader point.

In August 2015, *FrontPage Magazine* published an open letter to Sarsour, penned by Danusha Goska. The letter begins with a list of Sarsour's positions and honors she has received and a quote in which Sarsour identified as a feminist because she is a Muslim. Goska then tells the story of Kayla Mueller, a young American woman who was a humanitarian worker in Syria when she was captured by the Islamic State (IS) in 2013. Mueller died in IS captivity in 2015. Goska takes issue with Sarsour's insistence that the sexual assault and enslavement of women by IS fighters and leaders has nothing to do with Islam. The purpose of the letter is to demonstrate that Sarsour is a hypocrite who lies about the true nature of Islam and that she has no right to call herself a feminist either. The tone of the letter is condescending and accusatory; Goska quotes from the Qur'an and cites scholarly authorities for her claims about Islam and slavery; and in the end, she tells Sarsour that she could be saved if she recognized the true will of God and the prophets (Sarsour claims to be believe in). She does not say how.[30]

In January 2017, *The Federalist*, a conservative online magazine founded in 2013, published an essay by Shireen Qudosi, who is described as a "Sufi Muslim of Afghan and South Asian ancestry, and writer on Islam." In it, Qudosi rails against the Women's March, liberal feminism, and the Democratic Party's supposed embrace of Sarsour, and she hails President Trump as the quintessential representation of what has always moved America forward: productive controversy. The essay contains racist statements like this one: "An entire group of women, particularly women of color, have adopted the disability of self-victimization, even going so far as to ask 'white-women' participating in the march to observe and make space for women of color. " Qudosi describes Sarsour in these words:

> Venerated by leftists, Sarsour now rides the great beast of modern feminism much like the "god-King" Xerxes in "300." This weekend she and other heads of the Soros-connected movement protested against a democratically elected president. This is a Palestinian woman protesting about the democratic process in the freest country in the world.[31]

Profiled and maligned on websites like Counterjihad, Jihadwatch, and

30. Goska 2015.
31. Qudosi 2017.

many others, Sarsour is depicted as radical and extremist, naïve and cunning, hypocritical and dangerous – she is apparently the nightmare of right-wing and neo-conservative pundits and politicians.

Protest and controversy erupted as soon as Sarsour was announced as the CUNY commencement speaker. At CUNY, the opposition to her speaking related to her unapologetic championing of the Palestinian cause and many Jewish groups and individuals felt compelled to take a position.

Only a few weeks later, Sarsour spoke at the annual convention of the Islamic Society of North America (ISNA), the largest Muslim community organization in the country. In her speech at ISNA, Sarsour said,

> I hope that when we stand up to those who oppress our communities,
> that Allah accepts from us that as a form of jihad, that we are
> struggling against tyrants and rulers not only abroad in the Middle
> East or the other side of the world, but here in the United States
> of America, where you have fascists and white supremacists and
> Islamophobes reigning in the White House.[32]

Sarsour, on her part, is undeterred by the attacks and actively pushes back. In August 2017 she reiterated her commitments through a Facebook statement in which she linked her feminism to her "unapologetic love for Palestine and the Palestinian people," her "opposition to military occupation, colonization and land grabbing," her hijab, and her love for and adherence to her Islamic faith, challenging those who cannot "fathom to see women of color lead, inspire and win," who have faith "in a system that brutalizes people of color," and whose feminism "puts our lives in more danger." The post ends by saying, "YOU can keep your feminism. We promise you, we don't want it."[33]

Saving Muslim Women?

The events and people I have brought together in this chapter are puzzle pieces. Linked together, they form a disturbing picture of the shifting nature of gendered anti-Muslim hostility. Despite the many problems with saving Muslim women, it is clear that some Muslim women can no longer be saved. They have been cast outside the boundaries of savable victims of Islamic patriarchy and Muslim male violence and their bodies no longer matter (if they ever did in the first place). If casting Muslim women as victims was the only way to consider them fully human and entitled to safety, then this turn away is also a further step towards the dehumanization of Muslims in US

---

32. Abrams 2017.
33. https://www.facebook.com/linda.sarsour, August 3, 2017.

society. In the place of potentially savable victims, we find new castings of Muslim women: the Muslim woman terrorist, active shooter or supporter; the Muslim refugee woman who can no longer be trusted not to carry the same violent tendencies with her as her male counterparts; and lastly, the Muslim woman activist whose choice of political goals and causes threatens the very fabric of American conservative political discourse. She is proud to be a Muslim, she draws her moral values from her religion, she challenges the racist and anti-Black status quo of America, and she lays claim to a feminism that fights against patriarchy both within and outside of her Muslim communities. She reserves the right to build alliances, engage in multiple critique,[34] and recognize the systemic nature of racist, sexist, and neo-colonial exclusion and domination.

The consequences of these new constructions of Muslim women are frightening. Far beyond social media attacks, character assassination, and defamation, not to mention threats of sexual and other physical violence leveled against Muslim women activists, they form the foundation for the securitization of Muslim women. Virtually every Muslim woman can be designated a threat: at airport security, in public buildings, on the street, and in a mosque, and no Muslim woman can ever be completely trusted. Securitization also requires reducing Muslims to this specific aspect of their identities. These representations, as seen in the executive orders as well as FBI investigations, form the foundation for further state surveillance and the disciplining and control of Muslim bodes by the state. The presence of openly anti-Muslim and racist (and arguably sexist) policy advisors in the 2017 White House poses an increasing threat, not only to Muslim women, but all American Muslims, all people of color, and all those in the United States with social justice agendas.

The purpose of this chapter has been to chronicle the shifts in gendered anti-Muslim discourse, not only to tell the stories that need to be told, but to alert us as scholars and activists to the necessity of changing strategies to counter these developments and resist the continued dehumanization and securitization of US Muslims.

34. miriam cooke has elaborated on this concept: cooke 2000.

Works Cited

Abrams, A. 2017. "Women's March Organizer Linda Sarsour Spoke of 'Jihad.' But She Wasn't Talking About Violence." *Time Magazine,* July 6. http://time.com/4848454/linda-sarsour-jihad-comments-donald-trump.

Abu-Lughod, L. 2002. "Do Muslim Women Really Need Saving?" *American Anthropologist* 104:783-790.

——. 2013. *Do Muslim Women Need Saving?* Cambridge, MA.

Ali, W. E. Clifton, M. Duss, L. Fang, S. Keyes, and F. Shakir. 2011. "Fear Inc.: The Roots of the Islamophobia Network in America." Center for American Progress. http://www.americanprogress.org/issues/2011/08/islamophobia.html.

cooke, m. 2000. "Multiple Critique: Islamic Feminist Rhetorical Strategies." *Nepantla* 1:91-110.

Crenshaw, K. 1993. "Mapping the Margins: Intersectionality, Identity Politics, and Violence against Women of Color." *Stanford Law Review* 43:1242-1299.

Executive Office of the President. 2017a. Executive Order No. 13769 (Protecting the Nation from Foreign Terrorist Entry into the United States). 82 FR 8977 (February 1, 2017). https://www.federalregister.gov/documents/2017/02/01/2017-02281/protecting-the-nation-from-foreign-terrorist-entry-into-the-united-states.

——. 2017b. Executive Order No. 13780 (Protecting the Nation from Foreign Terrorist Entry into the United States). 82 FR 13209 (March 1, 2017). https://www.federalregister.gov/documents/2017/03/09/2017-04837/protecting-the-nation-from-foreign-terrorist-entry-into-the-united-states.

Goodwin, M. 2016. "They Do That to Foreign Women": Domestic Terrorism and Contraceptive Nationalism in *Not Without My Daughter.*" *Muslim World* 106:759-780.

Goska, D. 2015. "An Open Letter to Muslim Feminist Linda Sarsour." *FrontPage Magazine*, August 17. http://www.frontpagemag.com/fpm/259811/open-letter-muslim-feminist-linda-sarsour-danusha-v-goska.

Hammer, J. 2012. *American Muslim Women, Religious Authority, and Activism: More Than a Prayer* Austin.

——. 2013a. "Gendering Islamophobia: (Muslim) Women's Bodies and American Politics." *Bulletin for the Study of Religion* 42:29-36.

——. 2013b. "Center Stage: Muslim Women and Islamophobia." In *Islamophobia in America*, edited by C. Ernst, 107-144. New York.

Hu, E. 2010. "TX Rep. Louis Gohmert Warns of Terrorist Babies." *Texas Tribune*, June 28. http://www.texastribune.org/texas-mexico-border-news/arizona-immigration-law/tx-rep-louie-gohmert-warns-of-terrorist-babies.

Katz, J. 2015. "In Chapel Hill, Suspect's Rage Went Beyond a Parking Dispute." *New York Times*, March 3. https://www.nytimes.com/2015/03/04/us/chapel-hill-muslim-student-shootings-north-carolina.html?mcubz=3.

Love, E. 2017. *Islamophobia and Racism in America.* New York.

Mahmood, S. 2008. "Feminism, Democracy, and Empire: Islam and the War on Terror." In *Women's Studies on the Edge*, edited by J. Scott, 81–114. Durham.

Mahmood, S., and C. Hirschkind. 2002. "Feminism, the Taliban, and Politics of Counter-Insurgency." *Anthropological Quarterly* 75:339–354.

NPR 2010. "The Debate over Anchor Babies and Citizenship." National Public Radio, August 18. http://www.npr.org/templates/story/story. php?storyId=129279863.

Perry, B. 2014. "Gendered Islamophobia: Hate Crimes against Muslim Women." *Social Identities* 20.1:74–89.

Qudosi, S. 2017. "Linda Sarsour's Muslim Identity Politics Epitomize Feminism's Hypocrisy." *The Federalist*, January 24. http://thefederalist. com/2017/01/24/linda-sarsours-muslim-identity-politics-epitomize-feminisms-hypocrisy.

Schleifer, T. 2017. "King doubles down on controversial 'babies' tweet." CNN, March 14. http://www.cnn.com/2017/03/13/politics/steve-king-babies-tweet-cnntv/index.html.

Silverstein, R. 2014. "Clarion Project's New Islamophobic Film, 'Honor Diaries,'" *Tikun Olam*, March 27. https://www.richardsilverstein. com/2014/03/27/clarion-funds-new-islamophobic-film-honor-diaries.

Spivak, G. 1988. "Can the Subaltern Speak?" In *Marxism and the Interpretation of Culture*, edited by C. Nelson and L. Grossberg, 67-111. Champaign, IL.

Part Three

Marginalization and Activism

Muslim Detroit after Orlando:
The LGBTQ Question, Rituals of Inclusion, and Coalition Building across Racial and Religious Lines

Alisa M. Perkins

THE ORLANDO PULSE NIGHTCLUB shooting on June 12, 2016, resulted in one of the highest death tolls of any mass gun violence in modern US history. In the aftermath of the tragedy, thousands joined vigils that took place across the United States, which gave people a space to collectively mourn and express solidarity with Orlando victims and their families. Vigils also provided community leaders the opportunity to formulate coherent narratives about the violence in a space set apart from inflammatory media coverage.

On the evening after the shooting, about one hundred people gathered in Detroit's Clark Park for an event called "Orlando Vigil: Southwest Detroit Stands in Solidarity." Former Michigan State Representative Rashida Tlaib, who was soon to become one of the two first Muslim women in history to enter the US Congress, stood on a circular platform at the park's center, surrounded by community activists and religious leaders.[1] Her pre-teen son stood by her side, with both arms encircling her.[2] As she spoke, she began to weep, but her words remained clear:

> What's so hard with all this is that even as a Muslim I see what
> happens to so many people over the weekend, the dehumanization
> that happens, because of our faith, because of who we love. If my son
> was to love a man, I don't care. I will love him because love is love....
> So please, I want you to hug your children, but I want you to reach out
> to LGBTQ, the Muslim, Latino,... African American, our living victims
> of mass shootings.... In the legislature for six years, we've talked about
> gun control. We have talked about Charleston and those babies that
> died in the school.... No one should have to have a gun like that – no

1. I have retained the names of people whose statements are public. For interviews, all the names are changed.

2. Tlaib was the first Muslim American woman elected to the Michigan legislature and the second Muslim woman to serve in a state legislature. In a 2018 special election, Tlaib won Michigan's thirteenth congressional district – making her one of the first two Muslim women elected to Congress in US history.

one. You can support the second amendment; we can promote it, but not with an AK-whatever-the-hell-it-was.... Please, take on hate with your vote. Promise me you will vote.

In the opening of her speech, Tlaib asserts that the impulse toward dehumanization that spurred Omar Mateen to kill LGBTQ individuals over "who they love" sprung from the same source of hatred that drives people to degrade and destroy the lives of people based on "our faith," indexing Muslim Americans and other targeted faith-based minorities. Later, Tlaib refers to Muslims, Latinos, and African Americans as "living victims" of the mass shooting, linking them together as symbolic targets of the violence.

Like other community leaders in vigils across the United States, Tlaib pointedly identified herself as a Muslim during her speech. In an interview with her after the event, she explained that she did so partly to challenge narratives associating the shooter's motivation with Islam, such as the narrative voiced by then-presidential candidate Donald Trump.[3] By connecting the killings instead to social factors such as lax gun laws and American homophobia, Tlaib offered participants an actionable way to respond to the shooting, rather than remaining focused on the shooter's identity and personal motivations. As part of this, Tlaib alluded to The Campaign to Take on Hate, a national-level movement which, according to its website, works to "challenge this country's growing prejudice and persistent misconception of Arab and Muslim Americans" and "stands against bigotry toward all people."[4] Several Muslim American Take on Hate leaders stood near Tlaib on the stage as she spoke.

The shooter, Omar Mateen, was a Muslim. He had targeted a group of young, mainly Latinx LGBTQ individuals who were dancing at a club.[5] Mainstream press accounts associated Mateen's violence to a pathologized Muslim identity that caused him to despise his own same-sex desires and to externalize his turmoil with bloodshed.[6] These interpretations are problem-

3. Graham 2016b.

4. https://www.takeonhate.org/faq..

5. Lantinx is a gender-neutral alternative to Latino or Latina that some scholars and activists have adopted over the past few years. In this paper I use it when talking about populations and movements defining their identity with reference to marginalized gender and sexuality. At other times I use the term "Latino," following the patterns of use I observed among Latino/a/x community activists. See Ramirez and Blay 2016.

6. Ackerman 2016; Perez, Prokupecz, Shoichet and Porte 2016. Mateen claimed to have carried out the attacks in the name of ISIS and in response to specific American attacks targeting ISIS in Syria and Iraq. Some reporters emphasized Mateen's self-identification as a radicalized "Islamic soldier" in their analysis of the factors that motivated Mateen's violence. Alexander, Lawler, Sherlock, Akkoc and Graham 2016; Alter 2016. These reporters often fea-

atic on many levels, particularly because they cast endemically American forms of gun violence and homophobia as Muslim problems, obviating any kind of national self-reflection by scapegoating Muslims as "the other."[7]

While many news channels interpreted Mateen's act in an Islamophobic register, other sources sought to address the issue from multiple angles, some directly contesting the racializing frame. Some media channels featured the voices of LGBTQ Muslims.[8] Other sources provided interviews with scholars of Islam and religious leaders to answer doctrinal questions or to relay the histories of same-sex attraction in different Muslim cultures and societies.[9] Muslim American and LGBTQ activists engaged in many different forms of demonstration and expression in blogs, events such as public prayers for Orlando victims, and blood drives to offer various representations of solidarity.[10] This resulted in an unprecedented flow of information on the issue of Islam, Muslims, and same-sex attraction.

Questions about Islam, homosexuality, and othering boundaries are particularly salient ones in this age of increasing white nationalism and right-wing homophobic rhetoric. Studying how people find a way to respond to Islamophobia, racism, and homophobia together can help us understand the potential for strategic alliance formations among stigmatized groups. By gathering leaders of minority communities together to address the shooting, vigils that took place across the US allowed room for leaders and participants to imagine how Muslim, Arab, LGBTQ, Latinx, African American, and other minorities might represent shared struggles. For example, reflecting new attention to the importance of coalitional politics for Mus-

---

tured interviews with the shooter's father, Seddique Mir Mateen, who openly expressed his rejection of homosexuality to the press, supporting the ideas that homophobia had directly and personally impacted Mateen. Sullivan and Wan 2016. Reporters who stressed the possibility of Mateen's homosexuality centered their analysis on interviews with one of Mateen's ex-wives, with various individuals who claimed to have had intimate same-sex relations with Mateen, and with others who said that they interacted with him casually on online dating sites. Quoting official intelligence from the FBI, other outlets countered that there was no concrete evidence that Mateen's sexuality had played any role in the shootings. Man Who Says He Was Omar Mateen's Gay Lover Speaks Out 2016; Hennessy-Fiske, Jarvie, and Wilber 2016. The FBI also claimed that there was no evidence that Mateen had frequented LGBTQ clubs or had engaged with homosexual partners either online or in person. Hennessy-Fiske 2016.

7. Legal scholar Leti Volpp demonstates how the legacy of Orientalism links Muslim Americans to gender-based and sexuality-based violence. Volpp 2000; Volpp 2002. For a related analysis of how these tropes are attached to Muslims in Germany, see Ewing 2008.

8. Mehta 2016; Orlando Terror Attack Updates: Obama Meets with Victims' Families in Orlando 2016.

9. Jahangir 2016; DiFurio 2016; Jamieson and Neubert 2016; van der Krogt 2016; Markoe 2016.

10. Graham 2016a; Kuruvilla 2016; Durando 2016.

lim Americans, some recent scholarship employs the term AMSA to refer to groups and organizations sharing concerns across the spectrum of Arab, Muslim, and South Asian Americans.[11]

There were more than a dozen vigils held in the Detroit metro area after the Orlando shooting, and Muslim Americans played a prominent role in organizing and attending some of them. In some ways this was not surprising, given the high concentration of Muslim Americans in the area and their robust history of engagement in civic and political activism. But in another sense, this Muslim American visibility was completely unanticipated given the historical reluctance on the part of the area's Muslim community and religious leaders to publically acknowledge and support LGBTQ identities and concerns. Thus, in focusing on Muslim American public responses to Orlando, this chapter analyzes novel forms of coalition building.

The motivation to cross race, class, and gender lines expressed by Muslim American participants at the vigils exemplifies larger trends in Muslim American advocacy work taking place throughout the nation. Some Muslim American organizations are becoming more likely to seek alliances with other groups that they perceive having shared vulnerabilities under US white racial, economic, and cultural hegemony. Scholars such as Sunaina Maira link this trend in part to the shifting demographics of the Muslim American population, namely the coming of age of the "post-9/11 generation" who are sensitized to overlapping discrimination. Maira describes the consciousness of some young Muslim Americans and their peers as generating "alternative forms of politics that can provide a critique of Islamophobia, racism, and imperial violence as well as of neoliberal multi-culturalism, rights-based politics, and humanitarianism."[12] Her book catalogues these groups' changing engagement with intersecting "questions of civil rights, human rights, women's rights, and gay rights."[13] Some scholars describe how this trend toward identity politics and rights-based approaches may signify the dawn of a "new civil rights era" in Muslim American advocacy work.[14]

Further, the emerging alliances featured at the vigils exemplify what sociologist Eric Love describes as "transformational" coalitions.[15] Transfor-

11. Islamophobes frequently target Arabs and South Asians across religious lines (especially Sikhs) in their attacks. See Iyer 2015, 15. American organizations coming together as "Arabs" or "South Asians" often include a focus on pan-Muslim American concerns, as well as those relating to non-Muslims in the ethnic groups they serve. Maira 2016, 14–15.

12. Maira 2016, 3.

13. Maira 2016, 4.

14. Love 2017, 229. Hisham Aidi refers to the tendency of some Muslim Americans to identify with other marginalized minority groups as "racialization from below." Aidi 2014, 162–164.

15. Love draws his terminology from the work of Rev. Dr. William J. Barber II, President of NAACP's North Carolina chapter and Disciples of Christ pastor, who devoted several books and

mational coalitions imply the creation of shared agendas that entail risk, compromise, sacrifice, and the development of new forms of consciousness.[16] Muslim American and other activists I interviewed described how their work at the vigils produced a sense of intimacy, inter-dependency, and a shared identity with other vigil organizers and participants across race, class, and religious lines. They also explain the risk involved in taking on LGBTQ allies. This is especially the case because questions about Muslim Americans' stance on issues relating to LGBTQ visibility are part of a larger, ongoing debate within theological and popular Muslim American circles. There is also risk involved for Muslim Americans who wish to embrace African American and Latino American struggles and to articulate messages of dissent from the status quo. This is because some believe that Muslim American political struggles should remain centered in "respectability politics" or forging alliances with others who are already accepted by the mainstream.[17]

The vigils provided a means for the symbolic expression of these transformative coalitions through ritual process. Following urban anthropologist Roger Sanjek, I analyze the vigils as "public ritual events"[18] intended to express shared sentiment and advance political messages in symbolic registers. Such events work simultaneously on cognitive, affective, and emotional levels.[19] Anthropologist David Kertzer defines "ritual" as "symbolic behavior that is socially standard and repetitive."[20] He stresses the importance of symbol and ritual in enacting social change and expressing political meanings. For Kertzer, "symbols instigate social action and define the individual's sense of self. They also furnish the means by which people make sense of the political process, which largely represents itself to the people in symbolic form."[21]

---

articles to exploring the dynamics of coalition building. Bean 2013 cited in Love 2017, 145. See also Barber 2016; Barber and Wilson-Hartgrove 2016.

16. In contrast to transformational coalitions, Love describes transactional coalitions as relatively low-investment relationships developed between organizations. These coalitions are often developed around single issues. They may come into being around a particular act, such as signing a petition, with no promise or expectation of further commitment. Over time, transactional coalitions may develop into transformational coalitions if the parties involved mutually agree to move in that direction. Love 2017, 150–151.

17. Higginbotham 1994. For examples of how Muslim American respectability politics impacted communities and organizations, see Karim 2005; Karim 2009; GhaneaBassiri 2010, 230–241.

18. Sanjek 1998, 8; Sanjek 1992.

19. Drawing on Brian Massumi, Deborah Gould defines affect as intensities of feeling that underlie emotional, cognitive, and physiological expressions. Affect comes into being on a nonconscious plane, and these intensities of feeling turn into something else once they are exposed in words or action. Massumi 2002 in Gould 2010, 26.

20. Kertzer 1988, 7.

21. Kertzer 1988, 6.

Public ritual events usually take place in central locations. The public ritual events that Sanjek observed in his ethnography of Queens, New York, "broke the flow of ordinary events" by including formal behavior such as speeches, processions, candle lighting, and the sharing of food.[22] Deborah Gould explores the way that social movement leaders use such demonstrations to offer "emotional pedagogy" used to fuel political engagement.[23] Most importantly for my work, public ritual events like the Orlando vigils allow people to challenge boundaries between "us" and "them," "self" and "other" in symbolic and affective language.[24] In crafting these events, social actors create spectacles, intentionally drawing the attention of the press in hopes of changing local and national conversations. Taking symbolic and ritual dimensions into account, I show how the Orlando vigils both create and rehearse novel forms of coalition building and political dissent for Muslim Americans.

Muslim American Coalition Building

After Orlando, several community activists that I interviewed commented that the public display of coalition building between AMSA and LGBTQ groups was a novelty to them, even if they had been aware of such connections developing slowly and outside of the spotlight. By contrast, the will for Muslim Americans to reach across race, class, and religious boundaries in their post-Orlando advocacy work has a much older history. Evidence for this kind of race and class crossing for Arab, South Asian, and African American Muslim communities has been meticulously detailed by a range of scholars.[25] Yet, this scholarship also acknowledges that such cross-racial and interclass alliance formation has not been an especially prominent or consistent feature of Muslim American advocacy work through generations. One reason for this pertains to the way that national-level leadership for Muslim American advocacy groups has generally been dominated by Arab or South Asian Americans from relatively elite or white-aspiring classes. The option of "passing as white" for some, but not all, Muslim Americans has provided several routes for Muslim American organizations to ally with the dominant majority, to identify with racial minorities such as African Americans, or to opt for a separatist orientation.[26] This, of course, has not been an option for African American Muslims, who have a unique history of coalition formation across ethnic, racial, and religious lines.

22. Sanjek 1998, 8.
23. Gould 2010, 39.
24. Barth 1969.
25. GhaneaBassiri 2010; Dannin 2002; Iyer 2015; Howell 2014.
26. Abdulrahim 2008. See also Majaj 2000; Samhan 1999.

Erik Love describes the general tendency for Arab American and Muslim American organizations to have maintained a "centripetal" dynamic or inward-looking dynamic from their earliest histories as a complex phenomenon relating to national political factors.[27] In Love's analysis, the late 1950s civil rights era afforded a brief push for some Arab American organizations, such as the American-Arab Anti-Discrimination Committee (ADC), to organize across racial lines.[28] However, that age quickly ended with the rise of a period of supposed colorblind ideology in the 1970s and 1980s, which included government policies that actively discouraged or did not incentivize identity-based politics. Especially since 9/11, there has been an increased push on the part of Muslim American community activists and leaders to recognize the links between Islamophobia and racism, and thus to partner more closely with groups defined by race. The approach of public figures like prominent Arab-American advocate Linda Sarsour exemplifies this trend.[29]

Public Secular and Private Religious Vigils: Two Modes of Mourning LGBTQ Lives

The primary field site for this project on Orlando vigils was the metro Detroit area, including Southwest Detroit, Dearborn, and Ferndale. However, the first vigil I attended was in Kalamazoo, the city where I live and work, which is about two hours west of the metro Detroit area. I collected data on eight vigils in all: seven in the metro Detroit area and one in Kalamazoo, Michigan. I attended two of these vigils: the one in Kalamazoo, and one in Dearborn.[30] I interviewed seventeen people who took part in these vigils either as organizers, speakers, or attendees to understand the logistics, meaning, and impact of these events and their implications for understanding Muslim American coalition building.[31] I collected further information about the vigils from blogs, Facebook posts, and media sources. I also watched videos and analyzed transcripts of vigil speeches.

27. Love 2017, 62–65.
28. Love 2017, 154–159.
29. Love 2017, 204.
30. The vigil that I attended in Kalamazoo was organized by a group of community activists and held in a public park outside Kalamazoo City Hall. Jones 2016. It took place on the evening of June 13, a day after the event. Attending this event piqued my interest in carrying out a study of these vigils in the Detroit metro area, a place in which I have carried out fieldwork since 2007. By the time I could arrange a trip to Detroit, most of the vigils had already taken place, except for the one that I attended in Dearborn on July 22, 2017, which was organized by a group called Muslim Youth Connections.
31. Fourteen of the study participants were involved in one or more of the Detroit metro area vigils, and three were involved with the one in Kalamazoo.

Most if not all of the people I interviewed considered themselves community activists. Among these were members of civil liberties groups, anti-racist coalitions, and immigrant-rights groups. Also included were LGBTQ activists, municipal and state level politicians, and religious leaders affiliated with Sunni, Shiʿa, Catholic, and other congregations. I also interviewed activists and vigil attendees who identified as secularist or atheist. Study participants belonged to various ethnic and racial groups, including African American, Arab American, South Asian American, Latin American, and white.

I classified the eight vigils included in this study into two categories: five public secular vigils and three private religious vigils. I define public secular vigils as those that came together with the input of a broad range of community activists, politicians, and religious leaders. Mainly, the vigils that I classified as public secular ones took place outdoors, in locations such as parks, at the waterfront, or outside City Hall. One public vigil took place within a LGBTQ center, but the organizers of the event came from multiple organizations and communities. Event organizers of public vigils highlighted the LGBTQ identities of those who had been slain. They did this through including many signs and symbols of LGBTQ identity such as rainbow flags and by inviting prominent LGBTQ organizers to speak at the event.

I also gathered data on three private religious vigils. Two of the private religious vigils that I studied took place within Shiʿi mosques in Dearborn. A third took place at a school and was held by a Muslim youth group closely associated with a Shiʿi religious leader.[32] In an important way, these private religious vigils had a public aspect as well because they were open to all. But, in contrast to those vigils I classify as public secular ones, these private religious vigils were more tightly controlled by the organizations that hosted them. Organizers of events also made deliberate efforts to cross racial, religious, and class lines. However, as will be made clear in the following descriptions and analyses, certain kinds of expressions of solidarity were deliberately encouraged or discouraged to fit in with the vigil organizers' vision in a way that seemed more exclusionary than the organizational strategy found at the public secular vigils. These private religious events also took place indoors, contributing to the organizers' ability to influence the events.

Another difference between the public secular and private religious vigils concerned the presence or absence of Muslim religious leaders. While

---

32. The fact that Shiʿi religious organizations were more prominent than Sunni ones during the Orlando vigils reflects the numerical dominance of this group in Dearborn where they "outnumber Sunnis three to one." Howell and Shryock 2003, 446.

Muslim *community* leaders were key figures at both kinds of events, Muslim *religious* leaders limited their vigil involvement to private religious events. Only Muslim American community leaders who did not identify themselves as religious leaders took part in the public secular events. For example, there were no imams, mosque presidents, or mosque board members who spoke at the public secular vigils to represent their religious institutions.

Muslim religious leaders carefully billed their private vigils as memorials for victims of all recent mass shootings and not specifically for Orlando victims, although the names of the Orlando victims were recited. At these private religious vigils, leaders addressed crowds of Muslim and non-Muslim congregants, but without the banners of rainbow flags that were such a prominent element of the publicly hosted vigils. They also did not emphasize how this mass shooting was part of a longer, structurally supported history of violence against the LGBTQ community in the United States.

The contrast between Muslim American participation in the public secular versus private religious vigils in Detroit indexes larger, nation-wide debates taking place in the Muslim American community about how to represent and manage their relationships with LGBTQ individuals, organizations, and communities. In many ways, these debates closely parallel those taking place among Catholic and Protestant American communities. However, the debate is more complicated for Muslim Americans due to how they are positioned as stigmatized minorities in the United States. Movements for reform within the Muslim American community to express acceptance of LGBTQ identities run the risk of being coopted or conflated with liberal Islamophobic distortions linking sexual conservatism to un-Americanism and run the risk of perpetuating the good Muslim/bad Muslim binary.[33]

Like other religious communities, Muslim Americans across a broad spectrum of conservative and progressive positions condemned Mateen's act. Open letters of condemnation were signed by conservative and progressive leaders alike. Yet moves to take further steps toward identification, close alliance formation, and standing together publically with LGBTQ communities were controversial within the Muslim American community. In response to the new, highly visible forms of alliance formation, some Muslim Americans expressed a critique that Muslims Americans were going too far and not being careful or precise enough about the purposes and limits of their activism on behalf of LGBTQ groups.

For example, in a widely circulated open letter, Muslim American scholar Daniel Haqiqatjou cautions that activism to protect LGBTQ individuals against hate crimes should not be confused or conflated with acceptance of

33. Maira 2016, 4; Perkins 2010; Perkins 2016.

LGBTQ lifestyles on the part of Muslim Americans. Haqiqatjou writes: "The Orlando massacre has thrust the Muslim community once again into the national spotlight and this time the American people demand to know what Islam has to say about homosexuality and the 'LGBT liberation movement.'"[34] Haqiqatjou notes that there is something coercive about this exchange. For Haqiqatjou the question, "Does Islam support LGBTQ rights?" posed in the wake of Mateen's violent act is "itself unfair." Haqiqatjou cautions that hasty responses that uncritically echo the terms in which the questions are posed leave little room for any nuance or expression of difference. When Muslims answer yes or no, the American public will hear that "either Muslims are fully in support of the LGBT movement or they are no different from Mateen." Haqiqatou urges Muslim Americans to articulate a third option, in the form of a careful and qualified response showing what parts of LGBTQ recognition and rights Muslim Americans wish to support and which they cannot.

Executive Director of CAIR-Michigan Dawud Walid also critiques the new efforts to represent Muslim Americans' attitudes about homosexuality. In a public Facebook video he posted in July 2017, he discusses a Pew study that showed a huge spike among Muslim Americans in acceptance of homosexuality.[35] The Pew Study reports that 52% of Muslim Americans now said that homosexuality should be accepted in society, up from only 27% a decade ago.[36] Walid points out that the Pew report gives no information about how researchers elicited this information.[37] As for Haqiqatjou, for Walid one of the problems of these representational efforts is that they rely on conflating certain principles that are widely held by Muslim Americans, such as condemnation of violence against any human being, to a wholesale acceptance of alternative lifestyles and cultural shifts. In his talk, Walid discusses certain Muslim Americans' uncritical rush to portray themselves as accepting of all aspects of LGBTQ rights as a form of "aspirational whiteness" taking them away from core cultural and religious values.

Like several Muslim American community and religious leaders that I interviewed, here Haqiqatjou and Walid reflect a concern that some aspects of this new visibility of Muslim acceptance toward LGBTQ individuals can be seen as a kind of assimilationist behavior that legal scholar Khaled Bey-

---

34. Haqiqatjou 2016a; Haqiqatjou 2016b.

35. Walid 2017.

36. Forum on Religious & Public Life 2011; Bayoumi 2017; Kuruvilla 2017.

37. Walid asks, "Was the [Pew] question posed as, 'Do American people believe that homosexual people should have rights in society, should have civil rights, the right not to be harassed, or the right to have housing accommodations, the right to work?' Or, 'Do American Muslims believe that [people of] the same gender should be allowed to get married, to change their pronoun, or call themselves 'gender fluid' … or someone who's genetically a man … have female accommodations?'"

doun has labeled "conforming Islam." This type of behavior occurs when a Muslim American actor "alters and assimilates a disfavored Muslim trait, expression, or one's identity at large in line with positive counter-terrorism stereotypes," in hopes that this "mitigates or eliminates suspicion from the state" or for "personal benefit."[38]

Southwest Detroit as a Symbolic Location

"Orlando Vigil: Southwest Detroit Stands in Solidarity" took place in Clark Park on Monday, June 13, 2016, at six o'clock p.m. The vigil was attended by more than one hundred people. I focus on the Clark Park vigil for the remainder of this chapter because for all the vigils I studied, it featured the most visible coalitional work. Also, the way the vigil came together clearly reflected and advanced transformational coalitions already at play among these activists.

The highly diverse, working-class neighborhood of Southwest Detroit shares a long border with Dearborn and borders with Melvindale, Lincoln Park, and River Rouge. The 44,000 residents of Southwest Detroit live spread out over the region's twelve square miles. Known as the capital of Latin American life in Michigan, about fifty-seven percent of Southwest Detroit residents identify as having Hispanic ancestry on the census. The majority comes from Mexican American backgrounds, but others hail from or trace their ancestry to locales such as Puerto Rico and Central America.[39] The neighborhood also comprises many other ethnic and racial minorities, including African Americans, Arab Americans (mainly Yemeni and Palestinian), and Hmong. Working-class whites also reside in the area. This capital of Latin America in Michigan borders on Dearborn, the city considered the capital of Arab America in the United States. Some Arab Americans coming to the area who cannot afford to live in Dearborn gravitate to Southwest Detroit. This includes primarily Yemenis as well as some Palestinian Muslims.

Mexicantown puts Southwest Detroit on the map for outsiders. This commercial area attracts many from across the region, offering a range of Latin American cuisines, freshly made tortillas from the bakery, import stores, music, and festivals. Despite the relative vibrancy of this commercial district, Southwest Detroit's ethnically diverse population is facing a crisis: this area is experiencing intense gentrification and population displacement.[40] Community activists archly use the term "conquistadors" to describe the mainly white, moneyed new Detroiters who come into the

38. Beydoun 2017, 11.
39. Southwest Detroit Neighborhood Profile 2012, 3.
40. Hartigan 2005; Moskowitz 2017; Ross 2016; Montgomery 2016; Feeley 2016; Doucet and Smit 2016.

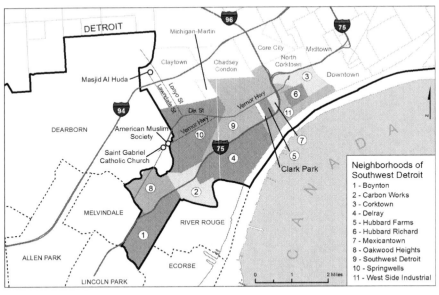

Maps provided courtesy of Jason M. Glatz, Michigan Western University Libraries Mapping Service, based on information from the Michigan Center for Geographic Information and the Detroit Department of Neighborhoods via data.detroit.gov.

neighborhood, buy up properties, and sometimes establish high-end businesses out of touch with extant residents' needs.[41] Detroiters across the city engage in heated debate over the benefits of gentrification in areas suffering from a lack of infrastructure, services, and resources. By contrast, the Southwest Detroiters I interviewed *unanimously* expressed opposition to the kinds of changes associated with gentrification. One local African American Muslim activist contested the idea that gentrification could benefit Southwest Detroit in a moral fashion:

> White washing isn't revitalizing. Revitalizing with the capitalist structure is not revitalizing. And if I don't see a push … for solidarity economics, there isn't a push for developing the most at-risk individuals or any attempt to pay homage to [the history of] this area. You are just pushing that out with new fancy establishments and restaurants and places that they cannot afford. That is not revitalizing, that is displacement. That is creating … an internal … refugee crisis in the US. That is how I see gentrification....] You are just making cultural warfare.

Besides displacement via gentrification, another crisis facing minority residents of Southwest Detroit, especially those from Mexico and from Muslim majority countries, is that they are increasingly becoming targets for surveillance, monitoring, and deportation. During the time of the Orlando shootings, in the lead-up to the 2016 presidential elections, Trump had already been promoting his ideas about forcing Mexico to pay for a wall separating it from the United States and a Muslim ban to filter out immigrants and refugees from Muslim majority nations. This greatly alarmed community activists, teachers, and youth workers from the area, who describe the trauma facing Southwest Detroit children whose families are targeted by such policies.

Described by one community activist as the heart of Mexicantown, Clark Park has long been known as a center for Latino American organizing and advocacy. This involves public demonstrations to secure rights and resources of Mexican-American and other immigrant communities. Such demonstrations support fair wages, unions, and access to education for immigrant groups. This organizing is led by locally-based groups like One Michigan for Immigrants Rights or regional groups like Pax Christiana.

41. Community activist and Michigan Coalition for Human Rights board member Bill Wylie-Kellerman observed this term being used by mainly white, new Southwest Detroit community residents to describe themselves. In his article, Wylie-Kellerman notes the disturbing aspects inherent in the supposed joke of white people self-referencing as "conquistadors" in the Latino context of Southwest Detroit. Wylie-Kellerman 2015.

Especially since Trump's presidential candidacy, Latin American and Arab groups in the area have used Clark Park events to reach out to each other in solidarity to work against a set of shared concerns. For example, since February 2017, a group of local and regional activists has held a "We Stand Together with Our Neighbors" weekly vigil every Friday afternoon at Clark Park to protest immigration policies targeting Mexican, Muslim, Arab, and other minorities, as expressed in the "No Bans, No Walls" placards that are regularly displayed by the participants.

The location of the Orlando Vigil in Clark Park was described by community activists as central to the event's success and meaning.[42] Ritual processes draw meaning and legitimacy from the power of the places in which they are situated. These places are often chosen because they are already loaded with symbolic meanings. By locating the vigil in Clark Park, one of the hearts of Southwest Detroit, vigil activists emphasized and honored the Latino identities of those who had been targeted.

Ritual can also bring new meanings to the space, symbolically transforming the old, just as a particular space can draw new meaning into the ritual. Some community activists stressed an almost complete absence of LGBTQ visibility among Latino Americans in Southwest Detroit. They compared the conservatism of Southwest Detroit's Latino American community to Arab and Muslim Americans in Dearborn and Detroit. By locating a vigil honoring Latinx LGBTQ youth in the center of Mexicantown, vigil organizers symbolically re-coded Clark Park and Latino Southwest Detroit as an LGBTQ-accepting place.

Besides its Latino American-identified community leaders, the vigil featured Muslim and Arab American community leaders from Dearborn, the wealthier city that shares a long border with Southwest Detroit. These leaders attracted a significant number of Muslim and Arab Americans from Dearborn to the event. The leaders standing together from a number of different backgrounds and the intermingling of different populations in the crowds provided symbolic and social expressions of crossing barriers and breaking boundaries across race and class lines.

The Clark Park Vigil as a Ritual of Transformation

Working within transformational coalitions entails a shift in orientation on the part of different allies as they learn to recognize each other's specific needs and values and adapt their own agendas in such a way as to reflect these. They are risky because any shift in an organization's agenda is

42. Kertzer 1988, 9. According to Kertzer, "Ritual action ... is often enacted at certain places and times that themselves are endowed with special symbolic meaning."

likely to alienate some members, causing friction and some degree of loss. Thus, transformational coalitions are highly relational. They entail familiarity, trust, and deep respect between the individuals representing each institution. People who invite one another to "stand together" on the same stage are symbolically authorizing the ideas espoused by their allies.

People whom I talked to about the Clark Park vigil, especially those from the communities most directly targeted by the violence, described a sense of shock, grief, rage, and fear when they heard about the shootings. These emotions drove some people to plan the vigil and others to attend. Organizers of the vigil used familiar forms of speech and recognizable gestures to help people find comfort and support as they share a unified focus. This included calling people to prayer, lighting candles, reciting names, releasing balloons, and speaking in official and ceremonial styles that echo liturgies, homiletics, and different traditions of mourning. This generated a sense of shared communication taking place on different levels, including the cognitive, the affective, and the emotional.

Arriving at a vigil such as the one at Clark Park, the participants are welcomed by the sight of familiar leaders standing together on a stage graced with banners, balloons, and rainbow flags. The leaders show vigil attendees that they are ready to speak for them, allowing those assembled to wordlessly grieve. Vigil organizers offer participants candles specially fit with foil to catch the drippings. These and other features help provide a sense of preparation, care, and order, helping to allow the crowd of hundreds to get swept away in emotion. People capture still and moving images of the event on cell phone cameras and circulate these on social media. News cameras and reporters are also there, eager to learn how the community is responding to the event. Organizers know that this is a chance to challenge the dominant narratives on local and national scales.

During the Clark Park vigil, the close relationship between those working across racial, ethnic, and gender lines were further cemented, brought onto the public stage in a vivid way, and witnessed by many perhaps for the first time. Alma, a Latino American woman who was a principle organizer of the Clark Park vigil describes her reaction as she saw the attendees for the vigil gather:

> It was quintessential for me ... when certain Latinos and people from
> the Arab community came. Like certain people ... who don't normally
> talk about that [homosexuality]. Then all of us on the stage together.
> Like, the array of color too. That was the most awesome, awe-
> inspiring moment. It was cross-generational.... It wasn't until a certain

moment that I was looking and said wow this is crazy. So many people said something about it [to me]. Like, the fact that they've never seen anything like this. It was powerful.

Some organizers and participants in the vigil experienced a sense of healing from attending the event. In her speech at Clark Park, community activist Consuela Lopez said:

> Those of us who have heeded the call that we are healers understand completely the responsibility and impact of being so.... We wisely know how to harness that power through establishing and cultivating harmonious relationships across invisible boundaries.... If this is not healing, then I don't know what else to call it. I am honored to know such true healers ... in our diverse community [who] showed solidarity with our Latino & Muslim family for our LGBTQ family. It doesn't end here today and not even tomorrow. We will continue to bond together.

Amal, a Muslim American community activist at the Clark Park vigil also included healing and boundary crossing in her description of the event. Amal described the range of feeling states she experienced during the vigil this way:

> I don't know, just feeling out of control.... Like, how do we stop this? ... There was this guy standing there holding a sign and just crying – I don't know who he was. I actually ... ran to him, and hugged him really tight, and I told him, I said, "I'm gonna fight for you. I don't know who you are, but know that you're loved, and that I'll work so hard to not allow something like that to ever happen to you." ... I think for many of us we were crying because ... this is our country and we just feel like someone just took a knife and just like slashed a part of who we are.... You just feel so much pain.

Amal explains how the vigil structure helped her organize some of her out-of-control feelings into fighting energy and into recognizable emotions of grief and love. She talks about crying with other vigil participants as part of a communal body in pain. This reflects the findings of Deborah Gould, who talks about the ability of social movement leaders to help members of oppressed groups to harness and channel affects, or inchoate intensities of feeling in the service of conscious and shared emotions and goals.[43]

---

43. "Social movement contexts not only offer a language for people's affective states, they also provide an emotional pedagogy of sorts, a guide for what and how to feel and for what to do in light of those feelings. Movements, in short 'make sense of' inchoate affective states and authorize selected feelings and actions while downplaying and even invalidating others." Gould 2010, 33.

Through their ritual speech, community leaders strove to put words to intolerable states, and to bind communities together in shared resolve for a better future.

Conclusion: Orlando Vigils as a Landmark in Muslim American Coalition Building

The Pulse nightclub tragedy raised new forms of public attention to the issue of Islam and homosexuality due to the Muslim identity of the speaker and the LGBTQ identities of the targets. The fact that the Muslim perpetrator of the violence and the mainly Latinx victims of the shooting were both racial minorities further shaped public response in terms of how these factors hailed certain civil leaders and citizens from these groups to respond to the events in particular ways. The event gave rise to new kinds information circulated by the press, social media, and community activists in face-to-face public gatherings. These new information flows included expressions of solidarity among Muslim and LGBTQ groups in ways that sometimes also entailed a crossing of race and class lines. This was particularly the case in the Clark Park Vigil in Southwest Detroit, due to the demographics and history of the place. This vigil was a site for the expression of complex forms of transformational coalition building among AMSA, Latinx and LGBTQ communities, in a way that captured certain local, regional, and national trends in Muslim American coalition building taking place in the contemporary United States. The public response to the Pulse nightclub shootings also resulted in certain Muslim Americans, including scholars and leaders, formulating critiques of these expressions. This critique sometimes called for a partial limit or slowing down of the way Muslim Americans expressed such alliances to make sure they are clear, precise, and compatible with the interpretation of their religion they wish to convey so that Muslim Americans do not further lose control of how they are being represented.

The Detroit area vigils in the wake of Orlando were sometimes portrayed as particular kinds of space set apart from – yet integrally connected to – everyday modes of relations, feelings, and actions. Vigils were depicted as a place in which the lines between the public and private, the personal and the political, the religious and secular were blurred to creative and energizing effect. In some narratives that I gathered, the Orlando vigils took on significance in the local imagination as a place for feeling together, in Gould's sense of the term, or healing together, in the words of some informants. For others, it was also a place in which to re-create or renew important emerging coalitions among oppressed minorities, especially in the age of Trump. Many participants described the roles Muslim Americans played in organizing and participating in these vigils as highly meaningful and key to their success. The Orlando vigils represent a landmark moment for Muslim American advocacy and organizing in the United States. The way that community activists describe the inter-relatedness of the issues confronting LGBTQ, Muslim, Latinx, African American and other minorities exemplifies the key salience of using boundary crossing as a framework to understand political activism for Muslims in America today.

Works Cited

Abdulrahim, S. 2008. "'Whiteness' and the Arab Immigrant Experience." In *Race and Arab Americans Before and After 9/11: From Invisible Citizens to Visible Subjects*, edited by A. Jamal and N. Naber, 131–146. Syracuse.

Ackerman, S. 2016. "Omar Mateen Described Himself as 'Islamic Soldier' in 911 Calls to Police." *The Guardian*, June 20, June 20. https://www.theguardian.com/us-news/2016/jun/20/omar-mateen-911-calls-orlando-shooting-fbi-release-isis.

Aidi, H. D. 2014. *Rebel Music: Race, Empire, and the New Muslim Youth Culture*. New York.

Alexander, H., D. Lawler, R. Sherlock, R. Akkoc, and C. Graham. 2016. "Orlando Shooting: Gunman Omar Mateen was a Closet Homosexual, Say Friends – As Wife Faces Charges after 'Helping Him Scope Out Attack'." *Telegraph*, June 14. http://www.telegraph.co.uk/news/2016/06/14/orlando-gunman-was-a-regular-at-lgbt-nightclub-pulse-before-atta.

Alter, C. 2016. "Ex-Wife Says Orlando Shooter Might Have Been Hiding Homosexuality From His Family." *Time Magazine*, Jun 15. Accessed September 21. http://time.com/4369577/orlando-shooting-sitora-yusufiy-omar-mateen-gay.

Barber, W. I. 2016. "The New Fusion Politics." *UU World*, January 18. http://www.uuworld.org/articles/new-fusion-politics.

Barber, W. I., and J. Wilson-Hartgrove. 2016. *The Third Reconstruction: How a Moral Movement is Overcoming the Politics of Division and Fear*. Boston.

Barth, F. 1969. *Ethnic Groups and Boundaries: The Social Organization of Cultural Difference*. Boston.

Bayoumi, M. 2017. "How the 'Homophobic Muslim' Became a Populist Bogeyman." *The Guardian,* August 7. https://www.theguardian.com/commentisfree/2017/aug/07/homophobic-muslim-populist-bogeyman-trump-le-pen.

Bean, A. 2013. "Moral Monday Movement Unleashes 'Linguistic Trauma'." *Friends of Justice*, December 10. https://friendsofjustice.wordpress.com/2013/12/10/how-the-moral-monday-movement-work-flips-the-script.

Beydoun, K. 2017. "Acting Muslim." *Harvard Civil Rights-Civil Liberties Review* 53.

Dannin, R. 2002. *Black Pilgrimage to Islam*. New York.

DiFurio, D. 2016. "Q&A: Islamic Scholar Omar Suleiman on the Quran and Homosexuality." *Dallas News*, September 21, June 16. https://www.dallasnews.com/opinion/commentary/2016/06/16/qa-islamic-scholar-omar-suleiman-on-the-quran-and-homosexuality.

Doucet, B., and E. Smit. 2016. "Building an Urban 'Renaissance': Fragmented Services and the production of inequality in Greater Downtown Detroit." *Journal of Housing and the Built Environment* 31.4:635–657.

Durando, J. 2016. "After Orlando Shooting, Muslim Americans Show Support for Victims." *USA Today*, September 25, June 12. https://www.usatoday.com/story/news/nation/2016/06/12/orlando-nightclub-muslim-reaction/85790320.

Ewing, K. 2008. *Stolen Honor: Stigmatizing Muslim Men in Berlin*. Stanford.

Feeley, D. 2016. "Detroit: Realities of Destructive Accumulation." *Alternate Routes: A Journal of Critical Social Research* 27.

Forum on Religious and Public Life. 2011. "The Future of the Global Muslim Population." Washington, D.C.

GhaneaBassiri, K. 2010. *A History of Islam in America*. Cambridge.

Gould, D. 2010. "On Affect and Protest." In *Political Emotions (New Agendas in Communication)*, edited by J. Staiger, A. Cvetkovich, and A. Reynolds, 18–44. New York.

Graham, D. A. 2016a. "The Complicated Pain of America's Queer Muslims." *The Atlantic*, September 21, June 14. https://www.theatlantic.com/politics/archive/2016/06/lgbt-muslims-orlando/486923.

———. 2016b. "Donald Trump Linked the Shooting to 'Radical Islam' and Used It as Evidence to Support His Proposed Muslim Ban." *The Atlantic*, June 13. https://www.theatlantic.com/politics/archive/2016/06/trump-speech-orlando/486878.

Haqiqatjou, D. 2016a. "An Open Letter to the Muslim Community in Light of the Orlando Shooting." *Muslim Matters*, June 16. http://muslimmatters.org/2016/06/16/an-open-letter-to-the-muslim-community-in-light-of-the-orlando-shooting.

———. 2016b. "Tough Conversations: Explaining the Islamic Prohibition of Same-Sex Acts to a Western Audience." Assembly of Muslim Jurists of America, Thirteenth Annual Imam Conference, Chicago, IL.

Hartigan, J. 2005. *Odd Tribes: Toward a Cultural Analysis of White People*. Durham.

Hennessy-Fiske, M. 2016. "FBI Investigators Say They Have Found No Evidence That Orlando Shooter Had Gay Lovers." *Los Angeles Times*, June

23. http://www.latimes.com/nation/la-na-orlando-gay-fbi-20160623-snap-story.html.

Hennessy-Fiske, M., J. Jarvie, and D. Q. Wilber. 2016. "Orlando Gunman Had Used Gay Dating App and Visited LGBT Nightclub on Other Occasions, Witnesses Say." *Los Angeles Times*, June 13. http://www.latimes.com/nation/la-na-orlando-nightclub-shooting-20160613-snap-story.html.

Higginbotham, E. B. 1994. *Righteous Discontent: The Women's Movement in the Black Baptist Church, 1880–1920*. Cambridge.

Howell, S. 2014. *Old Islam in Detroit: Rediscovering the Muslim American Past*. New York.

Howell, S., and A. Shryock. 2003. "Cracking Down on Diaspora: Arab Detroit and America's War on Terror." *Anthropological Quarterly* 76.3:443–462.

Iyer, D. 2015. *We Too Sing America: South Asian, Arab, Muslim, and Sikh Immigrants Shape Our Multiracial Future*. New York.

Jahangir, J. 2016. "Can Islamic Scholars Like Ghamidi Help LGBT Muslims?" *Huffington Post*, July 20. Accessed September 25. http://www.huffingtonpost.ca/junaid-jahangir/help-lgbt-muslims_b_11061884.html.

Jamieson, A., and M. Neubert. 2016. "Orlando Highlights Islam's Complicated Relationship with Homosexuality." *NBC News*, July 12. https://www.nbcnews.com/feature/nbc-out/orlando-highlights-islam-s-complicated-relationship-homosexuality-n594336.

Jones, A. 2016. "Call for love and acceptance rises at vigil for Orlando shooting victims." *MLive*, June 13. http://www.mlive.com/news/kalamazoo/index.ssf/2016/06/call_for_love_and_acceptance_r.html.

Karim, J. 2005. "Between Immigrant Islam and Black Liberation: Young Muslims Inherit Global Muslim and African American Legacies." *Muslim World* 95.4:497–513.

———. 2009. *American Muslim Women: Negotiating Race, Class, and Gender within the Ummah*. New York.

Kertzer, D. 1988. *Ritual, Politics, Power*. New Haven.

van der Krogt, C. 2016. "Friday Essay: The Qur'an, the Bible and Homosexuality in Islam." *The Conversation*, June 16. Accessed September 25. https://theconversation.com/friday-essay-the-quran-the-bible-and-homosexuality-in-islam-61012.

Kuruvilla, C. 2016. "American Muslims Send A Powerful Message Of Solidarity To Orlando Victims." *Huffington Post*, June 13. Accessed September 25. http://www.huffingtonpost.com/entry/american-muslims-send-a-powerful-message-of-solidarity-to-orlando-victims_us_575ef3d4e4b071ec19ee9fbe.

———. 2017. "American Muslims Are Now More Accepting of Homosexuality than White Evangelicals." *Huffington Post*, August 1.

http://www.huffingtonpost.com/entry/american-muslims-are-now-more-accepting-of-homosexuality-than-white-evangelicals_us_597f3d8de4b02a4ebb76ea3d.

Love, E. 2017. *Islamophobia and Racism in America*. New York.

Maira, S. M. 2016. *The 9/11 Generation: Youth, Rights, and Solidarity in the War on Terror*. New York.

Majaj, L. S. 2000. "Arab Americans and the Meaning of Race." In *Postcolonial Theory and the United States: Race, Ethnicity, and Literature*, edited by A. I. Singh and P. Schmidt, 320–337. Jackson, MS.

"Man Who Says He Was Omar Mateen's Gay Lover Speaks Out." 2016. *CBS*, June 21. https://www.cbsnews.com/news/orlando-shooting-man-who-says-he-was-omar-mateen-gay-lover-speaks-out-univision.

Markoe, L. 2016. "Muslim Attitudes about LGBT are Complex, Far from Universally Anti-Gay." *USA Today*, June 17. https://www.usatoday.com/story/news/world/2016/06/17/muslim-lgbt-gay-views/86046404.

Massumi, B. 2002. *Parables for the Virtual: Movement, Affect, Sensation*. Durham.

Mehta, D. 2016. "Orlando Shooting Has Significant Impact on LGBTQ Muslims, Toronto Activist Says." *thestar.com*, June 15. https://www.thestar.com/news/canada/2016/06/15/orlando-shooting-has-significant-impact-on-lgbtq-muslims-toronto-activist-says.html.

Montgomery, A. 2016. "Reappearance of the Public: Placemaking, Minoritization and Resistance in Detroit." *International Journal of Urban and Regional Research* 40.4:776–799.

Moskowitz, P. 2017. *How to Kill a City: Gentrification, Inequality, and the Fight for the Neighborhood*. New York.

"Orlando Terror Attack Updates: Obama Meets with Victims' Families in Orlando." 2016. *Los Angeles Times*, June 16, June 16. http://www.latimes.com/nation/la-na-orlando-nightclub-shooting-live-lgbt-muslims-mourn-1465758150-htmlstory.html.

Perez, E., S. Prokupecz, C. E. Shoichet, and A. L. Porte. 2016. "Omar Mateen Pledged Allegiance to ISIS, Official Says." *CNN*, June 12. http://www.cnn.com/2016/06/12/us/orlando-shooter-omar-mateen/index.html.

Perkins, A. 2010. "Negotiating Alliances: Muslims, Gay Rights, and the Christian Right in a Polish American City." *Anthropology Today* 26.2:19–24.

———. 2016. "Islam Is Not Our Enemy." *Anthropology-News* 57.11:95–102.

Ramirez, T. L., and Z. Blay. 2016. "Why People Are Using The Term 'Latinx'." *Huffington Post*, July 5. http://www.huffingtonpost.com/entry/why-people-are-using-the-term-latinx_us_57753328e4b0cc0fa136a159.

Ross, J. N. 2016. "Appropriating the Past: Urban Exploration and Loft Living in Deindustrialized Detroit." *Spaces & Flows: An International Journal of*

Urban & Extra Urban Studies 7.4.

Samhan, H. H. 1999. "Not Quite White: Race Classification and the Arab-American Experience." In *Arabs in America: Building a New Future*, edited by M. Suleiman, 209–226. Philadelphia.

Sanjek, R. 1992. "The Organization of Festivals and Ceremonies among Americans and Immigrants in Queens, New York." In *To Make the World Safe for Diversity*, edited by A. Daun, B. Ehn, and B. Klein, 123–194. Stockholm.

———. 1998. *The Future of Us All: Race and Neighborhood Politics in New York City.* Ithaca, NY.

Southwest Detroit Neighborhood Profile. 2012. Detroit.

Sullivan, K., and W. Wan. 2016. "Troubled. Quiet. Macho. Angry. The Volatile Life of the Orlando Shooter." *Washington Post*, June 17. https://www.washingtonpost.com/national/troubled-quiet-macho-angry-the-volatile-life-of-omar-mateen/2016/06/17/15229250–34a6–11e6–8758–d58e76e11b12_story.html?utm_term=.c3e5d750e414.

Volpp, L. 2000. "Blaming Culture for Bad Behavior." *Yale Journal of Law and the Humanities* 12.

———. 2002. "The Citizen and the Terrorist." *UCLA Law Review* 29:1575–1600.

Walid, D. 2017. "Regarding American Muslims Being More Accepting of Homosexuality than Evangelicals." Video post of D. Walid (August 2). https://www.facebook.com/dawudwalid/videos/1811540542492483.

Wylie-Kellerman, B. 2015. "Gentrification and Race: Can We Have a Real Coversation?" *Detroit Metro Times*, April 28. https://www.metrotimes.com/news-hits/archives/2015/04/28/gentrification-and-race-can-we-have-a-real-conversation.

Rights versus Respectability: The Politics of Muslim Visibility in Detroit's Northern Suburbs

Sally Howell

> IONA [Islamic Organization of North America]
> members are not Americans. I mean, even I get
> scared when I drive by there on Friday. Have you
> seen what they wear? They dress like Osama Bin
> Laden. They all have those scary beards. At our
> mosque, we dress like Americans – professional,
> college educated Americans.
>
> "Hisham"[1]

HISHAM IS A PSEUDONYM for a young would-be spokesperson for the American Islamic Community Center (AICC) in Madison Heights, Michigan. We spoke in the summer of 2015, when the AICC was petitioning the City of Sterling Heights for a zoning variance to allow the congregation to build a new mosque on land zoned for residential use. What should have been a straightforward vote over a routine zoning matter became a hot-button political issue in Macomb County during the 2015 election season. Despite the area's long history of discriminatory practices based on racial and religious differences – including against a steady stream of mosque proposals in the cities of Warren and Sterling Heights – the AICC's leaders were caught off guard by the vitriolic opposition they encountered. Hisham's pejorative statements about another local Muslim congregation hinted at why the group was so surprised. Hisham's comments sought to frame the AICC members as far superior to the residents of Sterling Heights: "We are Lebanese," he said. "Unlike the rest of Sterling Heights, we are 90% doctors. We are very well educated. We all have college degrees and most of us have graduate degrees in medicine or engineering." His implication was clearly that once the city's residents knew about the wealth, educational attainments, and professionalism of the congregation, not to mention their Lebanese heritage and trim beards, they would welcome the AICC with open arms.

---

1. Anonymous interview with the author, 2015, Sterling Heights, Michigan.

While the AICC's savvier spokespeople were never so naked in their claims, and while it is clear that they invested a great deal of sweat equity in satisfying, indeed exceeding, the city's zoning requirements, it is also true that this appeal to respectability – to model citizen status – was the foundation of the congregation's strategy. Rather than "lawyer up," as several neighboring mosques did in the same period, working with lawyers from the Council on American-Islamic Relations (CAIR), the American Civil Liberties Union (ACLU), or the Michigan branch of the American-Arab Anti-Discrimination Committee (ADC), the mosque's leaders insisted that they had "done everything right" and did not need to appeal to civil rights law. Their hard work, faith in the system, and class-based confidence misled them into thinking they would be treated fairly.

Like cities, suburban spaces are increasingly sites of contest between strangers who encounter one other across lines of difference defined by religion and migration. In metropolitan Detroit today, the fastest growing populations of immigrants are Muslims, frequently well-educated and professional Muslims who eschew ethnic enclaves in favor of suburban living near work, good schools, or other amenities.

Macomb County's suburbs took their present shape in the 1950s and 1960s as the retreat of working-class whites then abandoning the city en masse. Famous as home to the "Reagan Democrats" of the 1980s, and now of the "Trumpsters," these suburbs are nonetheless rapidly becoming more diverse. Muslim congregations historically deployed a mix of "respectability" strategies to overcome the resistance they encountered in the area. Prior to the introduction of the Religious Land Use and Institutionalized Persons Act of 2000 (RLUIPA), they tended to lose these cases and abandon Macomb County altogether. More recently they have found success by working closely with the local civil rights establishment, including, as a last resort, the United States Attorney for the Eastern District of Michigan. This is an unsettling place for the county's Muslims to find themselves given their long established history in the region, their socio-economic success, and their recent history of conflicts with the Department of Justice, which has tended to engage with mosques more as potential threats than as ordinary houses of worship.[2] Yet as Hisham's initial quote about the "scary" looking Muslims of IONA illustrates, local histories of race-based and class-based conflict and of intra-Muslim community differences are equally significant in shaping the routes Muslim American communities follow on the path to creating halal spaces for themselves in the suburban landscape.

Respectability strategies, Frances White tells us, enable minority communities to "regulate" their "social and political behaviors," police their

2. Howell 2011.

own members, and illustrate to observers the extent to which their social values are coterminous with those of the mainstream.[3] Largely discursive in nature, such strategies work to suppress some stories or behaviors while carefully crafting others, generating narratives of the self and Other that make sense of collective experiences and shape group identities, but also tend to reinforce the status quo rather than confront the mainstream with its inability to accept difference. Brandon Robinson, for example, explores the "assimilation" of LGBTQ people into heteronormative society and institutions by disassociating themselves from behaviors traditionally associated with homosexuality. His emphasis is not on the shaming of others, but on the disciplining of self and the distancing of those who seek to pass as normative from others who are more insistent on their right to be different – regardless of how others perceive them.[4]

Mahmood Mamdani's exploration of the West's colonial projects that have insisted on dividing the Muslim world into "good" and "bad" categories – with good Muslims conveniently most resembling Western elites and bad straying in innumerable ways from this "norm" – makes clear that the stakes of respectability are as critical to Muslims like Hisham as they are to other minorities.[5] As Muslims have gained visibility in American public culture in the twenty-first century, navigating the line between good and bad, between respectable and insistent, or between belonging and simply being, has been challenging at every turn.[6] By focusing on the narratives of self and community that shape three suburban Muslim congregations in Detroit as they pursue the quintessential American dream – suburban complacency – I hope to illuminate both the limits of respectability strategies in a period of increasingly paranoid Islamophobia and the significant and long term spatial/political/racial consequences of this strategy. The "State" is implicated in this process at every level, extending, limiting, protecting, and challenging the rights of Muslims in a highly erratic, unstable process that conditions the terms through which they are perceived and encountered in the US as citizen/subjects.

Macomb County: Corporate and White Flight to the Suburbs

While Detroit is known as the Motor City, and its remarkable growth in the early twentieth century was tied directly to the mass production of the automobile and the many structural and economic changes that followed, it

3. White 2001, 4–5.
4. Robinson 2012.
5. Mamdani 2004.
6. Alsultany 2005; Bakalian and Bozorgmehr 2009; Bilici 2011; Cainkar 2011; Howell and Shryock 2003; Naber 2008.

is also true that auto manufacturers have been fleeing the city itself since the industry's first days.[7] The push into Macomb County began during WWII when Chrysler and General Motors opened war production facilities there in collaboration with the US Army. In 1949, GM broke ground on their Eero Saarinen designed Tech Center in Warren, and, in response, Warren's population almost doubled in the 1950s, from 43,000 to 89,000. By 1970, the population had mushroomed to 189,000, making it Detroit's largest suburb. Sterling Heights maintained its mostly rural character well into the 1970s, despite the location of a US Army/Chrysler jet engine facility (today a Fiat/Chrysler plant) that opened in 1953 and two Ford manufacturing centers that followed, opening in 1958 and 1969. While jobs were a major factor in the population growth of the area, it was also shaped by the white flight that escalated in Detroit during the 1950s as blacks were forced out of their historic enclave in Black Bottom by urban renewal. As Mayor Coleman Young described this, "[the] white exodus from Detroit had been prodigiously steady prior to the [1967] riot, totaling twenty-two thousand in 1966, but afterwards it was frantic. In 1967, with less than half the year remaining after the summer explosion – the outward population migration reached sixty-seven thousand. In 1968 the figure hit eighty-thousand, followed by forty-six thousand in 1969."[8]

Warren and Sterling Heights provided a new zone of white racial exclusion to families concerned about the growth of Detroit's black population. In 1970, when Warren's workforce was 30% black, its population was less than 1% black, which drew the attention of state and federal authorities working to bring racial integration and public housing to the suburbs. Warren's city council, and later the electorate, voted down public housing (then tied specifically to integration), and the city was forced to give up over $17 million in federal dollars in the 1970s for defying the Civil Rights Act of 1964 and the Fair Housing Act of 1968.[9] Many blacks who attempted to move into Warren, despite this hostility, faced "arson, broken windows, and threats from their hostile white neighbors."[10] A few months after the city's referendum on open housing, Warren was again in the news for its refusal to comply with another court order – this one designed to integrate the Detroit Public Schools with those of its suburban neighbors – cementing Warren's and Macomb's reputations as unwelcome, virulently anti-black communities.[11] The working class there became known as "Reagan Democrats" in the

7. Barrow 2004; Sugrue 1996.
8. Young 1994, 179.
9. Bell 2013; Farley et al. 1997, 199; Riddle 2000.
10. Bell 2013, 156.
11. See Riddle 2000.

1980s, after defying the UAW (and the expectation of pollsters) and voting for Ronald Reagan in 1980 and 1984. More recently, Donald Trump won Macomb County by almost 50,000 votes, even though Barack Obama also won the county in both of his campaigns.[12] More recently, the population has also diversified in terms of race and class. In 2015, for example, the population of Sterling Heights was 6.3% black and almost 8.3% Asian. It has among the highest percentage of foreign-born residents in the state (25.8%), with Iraqi migrants (most of whom are Chaldean) making up the largest single group of foreign-born residents and over 12% of the city's population.[13]

Seeking Respect Round 1: Islamic Association of Greater Detroit

In the early 1970s, the Detroit region was home to only a half dozen mosques. When new migrants began arriving in Detroit from India, Pakistan, and Bangladesh in the 1960s and 1970s, they quickly encountered and explored these Arab, Albanian, and African American congregations. This migration of South Asian families to Detroit was something new. Indian and Bengali men had lived in Detroit since the first decades of the twentieth century, but their numbers had remained quite small and this earlier migration did not generally include women. In the 1960s, a growing number of Indian and Pakistani students began to arrive to study at Wayne State University and the University of Michigan. Engineers, accountants, and other professionals were also attracted to Michigan by the booming auto industry and the economy it undergirded. Unlike the earlier arrivals, who were mostly working-class migrants and single men, the newcomers tended to come from privileged backgrounds and to bring their families with them. Only the brightest and best educated of their generation qualified for American universities. These South Asian migrants arrived in Detroit in an era of genuine demographic flux. Initially, they took up residence in the city itself and sought to make common cause with their fellow Muslims, but by the 1970s, the city looked to many of them as though it were coming apart at the seams. Once they had the means to do so and families to support and protect, they tended to escape Detroit for the suburbs of Oakland and Macomb Counties.[14]

Sayad Taqi, for example, moved to Detroit in July 1967, just in time to witness the city's civil unrest. Employed by the Federal Reserve in Detroit, he lived on Grand River Boulevard. While his neighborhood escaped the worst of the fires and violence, he was still concerned about the wisdom of remaining in Detroit. Once he married and returned to Detroit with a young

12. Roe and Sandler 2016.
13. United States Census Bureau n.d.
14. For details on these patterns of migration and mosque building, see Howell 2014.

bride, he allowed his friends to convince him to move into the suburbs. It didn't help that he was mugged right outside his apartment building.[15]

Similarly, Mirza Ahmed arrived in 1970. He lived in an apartment house on Cass Boulevard known as the "Pakistani House," due to the large number of Pakistani families who lived there. He reports having loved his life in the city. He could walk to work, his wife was near friends, and the community created a prayer space in the basement of the apartment and worshipped together daily. When his office was relocated to the suburbs, however, he too relocated his family.[16]

Another enclave of South Asian Muslims settled on the outskirts of Hamtramck on the city's east side. According to Nizam Uddin, an auto worker who settled in the area in 1976, their members initially worshipped at Masjid al-Mumineen, or in Dearborn or Harper Woods, depending on where they worked. Some of them joined the Yemenis who prayed together in Poletown, and some of them banded together and rented a basement space just across the street from the Dodge Main factory on Conant. Most of these Bangaldeshi immigrants worked for one of the automakers on the assembly line. In 1976, sixteen or so Muslim families purchased a former gas station on Mt. Elliot in Detroit and began worshipping there. They faced no resistance at the time. They named this nascent mosque Masjidun-Nur. Uddin, one of the founders of this mosque, remembers that most of the city's South Asian Muslims worshipped together there in the late 1970s before those with medical and professional degrees began moving out to the suburbs.[17]

Those who were in Detroit at the time remember an era of optimism among the city's Muslims. Their communities were all growing. Some were getting settled in as new Americans, while others were making themselves at home within a new faith.[18] The community still felt small enough for people to know one another. For a few years they created a series of community-wide holiday prayer celebrations that grew quickly from a high school gym to Cobo Hall, Detroit's convention center. These events brought together rich and poor, immigrant and American born, black and brown. They are remembered with great nostalgia for the sense of "ummaness" they created – a sentiment with which many of the region's Muslims remember the 1970s more generally.[19]

Eventually, however, as Detroit's decline became harder to ignore, and

15. Sayad Taqi interview with the author, 2016, Warren, Michigan.

16. Mirza Ahmed interview with the author, 2016, Warren, Michigan.

17. Nizam Uddin interview with the author, 2017, by telephone.

18. This is the period when the Nation of Islam began its transition under the leadership of Imam Warith Deen Muhammad.

19. Howell 2014.

as many of the South Asian professionals completed their graduate training and moved into full employment, most often in the suburbs, they began to buy houses further and further afield. Sayad Taqi moved to Madison Heights (a suburb next to Warren) around 1970. He remembers having been uninterested in religion until he and his friends began having children. Then they started meeting together in one another's homes for prayers, religious study, and a sense of community, just as the Bangladeshis had done in Hamtramck. Eventually this small circle of ten or twelve families decided that they too needed a mosque. After incorporating as the Islamic Association of Greater Detroit (IAGD), they drew a circle on a map around their various homes and began looking for a piece of land somewhere near the center. Warren, north of 12 Mile Road, is where they found their first parcel of land and sought a zoning variance for their proposed house of worship. Only a handful of the mosque's members showed up at the Zoning Commission hearing to make their pro forma case before the commissioners. They were shocked to encounter a crowd of angry residents.[20]

> Sayad Taqi: At that time I did not know anything, so I did not hire an attorney or anything. Oh, my god. Do you know how many people come? At least 3–400. I was scared – the hell out of me, you know. I said, "Oh my god, what did I do wrong?"

The mosque's founders were shocked by the racist nature of the hostility they received, which conflated them with Detroit and blackness quite specifically. In my interviews with several of the mosque's founders, I found a complete unwillingness to repeat the nasty, pejorative language they heard in Warren in 1976. "'Go back to Detroit. What are you doing here? This is our place.' And many other things. I cannot tell you...." was all Mr. Taqi would quote from these encounters.[21] The incident was so upsetting to the mosque's founders that they said, "Whatever the price of the land, this is not the right place to put a mosque." Pressing to understand more of the nature of the hostility they faced, I asked Mr. Taqi if this was due to anti-black racism, what we now call Islamophobia, or to his (and the congregation's) non-European origins.

20. Taqi interview; Ather Abdul Quader, Ghaus Malik, Sharif Gindy, and Shah Ali Akbar interview with the author and Akil Fahd, 2011, Rochester Hills, Michigan.

21. The "go back to Detroit" taunt suggests that Warren's residents associated the mosque's members with blackness and other forms of unwelcome difference they attributed to the city. As we'll see below, such statements are intended as slurs and are frequently used against Muslims. Given the heavy accents of many IAGD founders, it is worth noting that they do not remember people having told them to go "back where you came from," which might have suggested xenophobia rather than this more traditional form of racism.

ST: No Islam. At that time, people didn't know anything about Islam. They had no idea what was going on. You go over there and you say, "Allahu akbar," nobody knows what is Allahu akbar. "La illaha?" Nobody knows what is la illaha. But now, after 9/11, what happened is the whole United States, they know everything about Islam.... But this was 1976. They have no idea what is Islam.

And, to emphasize the racialist nature of the resistance the mosque met, Mr. Taqi shared a story about an incident that occurred at a house he built for his family in Sterling Heights a few years later.

ST: Yes, I would definitely say the racism. Because, let me tell you something. So I built a house in Sterling Heights.... I called my friends and said, "come on over." And you know in my office, there are a lot of black people over there, in government. So a lot of black people came, and they parked over there. It was a dirt road. I couldn't sleep that night. Three cars, all their car, they throwed excrement on them. On my street! So my next door neighbor, I can't tell you his name, he said, "Hey, why did you invite all those blackies here?" And I said, "Hey, they are my friends and colleagues. I work for the government." He said, "I work for a bank." I said, "I don't care where you work, these are the people in my department." He said, "I am sorry about that, please don't call them here anymore." So I went through a lot!

Experiences like this one were foundational for IAGD's early members as they sought to identify their place in Detroit's suburbs. By refusing to verbalize the hostile comments and arguments they encountered at the zoning commission meeting and in other contexts, they choose to erase them, their sting, and the memory that such statements were ever directed toward them as immigrant Muslims. Rather than acknowledge such statements, a prospect that might highlight similarities between their experiences and those of other religious and racial minorities, they prefer to disassociate themselves from such affinities. Mr. Taqi's statement above makes this disassociation even clearer when he illustrates how the cars of black co-workers were vandalized by his new neighbors, while his was not. Thus the narrative asserts Mr. Taqi's own acceptance, his own security within this "all-white" suburb despite the experiences of the mosque as an institution. This is precisely where the history of IAGD becomes an example of a respectability narrative rather than something more defiant.

Similarly, after the IAGD's second attempt to build in Macomb County was equally unsuccessful, the congregation instead settled on a large piece of farmland out in the "boondocks," twenty-one miles north of Detroit in what was then Rochester Township in Oakland County. The board members prayed over this and agreed to let the purchase move forward, even though it was distant from all of their homes at the time. As Athel Abdul Quader described the decision-making process behind this purchase, they settled on this piece of land because there were only two or three neighbors there to potentially object. "And we made it a point, right from the get-go, to meet each one of them."[22] The group attended local festivals and shared information about their plans with the community. They spent a great deal of time with the mosque's neighbors, explained in detail their parking and other needs, and even paid to bring in a new water line that the neighbors too eventually benefitted from. They included their new neighbors in the community's holiday celebrations. In their earliest days, these same neighbors helped IAGD mow their fields and otherwise manage the property. They also helped smooth the concerns of other area residents and village administrators over the planned mosque, and, over time, they gradually sold several adjoining properties to the mosque, ensuring its ability to grow and evolve.[23]

IAGD is now one of the metro area's largest and most active mosques. Its board, imams, and members have contributed significantly to national organizations like the Islamic Society of North America and CAIR. They have created a local Muslim American policy organization, the Institute for Social Policy and Understanding, and they support inner-city health and urban development organizations like the Huda Clinic and Dream of Detroit. Their retreat beyond the reach of white working class hostility provided them with a safe space from which to raise their families, practice their faith, and invest in these many national and local institutions. It is equally true that their retreat from Macomb denied the Muslims who lived and worked there the type of visibility that would have encouraged further growth and settlement of the Muslim establishment there.

Seeking Rights: The Islamic Organization of North America

The IONA congregation took shape in the early 2000s. The mosque's leader, Imam Mustapha Elturk, is ameer of the Tanzeem-e-Islami movement in the United States, a Pakistan-based dawa movement that seeks to encourage Muslims to live a Quran-centered life. At the time, his congregation was small, but growing, and contained a diverse mix of mostly South Asian and Arab migrants and their US-born children. They began looking for a home in Macomb County largely because they saw that the area had no existing mosque. They spent several years trying to find the right property and were

22. Quader et al. interview.
23. Quader et al. interview; Taqi interview.

rebuffed on multiple occasions by zoning boards, sellers, and other city managers. In 2005, they signed a deal with a local physician to purchase his medical complex and convert it into a mosque – on Ryan Road in Warren. Ryan runs straight north from Hamtramck's now very diverse Muslim enclave, through black neighborhoods in Detroit, and then past a steady stream of highly visible Ukrainian, Polish, "Yugoslav," and finally Chaldean business districts in Sterling Heights. Given this display of diversity, Elturk was disappointed when a local neighborhood association near the building IONA purchased, and other anti-Muslim activists in the city, tried to block their renovation project (and thus prevent the establishment of the mosque).

When the mosque's plans came under attack, however, Elturk was a bit less shocked than his predecessors had been. In the aftermath of 9/11, anti-Muslim sentiments had become much more common. The mosque's opponents spoke in language that only thinly couched their anti-black racism and outright fear of and hostility toward Muslims. Thus when the zoning commission convened for a second time, Elturk and his congregation came prepared. Members of the neighborhood block club immediately behind the property complained about parking and traffic congestion, argued that a call to prayer would violate the city's noise ordinances, and asserted that a "storefront" mosque would transgress city aesthetic standards. Others simply shouted at the congregation to go back where they had come from ("hell," as one man suggested), asked how they would be able to distinguish worshippers from members of al-Qaeda or others organizing a terrorist plot, and suggested that human sacrifices might be practiced at this (as presumably at other American) mosques.[24] But Elturk made sure that a wide array of supporters were also on hand. Several interfaith activists, especially Christian clergy from Warren and Jewish activists from neighboring communities, were articulate spokespeople on behalf of the mosque, as was the Executive Director of CAIR-Michigan, Dawud Walid, and the mosque's attorney Shereef Akeel (a civil rights attorney). The Planning Commission nonetheless voted against IONA's renovations and sought to block their movement to the city. After this vote, but before the Commission had adjourned, Warren's city attorney pointed out to the commissioners that they were in clear violation of the 2000 RLUIPA Act and would be unable to defend their decision legally – potentially costing the city hundreds of thousands of dollars to defend a decision based on straightforward religious discrimination.[25] At this point,

24. These examples are taken from my notes from the commission meeting. I have published a lengthier essay on Elturk's and IONA's experiences in Warren in Howell 2011.

25. I want to point out here that professional employees of these cities routinely seek to work with mosques and accommodate their needs and petitions. In this, they differ significantly from elected officials and those appointed to serve on many of the zoning commissions described here.

the head of the planning commission, Gus Ghanam (a Lebanese American Christian), reversed his vote, giving IONA the 5–3 majority it needed. As a postscript to this evening of high drama, Elturk announced,

> We see the outcome of this meeting as favorable, but it underscores the need for deeper understanding between Muslims and the community. It is natural for people to be apprehensive when someone new moves in. We will treat our neighbors with the utmost respect…. [G]ood relations with neighbors is a requirement of Islamic belief."[26]

The story does not end there, however. Once the mosque finally opened, Elturk began hosting open houses for both the interfaith crowd who had been outspoken in supporting the mosque and the block association who had been outspoken in resisting it. These experiences, both negative and positive, helped convince the imam that he needed to focus more of his energy on interacting with the larger American society. In the intervening years, he has become a leading interfaith activist in the region. He heads up the new Muslim chaplaincy program at Detroit Ecumenical Theological Seminary. He is a leading and reliable participant in the Michigan Roundtable for Diversity and Inclusion and on the Michigan Muslim Community Council. Closer to home in Warren, Imam Elturk was part of an alliance that passed the Interfaith Covenant for Freedom, Equality and Justice in 2008 and in 2010 succeeded in getting Warren's mayor and city council to sign a similar resolution.[27] When I visited IONA in December 2014, I was not surprised to see Elturk's desk loaded with plates of homemade Christmas cookies and other holiday treats the neighbors had dropped by for him. Clearly the mosque was seen as a good neighbor by many area residents.

But not by all. The following summer IONA faced a second set of challenges and zoning hearings when it sought to build a playground on an empty lot adjacent to the building. Several neighbors rose up in opposition to the plan and mosque members again had to sit through zoning commission meetings in which they were accused of being terrorists among other indignities. Elturk was physically assaulted by one individual whose property abuts that of the mosque. IONA again hired attorneys to defend their case, who filed a "Request for Admissions and Request for Production of Documents" with the City of Warren in 2015 that reads like a RLUIPA test case. Among other information, they sought to discover the number of churches, synagogues, mosques, and schools in the city with playgrounds on adjoining lots. They inquired as to whether any of these past efforts were challenged. The case was quickly settled.

26. Commission meeting notes.
27. Mustapha Elturk, personal communication with the author, October 20, 2017.

By standing up for itself as it did, IONA opened the door to new mosque development in Warren. Six new groups have opened there following IONA's 2005 groundbreaking. Today IONA is surrounded by a small array of businesses that cater to the Muslim community – a grocery store, halal butcher, travel agency, realtor, restaurant, etc. Similar restaurants and grocery stores pepper the landscape along Ryan Road now in Warren. An Islamic parochial high school, several Muslim-oriented charter schools, and several Muslim-owned daycares have also opened in the area. Warren is now a visibly Muslim community. As Elturk put this to me recently, "we've broken the barriers and tore down the walls of hate and bigotry, but there are still some bricks laying around that need to be removed."

Seeking Respect, Round 2:
The American Islamic Community Center

AICC is a predominantly Lebanese Shiʿi congregation that first formed in 2003. Some of the more established families of the congregation trace their roots back to the earliest migration of Arabs to the Detroit area, but the majority of the mosque's members are immigrant families that arrived in the post-1965 era. Some came from Iraq on student visas to study in professional programs at Wayne State University or the University of Michigan. Others fled the Lebanese Civil War and its aftermath. They tend to have migrated from Beirut rather than the countryside, and with educational or economic capital to soften their landing in the United States. As their numbers in the northern suburbs grew, the community tired of driving to Dearborn for religious services, and gradually felt a bit estranged from the Dearborn community as well.[28]

In 2004, they purchased a 10,000 square foot social hall in Madison Heights and began worshipping there. Unlike their co-religionists in neighboring Warren, who repeatedly ran afoul of zoning commission and city council decisions, AICC felt welcomed by the municipal authorities in Madison Heights. But the congregation quickly outgrew its small facility and became frustrated over their inability to provide educational and recreational activities for the growing number of families with young children who joined their ranks. In 2013, they began to look for a larger home. Because most of their members lived in Sterling Heights, they tried to purchase an existing church there. "Every time we tried to buy an existing building, usually when they knew it was going to be a masjid, for some reason they wouldn't sell no

---

28. This information is drawn from an interview I conducted with Jeff Chehab and several members of the Board of the AICC in September 2015.

more. It would go off the market, so it was very complicated," Jeff Chehab explained to me. (Mr. Chehab was the mosque's main development officer and spokesperson during their 2015 conflict with Sterling Heights.) Their search moved to commercial and industrial properties, but their efforts to get these rezoned for religious land use were repeatedly shot down by city administrators. Finally, they found a 5-acre lot on 15 Mile Road that was zoned residential. Working very closely with Donald Mende, the Sterling Heights city planner, and other city professionals, the group developed plans for a facility with a gym and social hall, a day care, an attractive prayer hall with a large dome, and thirty more parking spaces than the city required. They felt that they had done everything right.

> Jeff Chehab: It was because we were within 100 percent of the rules.
> It was difficult because every objection that the city was gonna make
> was taken care of. We've covered everything. We had. We crossed
> our T's. We dotted our I's; did our homework. We signed a purchase
> agreement with the seller. We've done everything that it was almost
> impossible for the city to say no.

And yet.

> JC: Maybe one week before – I think nine days or ten days you have
> to give notice and put the [public notice] sign outside. That's when
> everything spun out of control, just crazy. Everything just happened.
> This thing took a life of its own. For whatever reason, some people
> do it for political motivations. People decided to do these petitions.
> Some people have legitimate reasons. Some people just want to be
> entertained.

Mr. Chehab and the congregation of the AICC found themselves at the center of an international media storm. "Proposed mosque in Detroit suburb draws sharp opposition: Members of an Iraqi Christian community are using anti-Muslim rhetoric to stoke fears about a proposed mosque," read one headline.[29] Yes, it was the Chaldean community that launched a petition against the rezoning request – their second such attempt to block a mosque in Sterling Heights. The Facebook group Chaldean Nation led the charge. "Do not let the biased Sterling Heights planning commission approve building a huge mosque in the heart of #Chaldean town in Michigan. They are insensitive to the Chaldean genocide in Iraq by Islamic Radicals," read one flyer for a demonstration at the site of the proposed mosque.[30] Both Mayor

29. Friess 2015.
30. Chaldean Nation Facebook Post, August 28, 2015.

Michael Taylor and his opponent, Paul Smith, used the controversy to appeal to Chaldean and other anti-Muslim voters. Taylor first posted about the matter on Facebook, saying, "My heart breaks for the Chaldean people in Iraq and throughout the world who are being terrorized by Islamic terrorists. I will do EVERYTHING in my power to protect, support and defend the Chaldean population in Sterling Heights. I had nothing to do with this mosque and do not want it built here."[31]

At the first zoning commission meeting to address the mosque's petition, Mr. Mende walked the commission through the mosque's plans for the site, making it clear that the building not only complied with all city codes and requirements, but exceeded their standards on all counts. He also made it clear to the commission that the request by the mosque for the variance was standard practice for the city and that any objections to the plan would surely run afoul of RLUIPA. He repeatedly cautioned the commissioners about their questions and suggestions when these implied that the mosque's petition was being treated differently than recent requests made by Christian congregations for similar variances.[32]

In the public comment portion of the hearing, fifty people spoke in opposition to the mosque while seven, all members of the congregation, spoke in its favor. Those who opposed the mosque made reference to parking and traffic concerns, to fear of late night noise and declining property values, and to potential harm to the social fabric of the neighborhood. They also asked the audience to "remember 9/11" repeatedly. One gentlemen said,

> I would like to appeal to this commission to deny the building of the mosque on the basis that – I will not use ethnic slurs or racial or any other forms – but you did not say anything about politics. If I was to go to Iran and appeal to them to build a Christian church they would all say no. I expect this commission to say no.

A Chaldean woman who lives across the street from the mosque site suggested that she would not build a church in Dearborn, therefore Muslims should not build a mosque in front of her house. "They can go to Dearborn!"[33]

31. Cwiek 2015.

32. This testimony was transcribed from the Sterling Heights Zoning Board of Appeals Meeting: 8/13/15 Video-on-Demand (accessed on August 15, 2015).

33. This appeal should be familiar to readers from the earlier campaigns where Muslim congregations were told to return instead to Detroit. Again, this taunt is clearly meant to mark Sterling Heights as a non-Muslim space where Muslims are not welcome. Unlike in earlier articulations, this statement implies Islamophobia was at the root of community hostility.

Speaking on behalf of the mosque, Mr. Chehab tried to be matter of fact:

> As Don Mende mentioned, we've been working with him for the past year. We don't plan on doing any external speakers: no call to prayer; no outside noise. We don't plan on being a nuisance to the residents or any other citizens and we are very well financed, so if we are granted this permission, we will have no problem financing this project and finishing it on time. Our group mostly will be using this facility for Friday prayer from 12–2. And during Ramadan programs which usually happen in the evening.

Ali Hijazi spoke about ten minutes later. He mentioned how well educated the congregation is and praised the city for being well governed by well-intentioned, professional people. He mentioned that the location of the mosque in town will reduce rather than increase traffic for the city, as their members will not have to cross town to travel somewhere else. He also mentioned the community's right to worship in a family friendly environment close to their homes. But as the tensions mounted in the meeting, the mosque's members were forced to address the bigotry they were encountering. Hussein Sobh, after mentioning that he had lived peacefully in the city for forty years, said:

> The thing that concerns me is that we still have a lot of misunderstanding about the culture. We are asking for a small piece of the pie, not the whole pie. This country is a melting pot. And how are you going to melt the pot and bring people together to live in harmony when every single time people relate us to 9/11? We are not asking much, just a place to worship, a place to gather, but you find a lot of objections for no reason at all. So if we live in this country, we have the professionals, doctors in the community, engineers, MBA. We have all kinds of professionals. I have three doctors in my house, myself. So I would appreciate it if we could consider this not out of any bias or hate toward us.... You should be able to open a church, a temple, a synagogue, a mosque anywhere you desire to. Including here. People are entitled to their religious freedom.

This comment, at least, was met with applause.

The zoning commission decided to postpone their vote on the matter for thirty days over the objections of Commissioner Stefano Militello, who said, stating the obvious, "if this was a Catholic church ... we wouldn't be doing this."

In the hiatus between these two meetings, when the media attention to the case was growing daily, I asked Mr. Chehab why the mosque was not speaking to the press. He responded, "Since the planning commission asked for the one month delay, we haven't said anything official, because no matter what we say it's gonna ... be used against us."

I suggested the group reach out to CAIR-Michigan, whose spokesperson was already involved in the media and in touch with the Department of Justice in regards to the case, as were other civil rights groups in the area. I mentioned IONA's success in Warren in 2006, when CAIR, the local interfaith community, and civil rights lawyers were effective in turning the tide against IONA's opponents.

> JC: Well, I'm thinking about it. Okay. At this stage in the game, we've been dealing with the city for almost a year now, Don Mende and his staff. We've been here for a very long time in this. I've probably been here more than most people who are in the city. He hasn't signaled anything, or the staff, or the city council, or the zoning board, even the slightest hint that they're gonna reject us, and they've been very cooperative in working with us....
>
> Why should we bring in an arsenal of people to stir the pot even more? It's strategy. We're not gonna sit there and provoke anybody. We're not gonna have CAIR bombard these people or these other organizations, put pressure on them. They haven't given us a reason to sit there and do that, so why start something?

Mr. Chehab was correct to point out that his silence here was part of a strategy – a respectability strategy. Play by the rules and the rules will work for you. Do not call attention to yourself. Emphasize your shared values and compatibility with the larger society. When the mayor asks you to make your mosque look less Middle Eastern, assure him that you will look into this. In this model, to insist on one's rights as a religious minority is to call oneself out as a minority, as an Other. It is to acknowledge the open hostility that had, at this point in the controversy, forced mosque leaders to seek police protection for their families and compelled them to send the woman whose property they were in the process of buying – a home she had lived in for over sixty years – up north for several weeks in order to protect her from her angry neighbors.[34] In the face of such vehement opposition, AICC's cooperative and trusting strategy seemed destined to fail.

The second zoning commission meeting took place on September 13. The public meeting hall was filled, as was an overflow space where people

---

34. Chehab et al. interview.

could watch the proceedings on a closed-circuit television. A crowd of several hundred more people waited outside. On this occasion, city officials refused to accept public comment on any matter other than the proposed height of the mosque's dome and minarets, which the AICC's architect had revised slightly from the earlier meeting. The aim was clearly to avoid prejudicial statements like those presented earlier. At the end of the allotted time, the commission abruptly cut off questions and comments, called the vote without discussion, and unanimously voted down the mosque's request. The (predominantly Chaldean) crowd was euphoric. They broke into cheers and ululations. As the mosque's stunned supporters quietly exited the building, a large dubkeh line formed in the parking lot dancing for joy. Others jeered and spit at hijab-wearing women. The police had to intervene to protect an imam in the crowd. The mosque's board was clearly shocked at both the outcome of the hearing and at the crowd's open and aggressive hostility.[35]

The intensive media coverage the AICC case had received made it difficult for the group to abandon their plans and search for a new site. They hoped that once the city council and mayoral elections were behind them, the city would reconsider the vote. When this did not happen, they finally filed a lawsuit in September 2016, just as the US Attorney for Eastern Michigan, Barbara McQuade, began to build a RLIUPA case on behalf of the mosque. It was easy for her staff to assemble evidence of discrimination given the public, frequently racist comments made in opposition to the mosque by Mayor Michael Taylor, city council members, and those on the Zoning Board of Appeals. The Department of Justice case was announced on December 15, 2016, shortly after Donald Trump's election to the presidency and roughly a year after he first announced his intention to bar Muslims from entering the United States. The cases were settled out of court just a week before Barbara McQuade was asked to step down from her position as US Attorney by the new president. The AICC had finally won the right to build a mosque in Sterling Heights. They are working now with IONA and with other mosques in the area to do a better job of outreach and public education. This is important because their would-be-neighbors continue to oppose the construction of a mosque on 15 Mile Road in Sterling Heights.[36]

Conclusion

The AICC board's decision, and that of other mosques before them, to defend their dignity rather than their rights is understandable. A prosperous congregation, they do not feel the hostility they have faced is warranted.

35. The author was in attendance at this meeting.
36. Fournier and Hicks 2017; Warikoo 2017.

And they are quick to point out that their Shiʿi community in Iraq has also suffered at the hands of ISIS and other extremist groups. This is something they have in common with Chaldeans. But respectability politics do not empower Muslims to fight back on their own terms – to insist on their right to worship and otherwise establish themselves on the local landscape in a visible, organized fashion. It is not clear that IAGD had this option in the 1970s. Without RLUIPA, could they have succeeded at opening a mosque in such a racially charged environment?

What is certain is that the consequences of their failure to do so have been significant for the Muslim community in Michigan as a whole. IAGD and other mosque communities that also tried to open in Warren in the 1970s and 1980s were so discouraged by the anti-Muslim sentiment and racism they encountered in Macomb County that they went elsewhere or worshipped quietly in one another's homes. Rather than confront the racism and bigotry they faced, they went out of their way to avoid future conflict. This strategy had the collective impact of accommodating anti-Muslim activists rather than challenging them. It made the Muslim community in Macomb County virtually invisible, which encouraged area residents to misidentify Muslims and to think of Muslims as outsiders rather than their neighbors. It also delayed the participation of local Muslims in interfaith activity in the region, as well as in more secular forms of coalition politics. While the Chaldean community in Sterling Heights opened several churches and scores of ethnically identifiable businesses, giving the city a recognizable Middle Eastern feel, the Muslim community there was simply not visible until very recently.

AICC's facility in Madison Heights and IONA's in Warren have both been vandalized on several occasions, robbed, and otherwise broken into. AICC did not report these incidents to the media or the local police. "The city is busy with bigger, more important crimes and matters," I was told as explanation. By contrast, IONA's visibility brought with it the support of their neighbors and likeminded activists. IONA has been able to claim public space in Warren as legitimately Muslim space. An ethno-religious marketplace has now sprung up around their mosque – a halal marketspace. And new mosques are following IONA's movement into the community. There are now seven mosques in Warren, whereas in 2005, there were effectively none. New mosques are opening in Madison Heights and will soon open in Sterling Heights as well. Rights politics are designed to support and empower this kind of visibility and the social, political, and even market forces that shore it up. Respectability politics, quite simply are not. For this reason it was reassuring to see the DOJ go to the defense of the AICC. Like it or not, their case has set an example. The hostility they faced is not likely to diminish soon. But neither is their unsolicited visibility nor the coalitions of which they are increasingly a part.

Works Cited

Alsultany, E. 2005. "The Changing Profile of Race in the United States: Media Representations and Racialization of Arab- and Muslim-Americans Post-9/11." Dissertation. Stanford.

Bakalian, A., and M. Bozorgmehr. 2009. *Backlash 9/11: Middle Eastern and Muslim Americans Respond.* Berkeley.

Barrow, H. 2004. "'The American Disease of Growth:' Henry Ford and the Metropolitanization of Detroit, 1920–1940." In *Manufacturing Suburbs,* edited by R. Lewis, 200–220. Philadelphia.

Bilici, M. 2011. "Being Targeted, Being Recognized: The Impact of 9/11 on Arab and Muslim Americans." *Contemporary Sociology: A Journal of Reviews* 40.2 (March):133–137.

Bell, J. 2013. *Hate Thy Neighbor: Move-In Violence and the Persistence of* Racial Segregation in American Housing. New York.

Cainkar, L. 2011. *Homeland Insecurity: The Arab American and Muslim American Experience after 9/11.* New York.

Cwiek, S. 2015. "Sterling Heights mayor backpedals on mosque comments." *Michigan Public Radio,* September 2. http://michiganradio.org/post/sterling-heights-mayor-backpedals-mosque-comments.

Farley, R., S. Danziger, and H. Holzer. 1997. *Detroit Divided.* New York.

Fournier, H., and M. Hicks. 2017. "U.S. Atty: 'Proud' of mosque settlement." *The Detroit News,* February 22. http://www.detroitnews.com/story/news/local/macomb-county/2017/02/22/sterling-heights-oks-settlement-mosque-lawsuits/98238840.

Friess, S. 2015. *Al Jazeera America,* September 8. http://america.aljazeera.com/articles/2015/9/8/proposed-mosque-in-detroit-suburb-draws-sharp-opposition.html.

Howell, S. 2011. "Muslims as Moving Targets: External Scrutiny and Internal Critique in Detroit's Mosques." In *Arab Detroit 9/11: Life in the Terror Decade,* edited by N. Abraham, S. Howell, and A. Shryock, 151–185. Detroit.

———. 2014. *Old Islam in Detroit: Reimagining the Muslim American Past.* New York.

Howell, S., and A. Shryock. 2003. "Cracking Down on Diaspora: Arab Detroit and America's 'War on Terror.'" *Anthropological Quarterly* 763:443–462.

Mamdani, M. 2004. *Good Muslim, Bad Muslim: America, the Cold War, and the Roots of Terror.* New York.

Naber, N. 2008. "Introduction: Arab Americans and U.S. Racial Formation." In *Race and Arab Americans Before and After 9/11: From Invisible Citizens to Visible Subjects*, edited by N. Naber and A. Jamal. Syracuse, NY.

Riddle, D. 2000. "Race and Reaction in Warren, Michigan, 1971 to 1974: 'Bradley v. Milliken' and the Cross-District Busing Controversy." *Michigan Historical Review* 26.2:1–49.

Robinson, B. 2012. "Is This What Equality Looks Like?: How Assimilation Marginalizes the Dutch LGBT Community." *Sexuality Research and Social Policy* 9:327–336.

Roe, J. and S. Sandler. 2016. "Resurgence of the Reagan Democrats." *The Detroit News*, November 14. http://www.detroitnews.com/story/opinion/2016/11/14/reagan-democrats/93852740.

Sugrue, T. 1996. *The Origins of the Urban Crisis: Race and Inequality in Postwar Detroit*. Princeton, NJ.

United States Census Bureau. N.d. "American Community Survey: 2011–2015 ACS 5-Year Data Profiles." https://www.census.gov/acs/www/data/data-tables-and-tools/data-profiles/2015.

Warikoo, N. 2017. "Judge denies request to halt building of Sterling Heights mosque." *Detroit Free Press*, June 30. http://www.freep.com/story/news/local/michigan/macomb/2017/07/01/sterling-heights-mosque/443050001.

White, F. 2001. *Dark Continent of Our Bodies: Black Feminism and the Politics of Respectability*. Philadelphia.

Young, C. 1994. *Hard Stuff: The Autobiography of Mayor Coleman Young*. New York.

Politics, Immigration, and Ethnic Mobilization: The Predicament of Iranian Immigrants in the United States since the Iranian Revolution

Mohsen Mostafavi Mobasher

Introduction

ON JANUARY 27, 2017, DONALD TRUMP signed an executive order entitled "Protecting the Nation from Foreign Terrorist Entry into the United States." The order barred admission to the United States of all individuals with non-immigrant or immigrant visas from seven Muslim majority countries – Iraq, Iran, Libya, Somalia, Sudan, Syria, and Yemen – for ninety days. The ban also barred entry to all refugees from anywhere in the world for 120 days and placed an indefinite ban on refugees from war-torn Syria. Hours after Trump signed the executive order, thousands of protesters gathered in airports across the country. Two days later, federal lawsuits were filed on behalf of travelers who were detained in US airports. On February 3, 2017, US Federal District Judge James Robart issued a restraining order to immediately halt Trump's executive order nationwide, allowing travel to proceed as it did before the executive order was implemented. The same day, Hawaii filed a lawsuit asking the court to block implementation of Trump's travel ban. Trump's administration filed an appeal, arguing that the executive order is a matter of national security and only bars immigrants from countries with ties to terrorism.

After multiple legal challenges, Trump signed a revised executive order that removed Iraq from the list of "banned" countries, omitted the indefinite ban on Syrian refugees, and allowed those already in possession of a valid visa to enter the country. Much like the first executive order, the revised ban on Muslims was challenged. Several US District Judges argued that the revised order was discriminatory against Muslims. As such, a temporary restraining order that prevented the travel ban from being implemented was issued in March 2017. Despite all the legal challenges, lawsuits, and public outrage, the Supreme Court developed new guidelines and allowed implementation of parts of Trump's temporary travel ban on June 26, 2017. Under the new guidelines applicants from the six listed countries who intend to travel to the United States have to present proof of a relationship with a close family member including parents and siblings or a connection to an entity such as a university in the United States.[1]

This is the not the first time that Iranians have been victims of discriminatory US immigration policies. Long before Trump's ban, Iranians were subject to exclusion, expulsion, detention, and deportation. Since the Islamic Revolution and the ensuing American Hostage crisis in Iran in 1979, Iranian immigrants in the United States have continually been demonized, stigmatized, and politicized. Despite their remarkable educational and financial achievements, impressive high rate of entrepreneurial activities, and overwhelming participation in the high paying sectors of the economy, as well as the dearth of evidence of their involvement in terrorist activities, Iranian immigrants in the United States are often perceived as a suspect group, are penalized for the actions of their home government, and are victims of civil rights violations, discrimination, prejudice, negative persistent media stereotypes, and racial profiling. This chapter emphasizes the political nature of immigration, underscoring the cumulative impact of political tensions between Iran and the United States since the Iranian Revolution and the American hostage crisis. It also explores the evolution in reactions of the first- and second-generation Iranians to the prevailing Iranophobia and the discriminatory and exclusionary immigration policies and practices of the United States over the past four decades.

US-Iran Political Relations since 1953 and Iranian Migration Trends to the United States

No one knows the exact number of Iranians who have left the country since the 1979 Revolution and the total number of Iranians who live outside of Iran. What is known, however, is that never before in Iranian history have so many Iranians from all walks of life been uprooted and dispersed so widely geographically. The revolution was certainly a turning point with indelible social, cultural, and political consequences. Although disputed, the Iranian government estimates the number of Iranians who live and work outside of Iran to be between two and four million. Other reports by international organizations such as the United Nations and independent scholars estimate the number to be between three-and-a-half and four million.[2]

The United States has the largest Iranian population outside of Iran. Most scholars divide the migration history of Iranians to the United States into two demographically distinct stages, the 1979 revolution being the di-

---

1. McGraw, Kelsey, and Keneally 2017.
2. Aidani 2010; Sheffer 2003.

viding point. The large-scale exodus of Iranians over the past four decades has been related to a cumulative combination of major post-revolutionary political and economic changes in Iran, the 1980–1988 war between Iran and Iraq, the dramatic transformation of socio-cultural life, and Iran's unpredictable socio-political future. Therefore, much like Iranian immigrants in other countries, the majority of Iranians in the United States left Iran during and after the 1978–79 revolution. The migration of Iranians to the United States before the revolution was much smaller in scale and more homogeneous in composition. It was also motivated by a different set of economic, political, and social forces. Whereas the pre-revolutionary migration of Iranians to the West, particularly the United States, was rooted in the economic expansion and modernization projects initiated by the shah of Iran after his restoration to power through a CIA military coup in 1953, the post-revolutionary exodus of Iranians was prompted by the downfall of the shah and the subsequent chaotic social, political, and economic consequences of the revolution, including the monopolization of power by clerics and religious leaders, the Islamization of the country, and the disastrous consequences of the Iran-Iraq war.

From the 1953 Coup to the 1979 Revolution

After the overthrow of the democratic government of Prime Minister Mosadegh in 1953 and the return of the shah to Iran, the United States became the dominant foreign power in Iran politically, economically, and culturally. The new US-Iran alliance after the coup was a turning point in the migration of Iranians to the United States. As a result of the strong ties between the two countries, which lasted until the overthrow of the shah in 1978, the Iranian government initiated a series of rapid economic expansions, modernization projects, and cultural reforms. Iran's march toward modernization combined with the rapid economic expansion and investment in industrialization, modern technology, and military buildup in the 1960s and 1970s created a huge demand for skilled workers and encouraged thousands of Iranians to immigrate to the United States for the purpose of acquiring technical skills and advanced education. Moreover, the shah's heavy investment in military buildup and hardware not only turned Iran into a major US ally in the Middle East but also facilitated an exchange of government officials and encouraged thousands of Iranian nationals to visit the United States temporarily for pleasure, business, or both. As a result of the increasingly positive US-Iran ties, between 1960 and 1970, 11,410 Iranian government officials and 28,489 other Iranians visited the United States. The comparable numbers for 1971 through 1977 were 25,984 and 140,539, indicating an annual average of 3,712 government officials and 20,219 visitors. Furthermore, a large number of young Iranians migrated to the United States in the 1960s and 1970s for education. Between 1960 and 1977, around 82,288 Iranian students were studying in US colleges and universities.[3] In the 1977–1978 academic year, as many as 36,220 Iranian students were enrolled in American universities and colleges.[4]

Each year, thousands of Iranian elites, upper-middle class professionals and entrepreneurs, students, and tourists immigrated to the United States without any legal difficulty. Moreover, the strong US-Iran relations combined with an increased flow of middle- and upper-middle class Iranian professionals to the United States not only promoted a positive image of Iran as an ancient civilization rapidly marching toward modernization and industrialization, but also encouraged thousands of Americans to visit Iran regularly. Consider, for instance, the Iran Air ads shown below. These ads were printed in various popular US magazines and offer positive portrayals of Iran: Iran is described as a "fascinating land of old pleasures and new promises"; a country with "fabulous ski slopes, warm blue seas, delicious caviar, and luxurious hotels" that "offers many rewards"; and as the "crossroads of the world."

Images of Iran in the United States before the Iranian Revolution

All this was suddenly changed after the Iranian Revolution and the American hostage crisis in 1979.

---

3. Mobasher 2012.
4. Hakimzadeh 2006.

From the 1979 Iranian Revolution to the Present

The Iranian Revolution drastically changed the pattern and nature of Iranian emigration to the United States. During the 1978–79 revolutionary upheavals, more than 190,000 Iranians entered the United States as non-immigrants. Of this number, only about 46,000 (24 percent) were students. The rest were members of the pre-revolutionary ruling class, religious minorities who left Iran for fear of political and religious persecution, and other individuals who left Iran for fear of the uncertain post-revolutionary consequences. Unlike the pre-revolutionary immigrants, post-revolutionary immigrants were more diverse and included a large number of high level experts and specialists in various scientific and technical areas, industrialists and merchants, entrepreneurs, writers and literary figures, artists, filmmakers, entertainers, journalists, students, and self-employed professionals. Politically, they consisted of former members of the parliament, ministers, and high ranking officers as well as political activists with different ideologies. Given that Islam is the official state religion in Iran and 90–95 percent of Iranians are associated with Islamic beliefs, the majority of post-revolutionary Iranians who entered the United States are Muslims. However, members of the other religious faiths such as Baha'is, Jews, Zoroastrians, and Christians, although small, also emigrated from Iran.[5] In addition to its diverse socio-economic, political, religious, and ethnic make-up, the population of Iranian immigrants in the United States is composed of a large number of women, elderly Iranians, and second-generation Iranians. As indicated in the US census reports, although a substantial number of Iranians in the United States are first-generation immigrants who were born and raised in Iran, the number of second-generation Iranians who were largely born and socialized in this country is growing rapidly. Similarly, the number of Iranian women who have been leaving Iran after the revolution has also climbed significantly. While some Iranian women left the country in pursuit of educational and professional goals, others emigrated because of a lack of freedom and their opposition to the policies of the Iranian government toward women. Still others resettled in the United States as fiancées and wives of Iranian men. This was particularly common during the Iran-Iraq war when long distance marriages were the only viable option for many young Iranian men who were unable to return home because of fear of military conscription. Consequently, for the first time in the migration history of Iranians to the United States, women outnumbered men.

Notwithstanding the significant decline shortly after the revolution, an

5. Bozorgmehr and Sabagh 1988; Bozorgmeher 2007; Mobasher 2012.

average of 11,864 immigrants and 22,635 non-immigrants from Iran have entered the United States annually since 1980. According to census reports, there were 422,664 individuals of Iranian heritage living in the United States in 2008. This constituted 0.14 percent of the total US population. The number of Iranians in the United States increased to 486,994 in 2015, of whom almost two-thirds (64.2%) are foreign born.[6] In addition, the 2015 American Community Survey (ACS) data indicate that 30 percent of Iranians in the United States have a bachelor's degree and another 32 percent have a graduate or professional degree. Moreover, a little over 60 percent are employed in management, business, science, and art occupations with a median earning of $73,549 for Iranian men and $53,207 for Iranian women, and a median home value of $509,700. Despite this remarkable socioeconomic status, Iranian immigrants have been victims of hostility, prejudice, and ongoing discrimination due to the political tension between Iran and the United States since the American hostage crisis in 1979. Immediately after the crisis, the image of Iran in American media changed from an "island of stability" and an ancient civilization with a rich cultural heritage to a "fanatic, terrorist country dominated by a crazy group of mullahs."

Photos by Marion Trikosko. In the collection of the Library of Congress.

Similarly the US immigration policy toward Iranians changed from a receptive and open door policy to a non-receptive and restricted immigration policy. As such, Iranian diplomats and military trainees were expelled, tight restrictions on visas issued to Iranians were imposed, visas previously issued to Iranians were revoked, and Iranian students were asked to report to the local Immigration and Naturalization Service (INS) offices. Moreover, there was a wave of backlash protests and a sudden increase in prejudice, discrimination, racial profiling, and hate crimes against Iranians in US cities from coast to coast. For example, some state universities either stopped

6. American Fact Finder n.d.

enrolling or voted to bar Iranian students from classes. Other schools doubled tuition for Iranian students. In addition, Iranian owned businesses were boycotted and occasionally Iranians were refused service at restaurants and retail stores.[7]

The perception of Iranians and Muslims as barbaric and uncivilized was intensified after the horrific 9/11 terrorist attacks. Immediately after 9/11, George Bush labeled Iran a sponsor of terrorism belonging to the "axis of evil." This new label not only deepened and added fuel to the existing anti-Iranian attitudes of Americans but also justified the implementation of new immigration policies against Iranians and other Muslim groups. One example is the National Security Entry/Exit Registration System (NSEERS), which was launched in 2002 and was reminiscent of the INS reporting requirement for Iranian students during the hostage crisis.[8] Over a decade and a half after 9/11, the story of Iranian immigrants remains unpleasant, and the distorted generalizations and stereotypes about Iranians continue to be propagated in the United States. Yet despite the new immigration restrictions and the current Iranophobic narratives, there is in fact reason to be optimistic about the future, especially when one considers the increasing political participation of Iranian Americans, particularly the second generation, in civil rights activism and the overall improved relations between the United States and Iran.

Iranian American Responses

The political reaction of Iranian immigrants in the United States after the hostage crisis was relatively weak and ineffective. The crisis and its massive political, social, and economic backlash took many Iranians by surprise. In less than two years – between the overthrow of the shah and the hostage crisis – US-Iran relations had deteriorated dramatically. The psychological trauma of the crisis combined with the absence of adequate political and human-capital resources, unfamiliarity with the US political structure and legal system, and lack of legal protection for the majority of Iranians who had entered as non-immigrants limited Iranians from legally challenging the US government for its discriminatory immigration policies and civil rights violations. Moreover, the stressful cultural adjustment for new immigrants, their preoccupation with the Iranian Revolution and its consequences, and their lack of a unified voice because of sharp political divisions between opponents and supporters of the revolutionary government meant that Iranians would remain politically passive as a collective group. With

7. Mobasher 2012.
8. Mobasher 2012.

the exception of two lawsuits filed by the National Emergency Civil Liberties Committee and the Confederation of Iranian Students with support from the American Civil Liberties Union, there were no major legal challenges to the treatment of Iranian immigrants. One such lawsuit was filed in response to President Jimmy Carter's order to require all Iranian student visa holders to report to immigration officials or face deportation. A federal judge ruled the crackdown on Iranians illegal and unconstitutional, arguing that Carter's order was based on national origin and violated the equal protection clause of the Constitution. Government lawyers appealed and a three-judge panel of the US Circuit Court of Appeals ruled that in this "time of international crisis" the government had the right to single out Iranian students and deport students who were in the country illegally. The government continued investigating Iranians and the INS resumed reviewing visas of students and holding deportation hearings.

Iranian American Responses to 9/11

After the 9/11 attacks and the emerging new wave of backlash against Iranians and other Middle Eastern immigrants, Iranian Americans took a more active stance in defending their civil rights and liberties. Unlike the relatively passive reaction of Iranians during the hostage crisis, after 9/11 Iranians were more united and inspired to participate in the political processes of their host society. They organized massive protests, filed lawsuits, and created grassroots civil liberties and educational organizations across the country. In response to the detention and inhumane treatment of 900 legal Iranians who voluntarily appeared at the INS office in Southern California to register for the post-9/11 NSEERS program, for instance, more than 2000 Iranians protested outside of a Los Angeles federal building carrying signs reading, "Detain terrorists, not innocent immigrants" and "What is next? Concentration Camp?" Moreover to challenge the NSEER's registration process, in cooperation with the American-Arab Anti-Discrimination Committee (ADC), Council on American Islamic Relations (CAIR), and National Council of Pakistani Americans (NCPA), the Alliance of Iranian Americans (AIA) filed a class action lawsuit in federal court. With regard to the aforementioned creation of grassroots organizations, some of the most prominent examples include the National Iranian American Council (NIAC), Persian Watch Center, Iranian American Political Action Committee (IAPAC), National Legal Sanctuary for Community Advancement (NLSCA), Iranian-American Anti-Discrimination Council (IAADC), and Public Affairs Alliance of Iranian Americans (PAAIA). Almost all of these organizations are non-profit, non-partisan, non-religious, and apolitical, and are financially supported through donations and membership fees. The primary objectives of these organizations are to advance the political interests of the Iranian American community, disseminate information about hate crimes and discrimination, create a safety net, educate policy makers in DC about Iran and Iranian immigrant communities, and encourage Iranians to participate in political processes and to vote and lobby against federal policies that are discriminatory toward Iranian Americans. Finally, to gain more political visibility and empowerment, a number of first- and second-generation Iranians ran for political office at local, state, and national levels. Since 9/11, many Iranians have been elected and appointed to various political positions.

This remarkable post-9/11 mobilization has been largely undertaken by second-generation Iranian Americans. As indicated in the 2015 US census report, second-generation Iranians comprise 36 percent of the Iranian American population. As a group, they have had a completely different political socialization and have a deeper understanding of the US political system than their foreign born parents who grew up in a non-democratic society with minimal democratic political freedoms and participation. Moreover, unlike their first-generation parents who endured a language barrier, cultural adjustment, and a lack of legal protection and resources during the hostage crisis, second-generation Iranians are not only more resourceful culturally, socially, and politically but also are more passionate about US politics.

In the last several years, Iranian American advocacy groups and organizations have expanded their activities and have gained more visibility. In addition to empowering Iranian Americans, protecting their rights, and supporting local representatives and political candidates who are sensitive to their concerns and interests, they are also acting as cultural and political liaisons between Iran and the United States in the hopes of increasing dialogue between the peoples of both nations. What is striking about these organizations is that, in contrast with comparable Muslim advocacy groups in the United States, there is an absence of any emphasis on Islamic identity as a mobilizing force. Such organizations emphasize instead the Iranian/Persian national identity as a unifying force. This is mainly the outcome of the political construction of anti-Islamic Persian national identity by opponents of the Iranian government and the continued Islamophobia of American society.[9]

9. Mobasher 2012.

Iranian American Responses to Trump's Executive Orders

Since the election of Trump in 2017 and the rise of a new wave of anti-Iranian immigration policies, second-generation Iranian Americans have become more politically conscious and more determined to respond to the ongoing backlash. Two of the largest Iranian American organizations that have had a major role in challenging the new anti-Iran foreign policies and anti-Iranian immigration policies are the National Iranian American Alliance (NIAC) and its sister organization, the National Iranian American Alliance Action (NIACA). As indicated on its website, NIAC's vision is transnational in nature with cultural and political objectives. NIAC's cultural vision is to promote the Iranian American community and its historical and cultural roots in the United States. Its political goal, however, is to encourage Iranians to act as responsible and informed citizens and actively support and promote democracy in Iran.

Immediately after Trump's first executive order was signed, NIAC and four other prominent Iranian American organizations – the Pars Equality Center, the Iranian American Bar Association, the National Iranian American Council, and the Public Affairs Alliance of Iranian Americans – filed a joint lawsuit to block and reverse the Muslim Ban. They also released the following joint statement:

> The Executive Order illogically categorizes everyone of Iranian
> descent as a potential terrorist. According to the Cato Institute,
> there was not a single case of an American being killed in a terrorist
> attack in this country by a person born in Iran — or any of the other
> six countries specified in the Executive Order. Iranians were not
> among the perpetrators of 9/11 or the Oklahoma City bombings or
> the nightclub killings in Orlando, Florida, or any of the other horrific
> acts of terror that have taken place in the United States. To the
> contrary, Iranian Americans were counted among the victims in San
> Bernardino, as well as among the first responders on the scene.[10]

In addition to the lawsuit, NIAC pressured lawmakers and members of the US Congress to pass legislation to revoke the order, pursued several legal avenues to overturn the order, and encouraged Iranian Americans to share their personal stories with members of Congress and journalists and explain how they have been impacted by the ban. Since June 26, 2017, when the US Supreme Court lifted the freeze on Trump's Muslim ban, NIAC has been actively disseminating information concerning the Court's ruling. NIAC has

---

10. "Iranian-American Orgs File Federal Lawsuit Against Trump Travel Ban Executive Order" 2017.

also been educating Iranians about their rights upon entering the United States and interacting with US Customs and Border Protection (CBP). The extent of NIAC's success in counteracting the effects of the ban remains to be seen.

Conclusion

My goal in this chapter was twofold: first, to describe briefly how major transformative events in Iran since the 1953 CIA coup have impacted the migration trends of Iranians to the United States and US immigration policies; and second, to survey the responses of first- and second-generation Iranian immigrants to said policies. As we have seen, the entire migration experience of Iranians in the US is so strongly impacted by a series of critical political episodes and developments, from the 1953 CIA-supported coup d'etat and the shah's restoration to power, to the 1979 revolution and hostage crisis, to 9/11. The sudden political shift in US-Iran relations from friendly allies before the revolution to hostile adversaries after the revolution had a significant negative impact on the integration of Iranians into the United States. Alejandro Portes and Ruben Rumbaut remind us that immigration policies of the receiving society, conditions of the host labor market, and characteristics of the ethnic community as well as the combination of positive or negative features experienced at each of these levels profoundly shape the mode of integration for new immigrants.[11] Government policies not only determine the immigration flows and the forms they take but also affect the likelihood of successful immigration with economic opportunities and available legal options.

The political tensions between Iran and the United States and the subsequent sanctions and the widespread negative anti-Iran views in the United States not only fueled fears of Iranian immigrants but also demarcated Iranians' limit of inclusion and integration, nurtured and justified discrimination and prejudice against Iranian immigrants, justified the institutionalization of tough immigration and refugee policies against Iranians, and affected everyday life for Iranian immigrants in various ways. By imposing sanctions on the Iranian government, the United States unintentionally squeezed and penalized Iranian nationals and denied them the same opportunities that were provided to other dual nationals because of their Iranian descent.

Despite some diplomatic progress in US-Iran relations and the subsequent improvement in US immigration policy and the admission of a large number of Iranians during Barack Obama's presidency, the Iranian government is still viewed as a terrorist state and as a threat to the international

---

11. Portes and Rumbaut 2006.

community. At the time of this writing, the US Congress overwhelmingly has passed another bill, entitled the "Countering America's Adversaries Through Sanctions Act," intended to impose more sanctions on Iran.[12] This bill was passed despite the Joint Comprehensive Plan of Action (JCPOA) that was signed on July 14, 2015, between the P5+1 (China, France, Germany, Russia, the United Kingdom, and the United States), the European Union (EU), and Iran to ensure that Iran's nuclear program will be exclusively peaceful. Notwithstanding protest from the European Union, the new US legislation expanded the sanctions policy against Iran and imposed secondary sanctions "against non-US persons for conducting business with certain sanctioned persons or industries in Iran."[13]

Since the election of Donald Trump diplomatic relations between Iran and the United States have regressed and become more tense. Moreover, the Iranian community in the United States is divided on Trump's new foreign policy toward Iran. Immediately after Trump's election, thirty exiled Iranians labeling themselves as "dissidents" signed a letter appealing to the US president-elect to take a hardline stance toward Iran by repealing President Obama's policies of rapprochement, terminate the Iran nuclear deal, and reinstate the nuclear sanctions aimed at the Iranians. In their letter they said, "We hope under your leadership the United States helps the Iranian people to take back their country from the Islamist gang which has been in charge for the last four decades." They added that "the world without the Islamic Republic and the Islamic State is a better place."

Unlike the anti-government Iranian dissidents who asked Trump to be tough with Iran, a group of prominent Iranians signed an open letter urging the United States president-elect to retain Obama's policies toward Iran. The letter states, "Despite the fact that millions of Iranians disagree with many of the decisions made by their government, they welcomed the Iran nuclear deal."

Without a unified voice, the implementation of more sanctions against Iran, and the executive order banning travel from Iran, it is reasonable to believe that the number of Iranians entering the United States will decline substantially and Iranian immigrants in the United will be subjected to the same level of prejudice, discrimination, and profiling, if not more, in the coming years. Similarly, it is reasonable to believe that much as before, Iranians in the United States will continue to mobilize more political and legal resources to challenge the new anti-Iranian discriminatory immigration policies of the US government.

12. Gershberg and Schenck 2017.
13. Gershberg and Schenck 2017.

Works Cited

Aidani, M. 2010. *Welcoming the Stranger: Narratives of Identity and Belonging in an Iranian Diaspora.* Sydney.

American Fact Finder. N.d. "2015 American Community Survey 1 Year Estimates: Selected Population Profile in the United States." US Census Bureau, https://factfinder.census.gov/faces/tableservices/jsf/pages/productview.xhtml?pid=ACS_15_1YR_S0201&prodType=table.

Bozorgmehr, M. 2007. "Iran." In *The New Americans: A Guide to Immigration since 1965,* edited by M. Waters and R. Ueda. Cambridge, MA.

Bozorgmehr, M., and G. Sabagh. 1988. "High Status Immigrants: A Statistical Profile of Iranians in the United States." *Iranian Studies* 21:5–36.

Gershberg, M. T., and J. A. Schenck. 2017. "Congress Overwhelmingly Passes New Sanctions Against Iran, Russia, and North Korea." *Fried Frank,* July 31. http://www.friedfrank.com/index.cfm?pageID=25&itemID=7840.

Hakimzadeh, S. 2006. "Iran: A Vast Diaspora Abroad and Millions of Refugees at Home." *Migration Policy Institute,* September 1.

"Iranian-American Orgs File Federal Lawsuit Against Trump Travel Ban Executive Order." 2017. National Iranian American Council, February 9. https://www.niacouncil.org/iranian-american-orgs-file-federal-lawsuit-trump-travel-ban-executive-order.

McGraw, M., A. Kelsey, and M. Keneally. 2017. "A Timeline of Trump's Immigration Executive Order and Legal Challenges." *ABC News,* June 29. http://abcnews.go.com/Politics/timeline-president-trumps-immigration-executive-order-legal-challenges/story?id=45332741.

Mobasher, M. 2012. *Iranians in Texas: Migration, Politics, and Ethnic Identity.* Austin, TX.

Portes, A., and R. G. Rumbaut. 2006. *Immigrant America: A Portrait.* Third edition, Berkeley, CA.

Part Four

Rethinking Muslim Politics

Drawing Near to God's Pleasure:
A Dialogue on the Black Muslim Political Tradition and the Moral-Ethical Imperatives of American Islam

Donna Auston and Sylvia Chan-Malik

LMOST A YEAR following the election of Donald J. Trump to the American presidency – an election in which Trump stated that "Islam hates us" and used the "Muslim ban" as a central campaign strategy – Donna Auston and Sylvia Chan-Malik engaged in a dialogue regarding the political orientations of Black American Muslim communities. In their conversation, the two scholars discussed contemporary Black Muslim political formations and US Muslim politics more broadly, with a focus on matters of race and gender. A continual theme that emerged through the dialogue was how the moral-ethical imperatives of anti-racism, gender justice, and Black liberation have constituted Black Muslim political and religious traditions, and how these traditions are critical to understanding the contemporary dynamics of US Muslim communities and politics. The conversations took place on two separate occasions in early October 2017 and built on earlier conversations that took place at the April 2017 Michigan State University symposium on "Muslims and Contemporary US Politics." What follows is an edited transcript of their dialogue, in which the two scholars of race, gender, and Islam in the United States sought to articulate the contours of a Black Muslim political tradition and the moral-ethical imperatives animating what they view as past, present, and future.

In the first section, "From Which Islam Has Never Been Disentangled," Auston and Chan-Malik address the ways Islam is inexorably tied to Blackness in the US racial order and the ways Blackness is disavowed or elided in the construction of contemporary US Muslim political agendas. In section two, "How the Women Go, Islam Goes," the two scholars turn to the ways gender shapes US Muslim political formations and how intersections of race, gender, class, and sexuality are integral to constituting more expansive and inclusive visions of "justice" in US Muslim communities. In the final section, "Drawing Near to God's Pleasure," the conversation turns to the articulation of a Black Muslim political tradition and how this tradition may be articulated and positioned as a moral-ethical imperative for US Muslim politics in the twenty-first century.

"From Which Islam Has Never Been Disentangled"

Sylvia Chan-Malik (SCM): Donna, can you describe the impetus for your research? What are the questions that inform your discussions of Black American Muslims and Islam?

Donna Auston (DA): My work begins with the desire to untangle how questions of racial identity shape religious understandings. How do these two categories – race and religion – work in concert with one another to produce US Muslims' subjectivities? How do questions of citizenship factor into the discourse about whether or not Islam is reconcilable with US identity? As an African American Muslim, I think about these questions differently. For example, assimilation is not a thing that concerns me. As an African American, I'm technically a citizen, though a citizen with an asterisk. Thus, while questions of whether or not Muslims are "home" in America, or Islam is compatible with American values are always awkward and problematic, for African American Muslims, they are a complete non-starter. I come from people who produced hip-hop, blues, and jazz. These are Black contributions to American culture, which are heavily inflected by Muslim participation and presence, by Black social protest and naming practices. The Black Muslim experience in American culture is so deeply embedded. So how do you disentangle Islam from Blackness? And why would you?

A question that comes up frequently in Muslim communities is, "Is it Islamically OK to be at a Black Lives Matter protest?" This is a striking question when you think about how Muslims will constantly reference Islam's emphasis on the preservation of life, as well as how Islam is an anti-racist paradigm, but somehow can't seem to apply these precepts to what's happening with the loss of Black life at the hands of the state. For example, I was in Newark for a protest on the day of Darren Wilson's non-indictment. And one of the things that tends to happen at protests is that people talk about the national cases, for example, Michael Brown and Eric Garner, but they also have their own local stories of police killing civilians, names that aren't familiar on a national scale. Around the same time as the Darren Wilson non-indictment, there had been a police shooting of a Black Muslim man named Abdul Kamal in Essex County, New Jersey. There have also been a number of other Muslim victims of police violence. So police violence is an issue that affects US Muslims directly. But when I'm in the mosque on Fridays, no one discusses this. It isn't understood as a crisis. So while I often encounter other believers struggling with their own anxiety, worry, and consternation over police brutality and violence, it is not being talked about at the mosque, it isn't the subject of a *khutba*. There's a total disconnect. Innocent men, women, children are being shot for no reason, and it doesn't register as a moral crisis amongst US Muslim leaders or in American Muslim religious spaces.

So what is behind this disconnect? Why doesn't anyone, including Muslims themselves, see Black Lives Matter as a *Muslim* issue? I see this as a result of how Muslims are only configured on the US political landscape in relation to terrorism, state surveillance, immigration, and homeland security. Thus, they are securitized subjects, and this subjectivity dictates the agenda of "Muslim" political concerns. So even beyond Black Lives Matter, we don't think of the environment, education, or healthcare as Muslim issues, as a part of US Muslim political concerns. This narrowness prevents the ability to build any broad-based platform for Muslim political activity. It's very limited: we're security concerns, we respond to that, and that's it. This is so disappointing, because as a Muslim, I know that there is enormous potential for a broad, informative, useful, productive, and *ethical* paradigm that could inform a wide range of Muslim positions that impact everyone's lives. But that doesn't happen.

SCM: Yes, and it also stems from a lack of knowledge on the part of non-Black Muslims regarding Black Muslims and African American Islam, as well as a general unfamiliarity amongst Americans of the actual history of Islam and Muslims in the United States. In particular, as African American Muslims have been in the United States for centuries, they have long navigated how to practice Islam within and against US racial contexts. Though through the 1960s most Muslims in the US were Black, the large-scale arrival of immigrants from South Asia and the Middle East after 1965 forever changed the demographics of US Muslim communities. And these new communities are often completely unaware of the experiences of African American Muslims, or even worse, they see these experiences as inauthentic or simply don't care. In turn, the presence of growing communities of non-Black Muslims has changed how Black American Muslims live and construct their identities, as they now must figure out how to respond to this ignorance, willful or otherwise, of their lives and experiences.

It's important to note that the very category of "US Muslims" as a collective group, or demographic, is a post-9/11 formation, since there was no demand for "US Muslim voices" or perspectives prior to that. But when US Muslims were asked to speak in a collective voice, it quickly became apparent how their subjectivities, opinions, and political positions were largely informed by categories of race, class, and ethnicity – not to mention gender – all of which led them to define "Islam" in different ways. Black Muslims had very different views on issues than Pakistani American Muslims, or Yemeni

American Muslims, etc. Thus, I think so much of the disconnect you speak of above – of how a multiracial group of US Muslims can be on completely different pages about what US Muslim political concerns are – is amplified by the fishbowl effect of the scrutiny Muslims have been subjected to since 9/11. We have really just been scrambling and responding to crisis after crisis ever since then, and there is so little meaningful intra-community dialogue that happens And this happens against a backdrop of an ongoing denial or ignorance of the history of Islam in the United States, as well as to the very ways race operates in this country, through logics of white supremacy, anti-Blackness, settler colonialism, etc.

A question I have, then, is, How do US Muslims engage history? And how does this shape their politics? Is there a distinctive Black Muslim politics? Because we have non-Black Muslim diasporic communities who come to the United States with notions of politics from their home countries and are very invested in what America can offer, in other words, the American Dream. Whereas for Black American Muslims, Islam has broadly arisen as a critique of and alternative to the nation-state. So there are very different notions of what "US Muslim history" is amongst these various groups. And this creates conflict.

DA: Absolutely. Part of my dissertation is trying to untangle what Black Muslim protest and politics looks like in this moment of racial crisis. But that reading has to be anchored in how we got here, in an intellectual and spiritual history of Black Muslim political-religious orientation. When Black African Muslim captives were brought to what became the United States as slaves – as chattel – *their spiritual practices became tied to a racial order from which Islam has never been untangled.* The presence of Muslims in the United States is always anchored inextricably to this racial order. To think about what Islamophobia looks like in a US context, one must go back to that time period. These histories have roots, they are racial ghosts, as written about by scholars like Avery Gordon and Anne Cheng.[1] So what we have now is that we're always somehow trying to *get away* from race, or *get past it, transcend* it, *get over it,* or *put it behind us.* But we've never actually really confronted it.

For US Muslims, there has to be a reckoning not only with the Islam of enslaved Africans, but how Islam re-emerged in the early twentieth-century United States through people like Noble Drew Ali, the Ahmadiyya movement, and, of course, later, the Nation of Islam.

SCM: At the historical moment when Noble Drew Ali, the Ahmadiyya movement, and Mufti Muhammad Sadiq enter the US cultural landscape in the

---

1. See Gordon 1997; Cheng 1997.

1920s and 30s, Black nationalism is gaining traction as a political ideology through figures like Marcus Garvey and Edward Wilmot Blyden. Islam and Black nationalism come to co-constitute each other, they link together notions of a Black diaspora and Black global struggle with Islam. In opposition to Christianity, Islam emerges as a religious orientation that names racism – and specifically anti-Black racism – as something that is morally and ethically wrong. Yet it also offers this universalist ethos that connects people across geographies.

DA: Leaders like Nobel Drew Ali, Mufti Muhammad Sadiq, and later Elijah Muhammad rendered Black struggle a global struggle – *a human rights struggle*. They never sought to discount race, but instead to make anti-Black racism legible on a global scale. That is such an integral part of a Black Muslim politics, such an integral part of being Muslim in the United States period: the idea that anti-Black racism is a global struggle.

SCM: As well as a deeply moral and ethical issue. A religious struggle.

DA: Exactly. I encounter this common question or assumption from people about my research: "Those early Black Muslim movements – they were more political than religious, right?"[2] But such questions fail to grasp how these things – politics and religion – hang together. Religion can be political, and one's politics can be religious. You can't really understand US Islamic movements without recourse to both of those paradigms.

"How the Women Go, Islam Goes"

SCM: In doing the research for my book, *Being Muslim*, I've found that this intersection between religion and politics is particularly pronounced for women, and specifically, Black Muslim women. For example, for Black working-class women who converted through the Ahmadiyya Movement in the 1920s, they may have been aware of Black nationalism and Marcus Garvey, but Islam was also something they had to incorporate into their day-to-day life. Being Muslim informed their modes of dress, what they ate, their manner of worship, and what rituals and traditions they incorporated into their lives. But they had to express all of these actions against racial and gendered contexts that devalued Black womanhood in specific ways, as hypersexualized, unintelligent, a slave/servant, that is, the Venus Hottentot, Sapphire, Mammy, etc. To put it another way, for them to speak their identities into existence as Muslims was an embodied affective practice that was likely guided by political motivations to challenge such stereotypes and the politi-

---

2. See Lincoln 1994.

cal ways of thinking that produced them. But this process was also always deeply intimate and spiritual. For Black women, Islam was a way to build a direct relationship with God and a global community, as well as to construct expansive horizons of being through which they could seek safety and sanctuary from debasements they encountered in the public sphere.

I've come to view these historical examples as critical to approaching the lives and struggles of contemporary US Muslim women across racial and ethnic boundaries. They demonstrate how US Muslim women have long been dealing with how women's bodies are always intensely politicized sites of struggle, and how racial contexts shape the contours of this struggle.

DA: Yes, and race and gender are always co-constituted. Gender is always such a prominent part of how American Muslims are figured as political subjects, as in the example of early Black Muslim women, as you mentioned, but also in foreign policy. The motivation for foreign policy decisions are so often articulated through women's bodies – anxieties about the nation and its borders. For Muslims, this is articulated around, particularly, the *hijab*, or headscarf. As many scholars have pointed out, the scarf is fetishized and becomes this epicenter of many battles over what Muslims are supposed to represent in terms of threat level and otherness.

SCM: Yes, the discourse of the veil.[3] And at the same time, that Islamophobes and others level these characterizations at US Muslim communities, there is a parallel, and equally uninformed, strain of discourse around gender within American Muslim communities. In this conversation, "feminism" is the enemy, and there is all this hand-wringing around, "Oh, the women are not covering and they're working, and they're feminists." Feminism is understood as a terrible blow to Islamic ideals, i.e. conservative interpretations of Islamic gender norms. So again, the fact that women are not adhering to certain types of norms acts as a symbol to many that there is something wrong. Women are always operating as a sort of an indicator of how Islam is doing: *how the women go, Islam goes*, or something like that [laughter]. Or on the flip, the women in Saudi Arabia have just been granted the right to drive, so externally, outside of those societies, people say, "Oh, Saudi Arabia is entering the modern era," or, "They finally caught up." As if they had previously existed in a different universe or a parallel time zone prior to that. Always, women are symbols of how advanced, strong, weak, corrupt, etc., a society or community is.

DA: So then to think about race, religion, and gender together in historical contexts reveals ideas of what women are supposed to be and what options

3. See Ahmed 1992.

are available to particular groups of women at certain times. As a Black Muslim woman, I often think about what I do and what my choices should be. In our present moment, we may look back on women in the Nation of Islam, and now, fifty years later, see their constructions of womanhood as archaic, oppressive, and patriarchal. But what were they intervening on in that time period? For Black women in the United States in the 1940s and 50s, taking care of, being devoted to, their own families was a luxury. For example, the women in my family worked as domestic servants for white people for generations. They had no choice – under slavery and then after that – but to take care of white people's kids, and many times at the expense of their own. So to assume these maternal, domestic roles in their own families and communities could be empowering; they were "freeing."

SCM: So what do you think about this growing anxiety around "feminism" in US Muslim communities? Many African American women and other women of color – whether they're Muslim or not, and including myself at times – are often wary of the term "feminism," because it's come to be defined so narrowly through white, second-wave precepts, even when we understand that's just a tiny portion of what "feminism" is. Indeed, so much of the antagonism and anxiety around "feminism" in American Muslim communities stems from a profoundly limited view of feminism as a political agenda *only* advocating individualism, workplace equality, abortion, rights, and sexual freedom. Yet the lives of Black women and women of color, as with the family members you were just talking about, actually continually express their agency and desires for gender justice in very strong ways, intersectional ways which I believe should also be understood as "feminism." But beyond an individualist paradigm, their desire for justice was and is holistic: it also means justice for their communities, for their children, their husbands, their partners, their brothers, which they understand as empowering themselves in the process. *We should see all of this as feminism*, instead of only using the term in ways that obstruct and erase the contributions of Black Muslim women and other women of color.

DA: Yes, and about the anxiety, I think there's a lot of soul-searching that's happening on a collective level in the US Muslim community because these issues of race, gender, and sexuality are pretty much at crisis point. In all my years in the Muslim community, there have always been conversations around what models of gender are appropriate for Muslims to adopt. But in the current political moment, US Muslim communities are collectively grappling not only with their position vis-a-vis the outside world, but also with its internal complexity and diversity. So what something like feminism might represent for me as a Black Muslim woman may be different from what it represents for a white convert or a brown Muslim woman from South Asia with different historical and cultural baggage. It's certainly interesting to watch. As an anthropologist, there's a lot of material for me to watch as this is unfolding, and it's not at all clear at this point where we're going to end up. But I am hopeful, I think, in spite of some of the difficult conversations that we are having, that there will be a more coherent and cohesive articulation as people begin to attempt to name and disaggregate things that aren't supposed to be conflated, like race, gender, and religion. We are starting to think about what it means to pay attention to our particular histories and our particular lived experiences, even if we all share one faith label.

SC: That makes me think about the different ways US Muslim women feel about the mosque or places of worship. Black women come to Islam because they sense the possibility of being fully human in their newly chosen religious spaces, to which they may bring in their own experiences as Black women and be accepted for who they are. They create gender-specific space where they can connect with other women and talk about issues of spirituality and faith. So a kind of safe space is created. Then, as more immigrant Muslims arrive in this country in the 1960s and 70s, what happens is that these spaces shift in terms of the racial and ethnic dynamics. Black Muslims get pushed aside, and so they feel marginalized in the very spaces that they labored so hard to create as spaces of solace. So that is also a disconnect, if you're an African American woman or a convert and you walk into a primarily non-Black and/or immigrant mosque, because you might feel culturally unaccepted and unable to find or build the kinds of connections that you were going to that religious space for in the first place.

DA: And this plays out in even larger ways. Because it *does* matter if your religious community affirms who you are, where you come from. At the very least, they should afford you a sense of a basic universal dignity as a human being, right? But there are people who will rob you of participation in that ideal on the basis of your racial or gender identity. And this also plays out in other ways, for example, in the spatial arrangements in mosques. What is available to a woman who comes to worship in a random mosque? What spaces does she have access to? How is she included in the communal worship activities of a particular sacred space?

But there are other ways that these types of issues play out that are tied in to bigger political issues, to one's political concerns as a woman. For example, what about when my concern for the well-being of my family and my community are not spiritual priorities of the religious community that I belong to? So if I am experiencing the devastation upon my family and my community wrought by mass incarceration because my sons, or my nephews, or my neighbor's children are being taken away by the state, what about that? That people in my family get caught up in a system that just circulates them in and out, that robs our communities of our best and brightest people? These are everyday issues that many Black communities live with.

I remember a friend of mine describing going to a masjid in Newark, and as they were coming out of the prayer, there was gunplay outside of the mosque. Other than my immediate concern for the person telling me the story, I just remember thinking about all of the children who might attend that mosque, all of the women now wrought with concern over the safety of their kids having to walk back and forth to a sacred space where they might have to dodge gunfire, or while going back and forth to school. And these concerns don't very frequently show up in Muslim political conversations. They don't show up in ways that allow for Black Muslims who deal with this violence frequently to be seen as victims, and not as pathological figures who are somehow more prone to violence than everyone else because of their inherent savagery. Certain racial ideas – of Black inferiority, Black savagery – erase the experiences of Black women and Black families. Which is all a long-winded way of noting how these problematic ideas about race and gender render vulnerable Black communities *even more vulnerable*. By rendering Black people illegible, the resources that they might need – whether political or religious – become even harder to access, which makes it harder for people to make sense of their traumatic experiences within religious spaces. And that – making sense of trauma, suffering – that is one of the things religious communities are supposed to do for you, right? They're supposed to give you comfort, provide tools that allow you to make meaning of your experiences. But these become unavailable because we're drowning in so many problematic ideas about race and gender.

SCM: What I hear you saying is that there isn't an intersectional – or perhaps a better word would be *holistic* – analysis of how to think about what US Muslim politics are. So for example, if we want to address gender inequities in the mosque, in our religious spaces, one response might be, "Let's just change the prayer arrangement within the mosque," for example, women and men stand side by side, or all in the same room, whatever. So that is a primarily gender-based kind of approach to thinking through a solution within religious spaces. But I hear you saying we also have to look at the larger context, for example, where the spiritual community is located, and acknowledge the issues that confront women, men, and children when they walk *outside* of the mosque. The desire for houses of worship to be safe, for the communities they are in to be safe – those are also issues that need to be

taken into account as we think through what it means to work for gender equity or racial equity more broadly in US Muslim communities. Because these
is a lot of conversation about mosque space, and that's really important to
talk about. But our religious imperatives as Muslims should go beyond the
mosque; they should lead to a more expansive way of thinking through how
attending to race, gender, and class produce religious imperatives that engage communities, that lead us "to come to know one another."

DA: To build upon that, I think when we're considering what a Muslim
political platform might look like, we must acknowledge how a desire for
respectability informs Muslim participation in US politics – this need to be
accepted, to be seen as "good." This desire for respectability considerably
narrows how an Islamic political paradigm for Muslims in the US might gen-
erate solutions for a wider group of people by focusing on what might be
called "family values" in American political terms. We employ notions of
normative Islamic ideals about gender, sexuality, and what family is supposed to look like, which wind up positioning Muslims in terms of political
issues as overly concerned with policing expressions of sexuality that are
deemed outside the framework of respectability. As a result, we lose sight of
what Islamic "family values" actually are, because that term aligns you with
a right, conservative platform. We lose sight of a conception of "family values" as indicating a platform that, for example, provides economic support
for families, for paid family leave, good health care, food stamps, etc.

If our ideals about gender are very flat and uncomplicated, that impacts how we can intervene upon this imperative to respectability. Because
by simply thinking about the same issues over and over (for example, the
veil, women in the mosque, etc.) in terms of respectability, we lose sight of
other things that actually are life-sustaining for people. With the religious
right in this country, you frequently see these weird contradictions in which
pro-life candidates are against abortion, but at the same time want to cut
food stamps and support the death penalty. Or they don't push for police
accountability when a child like Tamir Rice is killed. So in this current political moment, one of the things I'm seeing is how US Muslims are trying
to tease out where it is that their spectrum of value happens to lie in terms
of political alignments and political strategies. On the one hand, you have
Muslims who are pursuing alliances with a liberal, social justice platform,
for example, Black Lives Matter, LGBTQ rights, immigrant rights, etc. And
then on the other hand, you have an element that has become increasingly
vocal in calling for more moral alignment with what are traditionally seen
as conservative Republican family values.

SCM: Right. But for the latter group, it gets articulated as, "Stop trying to adapt Islam to this secular, liberal paradigm." They argue that "liberals" are trying to make Islam something that it isn't. For example, they'll say, "LG-BTQ issues can't be a part of Islam. There's no way."

DA: And those positions are interesting to me because gender and sexuality are always at the nexus of their arguments. Gender and sexuality determine whether something is moral in terms of an Islamic paradigm.

SCM: And in this logic, "feminism" becomes a catch-all for everything. It becomes shorthand for how Islam is under siege by the secular, liberal establishment, how Islamic morals have been destroyed, etc. "Feminism" is kind of the bogeyman, right?

DA: It's the bogeywoman. Can we be the bogeywomen? [laughter] But in all seriousness, when "conservative" Muslims critique feminism, they are never thinking about people like Sojourner Truth, Harriet Tubman, or any other Black feminists. This irrational fear of feminism amongst certain US Muslims is based on such a lack of knowledge of the full body of feminist thought and theory, and especially the feminism of women of color.

"Drawing Near to God's Pleasure"

SCM: I'd like to return briefly to the question of whether Black Lives Matter is Islamic as framed through US Muslim community discourse, much of it online. Perhaps one of the most heated debates to take place recently in US Muslim communities was around Sheikh Hamza Yusuf's comments regarding Black families at the Reviving the Islamic Spirit (RIS) Conference in December 2016. To summarize what occurred, Sheikh Hamza was asked questions about whether or not it was legitimate for Muslims to show solidarity with Black Lives Matter protestors or with the movement at large. His response to that covered a lot of ground, but he didn't say yes. He instead talked about the ways that systems of policing in the United States are some of the most just in the world and that Black-on-Black crime is an important factor in understanding police interactions with Black citizens. He also said he disagreed with BLM tactics in how they diverged from the "non-violent" approach of 1960s civil rights struggles.

DA: Yes, it was a big mess, obviously, because his comments sounded a lot like conservative talking points that typically are regurgitated in response to questions about why Black citizens are continually being shot, strangled, and brutalized by agents of the state. These tropes about Black criminality and Black pathology are typically used to justify this type of violence as the fault of Black people themselves. This was disconcerting for a lot of people in the US Muslim community. So this became a controversial moment. And then there were his follow-up comments. After initial push-back from the public about his original comments at RIS, he went on to issue what were intended to be clarifying statements, an apology of sorts, which in many ways just made it worse. In that particular set of comments, he said that racism was not the main issue facing Black communities, but rather it was the breakdown of the Black family, in other words, the Moynihan Report 2.0 – a way of thinking that completely ignores the ways structural racism negatively impacts Black families.[4]

My mother was a married woman living in Alabama when she was pregnant with my older sister. When it was time for her to give birth, she had to deliver my sister in a segregated hospital. It didn't matter how respectable she was, she still had to deliver her child into the world into a segregated and inferior hospital in Alabama in 1964. So when I heard Sheikh Hamza's comment (about the breakdown of the Black family), that was one of the first things I thought about. That experience is so profound to me not only because it impacted my mother, but my sister, who comes into the world segregated – this is how her life begins. So when you say that racism isn't the problem but the breakdown of the Black family is, I'm thinking, "Okay, how do you disentangle a story like that?" Because in spite of the fact that Black marriage was illegal according to US law for so long, my mother and her husband still formed a sacred bond of marriage; but this did not protect them against structural racism. The law of the land interferes and intervenes on Black lives in a way that stacks the deck against the stability of families. It is dangerous to trade out these more nuanced conversations about what the breakdown of the Black family actually means, in terms of lived experience, and instead, roll out these easy tropes of Black pathology as the natural order of things. And coming from a religious man who speaks about God's will, and how God designed the world, and how God wants you to be, for him to blame Black pathology for the issues Black communities are facing, this is problematic in so many ways.

SCM: It seems the insult of his comments was not only that they displayed a large distance between himself and the very real experiences of Black Americans and Black American Muslims, but also in how they conveyed his

---

4. For more on Hamza Yusuf's comments at the RIS convention, see Angail 2016; Evans 2017; Evans 2017; Miller 2017.

ignorance or misunderstanding of Islam's very history in the United States, in how he seemed to erase the fact that Black Muslims built the foundations of American Muslim identity and culture.

DA: I would agree with that. I also think there are a few more things that were in play there. On one hand, there's the orientation of Muslims – more broadly, but certainly within the American Muslim context – to religious authority. In other words, what type of relationship do lay Muslims have with their religious scholars? Is it dialogical? Can we converse with these scholars? Is there a space for critique and back-and-forth conversations? Or is this a very authoritarian, charismatic, I-say-you-do type of relationship? This at-times blind deference to authority is one aspect of what produced this controversy. On the other hand, this situation highlights the question of whether or not there is currently space for discussions about structural racism and anti-Blackness within sacred Muslim spaces in the United States. Do we make space for those conversations? Are we open to rearranging and restructuring our institutions to be more egalitarian and anti-racist? Is that an ethical and spiritual priority? Or is that "secular politics" that is some-how not legitimately a religious endeavor? So there's that. Finally, we must acknowledge that the person making these remarks is a white American. And so that also introduced a whole set of other issues in terms of unpacking what happened and then the conversations that came out as a result. One of the questions that I still have is, What is the spiritual imperative for white American Muslims in terms of anti-racism? What soul work do white Mus-lims have to do in order to be not just "not a racist" but actually anti-racist as a spiritual practice?

I think about how the Last Sermon of the Prophet Muhammad, peace be upon him, is an anti-racist message. As a believing Muslim, I take seriously the fact that he knew his time was near and he made his final message an anti-racist one, and actually one of gender-equity as well. And so it's baf-fling that these things (for example, Black Lives Matter) are tossed aside as secular, but as people like James Baldwin have asked, How are white people morally disfigured by racism? For me, that's a part of this conversation.

SCM: What becomes frustrating in conversations like the one around Sheikh Hamza regarding the role of race in US Muslim communities are when non-Black Muslims say to Black Muslims, "Stop being so narcissistic. You're just thinking about yourselves." What is so ignorant, so dangerous about such comments, is that I view African American Muslims as impelled to instigate conversations around race due to a deep sense of concern and care for their fellow co-religionists. It is out of their own lived experience and deep multigenerational understandings of the consequences of racism in the United States that these are warnings to the collectivity. They are driven by the imperative to say, "Look, we have been here. We have been engaging in how to live this religion in what Toni Morrison calls the 'wholly racialized society of the United States.' And this is what we have learned. So it is out of a deep sense of care for you as a fellow Muslim, that I am saying this to you: pay attention to racism." This is not naval-gazing, but an expression of care and concern for fellow Muslims and society as a whole.

DA: Right. These types of thinking prevent us from untangling things in any real way. This idea that there are secular concerns over here and there are religious concerns over there is something that is just not tenable because the ground zero of religion is the lived experience.

SCM: So in light of everything we have discussed in regards to how race and gender shape what we think of US Muslim politics, do you think there is any utility in trying to articulate and advance a Black Muslim political position? And if so, what is a Black Muslim politics and what would it look like? What is at stake in defining it?

DA: There is absolutely such a thing as a Black Muslim political position and tradition, and there should continue to be such a thing. A Black Muslim politics begins in terms of how we feel we can legitimately and spiritually respond to the political and racialized conditions that our bodies exist in. It asks, How can I effectively both practice my religion and remain true to God and also deal with "secular" concerns like racism and white supremacy? How can I effectively discuss and protest racism and white supremacy without committing some type of breach in my spiritual domain or practice? I see many of the earlier Muslim movements as having a much better handle on that question than we do. I think they were much more comfortable with the idea that your spirituality had an obligation to actually wrestle with these concerns in real, tangible ways. So through theology, through practice, through the organization of your mosque, through the organization of your families, through the development of communities, in every aspect of your life, these obligations to justice were moral imperatives of your faith. In these Black Muslim movements, it was not ethically possible to be a servant of God and live in an environment of extreme racial injustice without responding to that injustice in a proactive way.

My own research is concerned with trying to untangle what these moral imperatives are in our current political moment. In the United States, we're always at varying levels of racial crisis. But I think this is a particularly difficult moment. How do I disentangle what a Black Muslim political, spiritual ethos looks like right now? And how is this ethos showing up in this moment? How are Muslims living with what it means to be Black and what it means to be Muslim in the era of Black Lives Matter under Trump? I approach these questions as somebody who converted to Islam in the late 1980s through an attraction to the ways that social and racial justice, seemingly "secular-political" concerns, were articulated through Islam; this was what attracted me to Islam in the first place. I felt that by becoming Muslim I could change myself and I could change the world, simultaneously. Islam gave me the tools to combat my own ego and whatever other internal failings that I have as a person. But it also placed in my lap the responsibility for taking the ideals of justice and implementing them in the world in whatever ways were available to me.

What I would like to see going forward in US Muslim politics is a collective discourse that comes to terms with Black Islam as a liberation theology. There needs to be a more systematic articulation and then a building upon of those foundations that are already so well laid by our early Black American Muslim pioneers. For those communities of Black Muslims, Islam by definition was liberation theology. So I would like to see subsequent generations pick that up and take it further.

There's a *hadith* or a tradition of the Prophet Muhammad, peace be upon him, where he says that whoever sees an evil, she should change it with her hand. If she cannot do that, she should change it with her tongue. And if neither of those options is available, then – this is a paraphrase, of course – disliking it in one's heart is the minimum. This is the minimal level of where a believer should be. So being in the world and sitting in the midst of injustice of any type should not be an option for a Muslim. You can't be settled. You can't be settled and be moral. And this is my perspective. You can't be a Muslim in the world and be comfortable and/or well-adjusted to oppression. So based on the genealogy – the Black Muslim political tradition – through which I converted into Islam, *social justice is a moral imperative and an act of worship. It is as much an act of worship as prayer or fasting. We must put the establishment of justice on par with those particular ritual acts as effective means of drawing near to God's pleasure.* For me, that is what a Black Muslim politics in the United States has always been and needs to be going forward.

Works Cited

Ahmed, L. 1992. *Women and Gender in Islam: Historical Roots of a Modern Debate.* New Haven, CT.

Angail, N. 2016. "Hamza Yusuf and the Dangers of Black Pathology." *Muslimah Media Watch,* December 27. http://www.muslimahmediawatch. org/2016/12/27/hamza-yusuf-and-the-dangers-of-black-pathology.

Chan-Malik, S. 2018. *Being Muslim: A Cultural History of Women of Color in American Islam.* New York.

Cheng, A. 1997. "The Melancholy of Race." *The Kenyon Review* 19.1:49–61.

Evans, U. 2017. "Discussing Controversy: Hamza Yusuf at RIS." *American Learning Institute for Muslims,* December 27. https://www.alimprogram. org/articles/discussing-controversy-hamza-yusuf-at-ris.

Gordon, A. 1997. *Ghostly Matters: Haunting and the Sociological Imagination.* Minneapolis.

Lincoln, C. 1994. *The Black Muslims in America.* 3rd ed. Grand Rapids, MI.

Miller, R. 2017. "Black Muslims and the Politics of Respectability." *Sapelo Square,* February 1. https://sapelosquare.com/2017/02/01/black-muslims-and-the-politics-of-black-respectability.

The Idea of a Global Muslim Left

Junaid Rana

THE SCHOLARSHIP ON PROTEST RELIGIONS in North America has long noted that Islam is counted among them. Islam as holy protest has been described as oppositional, for example, and considered an antithesis to the system of white supremacy enabled by certain versions of Christianity.[1] The discrepancy between the practice of Christianity as a religion of divine justice and salvation belies the lived experience particularly in the context of slavery in the Americas. That white supremacy emerged out of Christianity, and then was folded into a particular form of racial capitalism,[2] should not be a surprise given how this system of dominance seeks to objectify all human existence including social and economic relations, as well as religious and spiritual life. And while the connection of white supremacy to Christianity as a force of oppression is at root a theological and political problem, the possibility of religion as a force to transform society toward a more emancipatory end should not be foreclosed. Such a conclusion has been the tendency of secular political traditions, in particular, leftist traditions that are suspicious of religion and even denounce it completely. In contrast to such dismissals, the example of liberation theology in the Catholic tradition, premised on the elevation of the marginalized, provides a point from which to imagine radical politics within religious approaches.[3] Similarly, the political figures of holy protest in the freedom struggles of the United States range from abolitionists to civil rights leaders to those involved, for instance, with the radical politics of the Black Panther Party.

Barely below the surface of accounts of political protest and dissent is the role of religion – particularly the salience of faith-based organizing. From the perspective of Islam in the North American model, the role of Elijah Muhammad and the Nation of Islam has been at the forefront of an oppositional, dissenting, protest religion and theological approach. Much of this tradition of protest theology in the United States emerged from Black Islam and has yet to be fully discussed and analyzed.[4] While Malcolm X has rightfully garnered much attention, there is a long line of thinkers

1. DeCaro 1996; Curtis 2006; Dannin 2002.
2. Robinson 1983.
3. See Cone 1975.
4. Jackson 2005.

and activists within the pantheon of Islamic thought that would square fully within what the late great scholar Cedric Robinson calls the Black radical tradition.[5] Similarly, the turn away from the Nation of Islam by Warith Deen Muhammad merits more fully a consideration of the experience of Blackness in traditional Islam. What such endeavors would inevitably lead to is a vibrant and complex debate of politics. A more complete discussion of these philosophical traditions and debates would clarify the development into a range of organized political factions and radical historical approaches.

And while understanding how Muslims engage in political philosophy is a vastly important exercise, the question of how those from the Muslim world are experimenting with political ideas is just as useful. Drawing on historical figures from the past can reveal much about the present but also contribute to future political projects. In this essay I present examples of these two different approaches in the historical figures of Malcolm X, or Malik Shabazz, and Dada Amir Haider Khan. The first engaged in the theorization of an ethics of Islamic liberation theology, and the second was an internationalist and anti-colonial radical who hailed from a village outside of Rawalpindi in present-day Pakistan. Each figure represented different periods of the twentieth century and they are not presented here as a progressive history, since the periods I discuss first for Shabazz are in the second half – in the 1950s and 60s – and for Dada in the first half. Indeed, the point here is that political formation consists of many different sources and origins. And as Edward Said famously argued, theories have an interesting way of traveling that does not guarantee a certainty of political outcome.[6] Here my interest is in tracing political formations of what might be loosely referred to as the Muslim left.[7] These are experiments in ideological and political philosophy, for lack of a better description, that have been difficult to track and have been submerged from political sight. As a politics that historically is anti-imperial, and at times anti-state, the result of such engagement is more generally internationalist. And while the term Muslim left might seem out of place and unintelligible, it is this incommensurability that is perhaps most politically productive.

It is with these thoughts in mind that I begin with the question of the possibility of Muslim politics in the contemporary moment, and more specifically the possibility of a broad range of politics that would include the notion of a Muslim left. As a challenge to the preordained social scripts of what has been made possible as a colonial vestige of politics, that is the poli-

5. Robinson 1983.
6. Said 1983.
7. Rana and Daulatzai 2018.

tics associated directly with state governance, I wish to probe what might be considered contradictory, but, in fact, is a kind of seamless politics. The legacy of Edward Said's great insight into the Muslim world that orientalism crafts a certain racial colonialism in which politics is subsumed in a dialectic of us and them, and is even complicated by Cemil Aydin's recent work into the conjuring of the term "Muslim world," speaks to the complexities of social and political practice between rivals, enemies, and even friends.[8] In both examples of conjuring orientalism or the idea of the Muslim world, colonial structures and imaginaries are used to obfuscate complexity and the fierce debate of ideas. What a term like the Muslim left makes possible is an insight into the politics and practices of those who have engaged in a distinct formation that is itself an underappreciated philosophical and theological tradition. And while such a term does not follow simple programmatic rules for who participates or is engaged with the Muslim left, this ambivalence is partly due to a sense of the non-organized organization of this category. The Muslim left, or for that matter the idea of Muslim socialism, or Muslim anti-colonialism, has not been a premise of how these politics have been understood, particularly from the vantage point of political theory. The lens has typically been far more secularized and universalizing in terms of understanding those who might be considered Muslim as engaging in anti-colonial politics or experimenting with communism or socialism. In the secularized form of the political, being Muslim is rendered incompatible with a range of struggles of decolonization, liberation, or social justice.[9] Even further, the idea of revolutionary thinking is one that is distinguished as a narrow or sectarian politics in, say, the example of anti-colonial Algeria or revolutionary Iran.[10] By calling these politics the Muslim left, I do not mean to say that there is something exclusively religious about such ideological positions, nor do I mean to deny the possibility of theological influence. Rather, it is to say that there is a political formation that has recognizable debates, theories, strategies, and a body of philosophical and ideological texts from which to engage with experiences and approaches to ideas such as anti-colonialism, anti-imperialism, anti-racism, anti-sexism, and other critiques of systems of oppression and dominance.

8. Said 1979; Said 1993; Aydin 2017.

9. For example, in the case of reading the work of Frantz Fanon, I have argued that while Blackness as a thematic has been theoretically productive, the issues of Arabness, Islam, and indigeneity are curiously absent, particularly in relationship to Fanon's clear political solidarity and work with Algerian anti-colonialism. See Rana 2017.

10. For example, the French philosopher Michel Foucault's interest in revolutionary Iran as creating a "political spirituality" is largely dismissed by the academic left. See Ghamari-Tabrizi 2016.

Take for instance the well-known Black revolutionary figure Assata Shakur. Long known as an inspiration of the Black liberation movement, Shakur represents the intersecting histories of Islam and liberatory politics in the United States. In her autobiography, *Assata*, she details the role that Islam had in terms of impact:

> I had always said that if i [*sic*] had any religion, it was Islam, but I had never practiced it. Because of Elijah Muhammad and Malcolm X, the Muslim influence over our struggle has been very strong, but it has always been difficult for me to accept the idea of an all-powerful, all-knowing god. And, i [*sic*] reasoned, how could i [*sic*] be expected to love and worship a god whose "master plan" included the enslavement, torture, and murder of black people?[11]

This profound statement by a key figure of Black revolutionary thought in the United States speaks to a range of issues. First, the significant role of the Nation of Islam in shaping US radical social movements whether through practitioners, political critique, or ideology. Second, and more complex, a sense of doubt related to the presuppositions of monotheism. Without going too far into whether this constitutes the category of the Muslim left that I am arguing for, this last point of a transcendental deity points to how theodicy is imagined in a Manichean world of good and evil. As I describe below, such critical thinking is an important aspect of social movements that have often been under-examined. And while Assata Shakur was not a Muslim per se, the impact of Islam on her and other Black revolutionaries is palpable. Later in the autobiography Assata recounts how during one of her trials "the Muslim sisters and brothers brought their prayer rugs and broke out into prayer in the hallway of the kourthouse [*sic*]."[12] As a form of protest that is integrated into the Black radical tradition, Islam is undoubtedly a key aspect of this history. And indeed there is yet much to recover in terms of the role that Islam played and continues to play in the Black revolutionary and liberation movements.

In the US context, the example of Martin Luther King Jr. as a figure of the Christian left, is a parallel of how to think of Malcolm X as emblematic of the Muslim left. Such a connection is part of the historiography I entertain by beginning with an elaboration of the theological and philosophical readings of Malik Shabazz's thought. What is remarkable about Martin and Malcolm within US politics is the way that they have been divorced from their faith traditions despite having a generative and immense influence on

11. Shakur 1987, 92.
12. Shakur 1987, 212.

a broad range of religious and political practice. It is precisely their religious beliefs that gave them a sense of justice in the world and point to a horizon of theodicy in the political future, yet their words are often detached from the religious provenance of their ideas and values to articulate a secular view of the world. Instead, my argument would have us think deeper about the religious convictions of their political positions, in order to imagine entire realms of political practice that have been thus far underappreciated. And while politics and religion have been separated as part of social practice, the development of political thought that is the result of an encounter with people, places, and specific philosophical debates requires further elaboration. In providing a glimpse of such historical possibilities I then turn to the time that Dada Amir Haider Khan spent in the United States that was formative in his development as a radical leftist. While Malik Shabazz is a well-known figure of Black liberation, whose legacy regarding his belief in Islam has often taken a back seat,[13] Dada is a lesser-known figure who had immense significance in the Global left.

Malcolm, the Muslim Critic of White Supremacy

Malcolm X is one of the great philosophers and theologians to come out of North America. He was not just a talented political leader; his ideas are at the heart of a politics and struggle for justice that are profound and inestimable in their reach. From the perspective of the Black liberation movement, it was his criticism of the system of white supremacy that is the foundation of the idea of America that gestured to a political Blackness that is aspirational. What has often been left out of the study of Malcolm X is how to study him in relationship to his ideas and thoughts of Islam. Malcolm X, El-Hajj Malik El-Shabazz, was after all a Muslim. He was a man who as a Muslim prayed to Allah and found solace in the religion of Islam. Initially his relationship to Islam came through the thought and writing of Elijah Muhammad; later through his travels around the world and his performance of the Hajj, his growth and political acumen expanded his critique of the condition of Black people toward a more broadly internationalist position that accounted for the liberation of all. Toward the end of his short life, his troubled relationship with the Nation of Islam propelled a range of transitions that crafted what Edward Curtis has called an Islamic ethics of liberation.[14] This idea of liberation was framed in relationship to his conceptions of politics as a Muslim in relationship to non-Muslims, and as a Muslim in relationship to

13. For example Manning Marable's (2011) biography sets out to historicize the life of Malcolm X but does little to elaborate his ideas and relationship to Islam.
   14. Curtis 2015, 776.

other Muslims. Such an Islamic ethics was simultaneously pan-African and pan-Islamic, and was centrally informed by Gamal Abdel Nasser's idea of pan-Arabism. As Curtis usefully argues, "this ethics was not a detailed political platform; it was a moral argument that the Muslim world had a religious obligation to fight for the freedom of all people of color, whether Muslim or not."[15] And as such, an Islamic ethics was not an abstraction to divine justice but the necessity of practicing a political life in public that was to the benefit of society as a whole, not in the sense of individual ideas of self-determination but collective forms of transformation. In the period after splitting with the Nation of Islam, Shabazz's growth thereafter was developed with the sense of Islam as "a religious and political system of liberation from white oppression."[16] The conditions from which white supremacy mobilized a dominance synonymous with colonialism and racial capitalism were such that Shabazz expanded his argument of liberation of Black people as part of an international struggle that ultimately was a struggle for all of humankind.

So what does a critique of white supremacy have to do with Islam? And how might we think of politics as a field of liberation practices that are also in tune with religious belief and faith? To address these questions I turn to Shabazz's speech "The Ballot or the Bullet," which was delivered in two consecutive weeks, first in Cleveland, Ohio, and then in Detroit Michigan. Here I am interested in the oft-cited passage in which Shabazz elaborates his political positioning and develops his analysis. I quote at length from both versions to examine the range of ideas and the differences in delivery. In the first version recorded in Cleveland, Ohio, at the Cory Methodist Church on April 3, 1964, he says,

> I'm not a politician, I'm not even a student of politics; in fact, I'm not a student of much of anything. I'm not a Democrat. I'm not a Republican, and I don't even consider myself an American. If you and I were Americans, there'd be no problem. Those Honkies that just got off the boat, they're already Americans; Polacks are already Americans; the Italian refugees are already Americans. Everything that came out of Europe, every blue-eyed thing, is already an American, and as long as you and I have been over here, we aren't Americans yet.
>
> Well, I am one who doesn't believe in deluding myself. I'm not going to sit at your table and watch you eat, with nothing on my plate, and call myself a diner. Sitting at the table doesn't make you

15. Curtis 2015, 776.
16. Curtis 2015, 777.

a diner unless you eat some of what's on that plate. Being here in America doesn't make you an American. Being born here in America doesn't make you an American. Why, if birth made you American, you wouldn't need any legislation, you wouldn't need any amendments to the Constitution, you wouldn't be faced with civil rights filibustering in Washington, DC, right now. They don't have to pass civil rights legislation to make a Polack an American.

No, I'm not an American. I'm one of the twenty-two million black people who are the victims of Americanism. One of the twenty-two million black people who are the victims of democracy, nothing but disguised hypocrisy. So, I'm not standing here speaking to you as an American, or a patriot, or a flag-saluter, or a flag-waver – no, not I. I'm speaking as a victim of this American system. And I see America through the eyes of the victim. I don't see any American dream. I see an American nightmare.[17]

The first point to note in this passage is Shabazz's refutation of politics, specifically in the practice of the US political system, the politics of politicians. Embedded in this reasoning is a different type of politics, one that is for those who are disenfranchised and shut out of a political system based in hypocrisy. Through an analysis and practice of negation Shabazz articulates that what is considered "American" and "Americanism" is a system from which he is a victim of exclusion and domination. The unspoken system here is white supremacy and racism that would make white immigrants part of America.

Then in Detroit, Michigan, on April 12, 1964, at the King Solomon Baptist Church just over a week later, he expands his thinking in what is often considered the definitive espousal of Shabazz's Black nationalism. In this portion of the speech a week later, Shabazz condenses his thoughts:

I'm no politician. I'm not even a student of politics. I'm not a Republican, nor a Democrat, nor an American, and got sense enough to know it. I'm one of the twenty-two million black victims of the Democrats, one of the twenty-two million black victims of the Republicans, and one of the twenty-two million black victims of Americanism. And when I speak, I don't speak as a democrat, or a republican. I speak as a victim of America's so-called democracy. You and I have never seen democracy, what we've seen is hypocrisy. When we open our eyes today and look around America we see America not through the eyes of someone who has enjoyed the fruits of Americanism, we see America through the eyes of someone who

17. Shabazz 2015, 655–656.

has been the victim of Americanism. We don't see any American dream, we've only experienced the American nightmare. We haven't benefited from America's democracy, we've only suffered from America's hypocrisy. And the generation that's coming up now can see it and are not afraid to say it. If you go to jail, so what? If you're black, you were born in jail. If you're black, you were born in jail, in the North as well as the South. Stop talking about the South. As long as you're south of the Canadian border, you're South. Don't call Governor Wallace a Dixie governor, Romney is a Dixie governor.

Twenty-two million black victims of Americanism are waking up, and they're gaining a new political consciousness, becoming politically mature. And as they develop this political maturity, they're able to see the recent trends in these political elections. They see that the whites are so evenly divided that every time they vote, the race is so close they have to go back and count the votes all over again. And that means that any block, any minority, that has a block of votes that stick together is in a strategic position. Either way you go, that's who gets it. You're in a position to determine who'll go to the White House, and who'll stay in the dog house. You're the one who has that power. You can keep Johnson in Washington DC, or you can send him back to his Texas cotton patch.[18]

Here a telling metaphor is the one that pairs democracy with white America, and jail with Blackness. Such a stark division is the epitome of how Shabazz describes another duality, one of the American dream, again reserved for whiteness, and the American nightmare that Black people suffer. The ferocity of his criticism of racism and white supremacy are often taken as secular critiques. But what if they were understood as theological, or even in the vein of what Sherman Jackson suggests as theodicy, or the idea of divine justice in the face of evil?[19] Approaching Malcolm's thought from this vantage point suggests a moral evaluation that draws on ideas of liberation that were an essential aspect of his popularity. Indeed, as Edward Curtis has argued such thinking was formative in Malcolm's move toward liberation theology.[20] Such was a politics that was neither Republican nor Democrat in the American sense of electoral politics but certainly raised issues of political critique that were *radical* and devoted to a conception of grassroots politics. Throughout these passages and at the heart of Shabazz's ethical critique throughout his writings, speeches, and sermons, is his indignant condemna-

18. Shabazz 2015, 678–679.
19. Jackson 2009.
20. Curtis 2015.

tion of hypocrisy, and in particular the contradiction of an American form of democracy based in the system of white supremacy.

It is important to note that at the beginning of both versions of the speech he starts with the statement, "I'm still a Muslim; my religion is still Islam."[21] His reaffirmation to his religious beliefs was in the context of his split with the Nation of Islam, despite maintaining his respect for the religious influence of Elijah Muhammad on his religious path. Such an important statement is easily forgotten in a speech that considered a manifesto of Black nationalist politics. Many of the iconic pictures of Malcolm X are those of him praying. Yet toward the end of the first version of the "The Ballot or the Bullet" speech, he makes a separation of religion and politics that is pragmatic:

> We keep our religion in our mosque. After our religious services
> are over, then as Muslims we become involved in political action,
> economic action and social and civic action. We become involved with
> anybody, any where, any time and in any manner that's designed to
> eliminate the evils, the political, economic and social evils that are
> afflicting the people of our community.[22]

Such pragmatism is a hallmark of Shabazz's ethical approach. For him, politics was increasingly internationalist and global, even before he split with the Nation of Islam. For Shabazz such distinctions are an important aspect of developing a political program as a Muslim intent on eliminating "evil," in which suffering is brought upon humankind. And while white supremacy is associated with America and Americanism, he also makes the distinction of discussing how figures such as Billy Graham mobilized the ideas of white nationalism as a gospel of the church.[23] In other words, what is not said explicitly in the passages I quote above is made into a more pragmatic analysis of politics and the factions of the system of white supremacy. Whereas Americanism stands in for the system of white supremacy, white nationalism is the patriotism of white belonging and white life from which Christianity enables the racial hierarchy of the status quo through pride in racial character. For Shabazz, from the viewpoint of the oppressed, there is something to be learned from the oppressor. He makes a point of saying he has studied figures such as Billy Graham and the evangelical church that espouse and reinforce the ideas of white supremacy through white nationalism. As iterations of political ideology and practice, Shabazz takes these notions to invert

---

21. Shabazz 2015, 654, 672.
22. Shabazz 2015, 666.
23. Shabazz 2015, 684–685.

them in terms of Black liberation and the struggle of Black nationalism. Not the simplistic notions of Black racialism that have often been placed erroneously in the thought of Shabazz, but the ability of a racial nationalism to be used toward uplift and betterment. This was not a rule of creating parallel structures, rather it maintains the revolutionary qualities in Shabazz's call to radicalism and decolonization throughout this speech.

As a Muslim who denounced the contradictions of the American system of white supremacy, Malik Shabazz argues that he cannot be an American, but rather must live in the nightmare called America. For him, the transformation from white supremacy could only happen through political awakening and consciousness. That such politics is unpredictable was part of his strength and ability as a political theorist to mobilize an opposition. And while Shabazz offers some profound framings of how we might think of the Muslim left in terms of political internationalism and radicalism, he offers a source to continually refer to and critique as a foundation of a political philosophy and theological reasoning.

Dada, the Anti-Imperialist Revolutionary

In the tradition of the of Cold War internationalism that Malik Shabazz engaged, Dada Amir Haider Khan, whose long career has been significant to the South Asian and global left, developed his political consciousness in significant ways in the early part of the twentieth century in the United States. The source material for much of this information comes from his invaluable memoir *Chains to Lose: Life and Struggles of a Revolutionary*. Written from the first-person perspective, the memoir details Amir Haider Khan's experiences as a traveler and his growing political consciousness. As a young teenager, he left his village outside of Rawalpindi, in colonial India, to join the British merchant navy, and shortly thereafter the United States merchant marine. He would then travel the world as a sailor, worker, and student, later to return to Pakistan in the aftermath of the 1947 Partition of the Subcontinent. The memoir *Chains to Lose* chronicles the development of Amir Haider Khan into a political agitator and committed international leftist. The memoir is written in the genre of a revolutionary biography that highlights his political awakening through a dialectical mode of writing. With this mode of descriptive writing and political analysis, Amir Haider Khan highlights the contradictions and disparities of social, economic, and political thought.

Soon after joining the crew of the S.S. Franz Ferdininand sailing from Bombay, a young Amir Haider Khan, barely a teenager, recounts how the crew was tested early when a Kashmiri from Mirpur met an early death by accident. After burying their crewmate at sea, a solemn mood overtook those on the ship. He reports that the melancholy was broken when a fellow crew member stated, "It was the destiny of the departed to be buried in this particular sea and it was the fulfillment of this destiny that the circumstances brought him here and nothing in the world could alter it." Amir Haider Khan was around fourteen or fifteen years old at the time. Marking his iconoclastic and rebellious attitudes early on, he responds to this statement with a criticism of destiny and fatalism:

> Never having been exposed to other ideas we all believed the dogma that birth, death and all the factors of our lives which governed these events were predestined, and all the reasons or causes were merely excuses or pretenses. Man was the helpless agent through which the great drama of human destiny was played. There was nothing more to it than the will of the inscrutable – the supernatural Allah. There was no fault to be found in the accident that caused the death of our shipmate and deprived his family of their bread-winner.
> But I believe that nothing in this world is immutable or written in stone. Consistent with this law there is nothing predestined about birth or death, and the factors governing these events are subject to modification or change.[24]

His renegade thought of countering dogma is a hallmark of his belief in social possibility, transformation, and justice. Such ideas reverberate throughout the memoirs and are a signpost of his approach to revolutionary change and the uplift of society.

As a young man traveling and learning from the world, his time in the United States is of particular interest in thinking through his political outlook. As an adept observer, in tune with the ideas of this period, the memoirs are remarkable for the narrative of political and personal transformation chronicled in his travels as he witnessed the upheavals of the twentieth century. In his later life, he affectionately garnered the moniker "Dada," or grandfather, by social movement intellectuals and leaders in South Asia. His early life in the United States overlapped with several significant figures and the crosscurrents of radical social movements in terms of internationalism, decolonization, anticolonialism, and the Black radical tradition. Dada crossed paths with Garveyites, labor radicals, and members of the Ghadar Party, the latter group based in San Francisco and Vancouver and engaged in long-distance anticolonial struggle against the British in India.[25] While in the United States, Dada spent significant time in Detroit and New York and

24. Khan 2007, 80.
25. For the histories of anti-colonial radicalism in the Ghadar Party see Sohi 2014 and Ramnath 2011.

even became a naturalized US citizen. As Vivek Bald has observed, Dada's short time in the US from 1918 to 1926 was exemplified by his encounters with other radicals that transformed "his conceptions of justice and injustice, broadened his racial consciousness, and sharpened his convictions as a political actor."[26] With the wide array of figures of the US and global left that Dada interacted, including Agnes Smedley, Joseph Mulkane, Lala Lajpat Rai, Budh Dhillon, and others, the memoir is written in a genre of socialist writing that is didactic and descriptive, providing insight into his method of anti-capitalist and anti-colonial thought. Dada's attraction to the platform of the Ghadar Party was crucial to his early political organizing and radicalism. As he traveled from his base of New York City, he distributed the literature of the Party, delivered political speeches on board ships, and was even tasked to smuggle firearms to India.[27] While New York marked his anti-imperial fervor and direct involvement in anti-colonial struggle, he developed his political acumen with reference to race and religion in Detroit, although in his memoirs it is also clear that this happened throughout his lifetime.

In Detroit, Dada came into contact with followers of Marcus Garvey and attended meetings of the Islamic Association organized by Duse Muhammad Ali, whom he referred to as Dost Mohammad Effendi.[28] These groups were brought together as an organization for oppressed people that brought together Blacks, South Asians, and Arabs in an early experiment of multiracial Islam.[29] While Dada did not gel with the group led by Duse Muhammad Ali because of sectarian and communal divisions that blamed the plight of colonial India on "Hindus" rather than imperial Britain,[30] he attended these meetings because of the congruence with his economic and social critiques. The group "[contrasted] with all the local white Christian churches in which the Negroes were not permitted even to offer prayer, the small Islamic group of diverse races was a sort of illustration of Islamic unity." When asked to speak to the group, Dada reports,

> At the time I was skeptical about all religions. Yet I did not know any rational argument against any of them. Hence, I said to the gathering that various religions taught various ways for the salvation hereafter though no one has returned to inform us of the other world. But in the present world, despite all sorts of beautiful teaching of all the other religions, it is only Islam that practices the real fellowship

26. Bald 2013, 140.
27. Khan 2007, 233–247.
28. Khan 2007, 467–479. Historian Sally Howell (2014) also writes about this period, 72–79.
29. Howell 2014, 75–80. See also Turner 1997.
30. Khan 2007, 478.

among all the human beings. The proof of this is right here amongst yourselves.[31]

What this comment reveals is the doubt concerning religious institutions, while still maintaining an analysis in the power of faith to unify disparate groups of people. Dada's disinterest for the group came from Duse Muhammad Ali's intention to build the organization as a "commercial enterprise."[32] Rather than a political agenda, the Islamic Association was interested in capturing a market of commercial activity akin to a model of third world capitalism. Although Dada's experience with Garveyism and the related model of Duse Muhammad Ali's Islamic Association did not yield sustained interaction, his time in Detroit reveals his positions regarding Islam and religion more generally. And while he easily spoke to the congregation about unity and fellowship, he would not compromise his principles that were anti-imperial, internationalist, and anti-capitalist.

What Dada provides here is a lesson for how to think of the complexity of the Muslim left. Soon after Dada's time in Detroit, he left for Moscow for an education at the University of the Peoples of the East, where he come into close contact with a range of figures of the Third World left, including the founder of the Indian Communist Party M. N. Roy. Half his life had not been completed, yet this formative time in the United States had come to a close. Dada Amir Haider Khan's convictions came from a number of sources, including his working-class and labor politics formed toiling at sea, but it was the encounter with like-minded people in the United States, whose political philosophies and approaches informed Dada's political life and trajectory.

The Provocation of the Muslim Left

One response to the idea of the Muslim left is that it is a narrowing of sectarian politics. On the contrary, I argue that it opens different and unexplored vistas and horizons for political theory, strategy, and practice. The figures of Malik Shabazz and Dada Amir Haider Khan are two among scores of examples from which to frame the multitude of debates, ideas, and experiments of the Muslim left. Malik Shabazz is an example of recuperation and reinvigoration of liberation ethics and Islamic liberation theology that as political theories and praxis provide a different axis from which to understand Muslim politics. Dada Amir Haider Khan is a rich character, whose ideas regarding anti-imperialism and a commitment to socialist and communist ideas are significant histories of the international global left that similarly provide

31. Khan 2007, 478.
32. Khan 2007, 479.

an example of struggling for a more just world. The range of possibilities of those we might consider in relationship to the Muslim left includes figures from around the world from this abbreviated roll call: Betty Shabazz, Houria Bouteldja, Jamil Abdullah Al-Amin, Sekou Odinga, Saadi Yacef, Ahmed Kathrada, Suheir Hammad, and so many others.[33]

In these two historical figures, Malik Shabazz and Dada Amir Haider Khan, I present two different possibilities of the global Muslim left. Each represents dramatically different experiences and relationship to Islam. But where they converge is a political theory and practice of radicalism that draws on left internationalism, a critique of white supremacy and racism, and anti-colonialist and anti-imperialist politics. For both, it was through their travels and encounters with others that led to expanded political visions. Shabazz and his extensive travels through the Arab world and the continent of Africa informed his growing internationalist vision and an alignment with the socialist factions of pan-Africanism and pan-Arabism. Similarly, for Dada Amir Haider Khan, his travel from colonial India as a merchant marine, which took him all over the globe, but in particular his time in the United States, politicized him in specific ways that led him to further education in Moscow and then back to South Asia in the second half of the twentieth century. The notion of the Muslim left is hardly definitive for either of them since their political ideas and practices are far-reaching and generative. Yet the term Muslim left returns to both figures a complex relationship of religion and politics that has often been undervalued and deemed impossible. In the contemporary moment, the challenge comes from the idea of how to engage in decolonial and revolutionary politics such as those that Houria Bouteldja has called for in the context of French politics,[34] and that in important ways is already taking place among Muslims in diasporic settings such as the United States.

33. See Rana and Daulatzai 2018; Daulatzai 2012; and an adjacent argument regarding Islam and Muslims in relation to the academic left, Rana 2017.
34. Bouteldja 2017.

Works Cited

Aydin, C. 2017. *The Idea of the Muslim World: A Global Intellectual History*. Cambridge, MA.

Bald, V. 2013. *Bengali Harlem and the Lost Histories of South Asian America*. Cambridge, MA.

Bouteldja, H. 2017. *Whites, Jews, and Us: Toward a Politics of Revolutionary Love*. Cambridge, MA.

Cone, J. 1975. *God of the Oppressed*. New York.

Curtis, E. 2006. *Black Muslim Religion in the Nation of Islam, 1960-1975*. Chapel Hill.

Curtis, E. 2015. "'My Heart Is in Cairo': Malcolm X, the Arab Cold War, and the Making of Islamic Liberation Ethics." *Journal of American History* 102.3:775–798.

Dannin, R. 2002. *Black Pilgrimage to Islam*. Oxford and New York.

Daulatzai, S. 2012. *Black Star, Crescent Moon: The Muslim International and Black Freedom beyond America*. Minneapolis.

DeCaro, L. 1996. *On the Side of My People: A Religious Life of Malcolm X*. New York.

Ghamari-Tabrizi, B. 2016. *Foucault in Iran: Islamic Revolution after the Enlightenment* Minneapolis.

Howell, S. 2014. *Old Islam in Detroit: Rediscovering the Muslim American Past*. Oxford and New York.

Jackson, S. 2005. *Islam and the Blackamerican: Looking toward the Third Resurrection*. Oxford; New York.

———. 2009. *Islam and the Problem of Black Suffering*. Oxford; New York.

Khan, D. 2007. *Chains to Lose, Life and Struggles of a Revolutionary: Memoirs of Dada Amir Haider Khan*. Edited by H. Gardezi. 2 vols. Karachi.

Marable, M. 2011. *Malcolm X: A Life of Reinvention*. New York.

Ramnath, M. 2011. *Haj to Utopia: How the Ghadar Movement Charted Global Radicalism and Attempted to Overthrow the British Empire*. Berkeley, CA.

Rana, J. 2017. "No Muslims Involved: Letter to Ethnic Studies Comrades." In *Flashpoints for Asian American Studies*, edited by C. Schlund-Vials, 101–114. New York.

Rana, J., and S. Daulatzai. 2018. "Writing the Muslim Left: An Introduction to Throwing Stones." In *With Stones in Our Hands: Writings of Muslims, Racism, and Empire*, edited by S. Daulatzai and J. Rana. Minneapolis.

Robinson, C. 1983. *Black Marxism: The Making of the Black Radical Tradition*. London.

Said, E. 1979. *Orientalism*. New York.

———. 1983. *The World, the Text, and the Critic*. Cambridge, MA.

———. 1993. *Culture and Imperialism*. New York.

Shakur, A. 1987. *Assata: An Autobiography of Assata Shakur*. Westport, CO.

Sohi, S. 2014. *Echoes of Mutiny: Race, Surveillance, and Indian Anticolonialism in North America*. Oxford.

Shabazz, M. 2015. *Malcolm X: Collected Speeches, Debates and Interviews (1960-1965)*. Edited by S. Atwal. N.p.

Turner, R. 1997. *Islam in the African-American Experience*. Bloomington, IN.

Index of Names

Abdel Nasser, Gamal, 206
Abdul Kamal, 186
Abdul Khabeer, Su'ad, 106n7
Abdul Quader, Athel, 157
Abdul Rauf, Faisal, 93
Abdul-Jabbar, Kareem, 36
Abu-Lughod, Lila, 104-105, 117
Abu-Salha, Razan, 108, 110
Abu-Salha, Yusor, 108, 110
Affleck, Ben, 83, 84-85, 92, 95, 98-99
Ahmed, Mirza, 154
Aidi, Hisham, 130n14
Akeel, Shereef, 158
Amin, Jamil Abdullah Al-, 214
Ali, Arshad, 106n7
Ali, Ayaan Hirsi, 94n47, 95, 97
Ali, Duse Muhammad (Dost Mohammad Effendi), 212-213
Ali, Mahershala, 72
Ali, Muhammad, 1, 36, 84, 86, 97
Ali, Noble Drew, 188-189
Alsultany, Evelyn, 3, 106n7
Anglin, Andrew, 10
Ansari, Anousheh, 72
Arendt, Hannah, 27, 38
Assad, Bashar al-, 59
Auston, Donna, 5, 185
Aydin, Cemil, 203

Bachmann, Michele, 74
Baird, Robert, 12-13, 12n14, 14
Bald, Vivek, 212
Baldwin, James, 197
Balibar, Étienne, 38-39, 43

Bannon, Steve, 9
Barakat, Deah, 108
Barakat, Farris, 108
Barakat, Suzanne, 108
Barber, William J., II, 130n15
Barthes, Roland, 37
Bayoumi, Moustafa, 117
Best, Ricky John, 109, 110
Beydoun, Khaled, 136-137
Bilici, Mucahit, 2-3
bin Laden, Osama, 74, 88, 149
Blyden, Edward Wilmot, 189
Bourdieu, Pierre, 43
Bouteldja, Houria, 214
Brown, Michael, 186
Burnett, John, 72n7
Bush, George H. W., 70
Bush, George W., 15-17, 18, 19, 60, 92, 175
    Bush administrative policies, 61

Carter, Jimmy, 176
Chan-Malik, Sylvia, 5, 185
Chehab, Jeff, 160n28, 161, 163, 164
Cheng, Anne, 188
Christian, Jeremy Joseph, 109
Clinton, Bill, 19n29
Clinton, Chelsea, 55
Clinton, Hillary Rodham, 19n29, 48, 49-50, 55-56, 57, 58-59, 61, 62, 94
    Clinton campaign, 92
cooke, miriam, 121n34
Cooper, Anderson, 1
Crenshaw, Kimberlé, 107

Crèvecoeur, Hector St. John de, 12
Curtis IV, Edward E., 3, 94, 205-206, 208

Dadkhah, Mohammad Ali, 97
David Horowitz Freedom Center, 74, 75-76
D'Harlingue, Benjamin, 87
Dhillon, Budh, 212
Daulatzai, Sohail, 106n7
Deeb, Lara, 106n7
Dost Mohammad. *See* Ali, Duse Muhammad

Eisenhower, Dwight D., 13, 14, 19, 60
Ellison, Keith, 36
Elturk, Mustapha, 157-160, 158n24
Ewing, Katherine Pratt, 79

Fadda, Carol, 106n7
Fairey, Shepard, 36
Falwell, Jerry, Jr., 74
Fanon, Frantz, 203n9
Farhadi, Asghar, 71-72
Farook, Syed Rizwan, 115
Fletcher, Micah David-Cole, 109
Foucault, Michel, 203n10

Gabriel, Brigitte, 74, 75n12
Gaffney, Frank, 74
Garner, Eric, 186
Garvey, Marcus, 189, 212
Geller, Pamela, 73
Ghanam, Gus, 159
GhaneaBassiri, Kambiz, 2
Ghouri, Ali, 27
Giddens, Anthony, 42-43
Gohmert, Louie, 112
Goodwin, Megan, 113

Gordon, Avery, 188
Goska, Danusha, 119
Gould, Deborah, 131n19, 132, 142, 143
Graham, Billy, 209
Graham, Lindsey, 112
Grewal, Zareena, 106n7

Hadid, Bobby, 34
Hammad, Suheir, 214
Hammer, Juliane, 4, 106n7
Haq, Zia ul-, 70
Haqiqatjou, Daniel, 135-136
Harlingue, Benjamin D'. *See* D'Harlingue, Benjamin
Harris, Sam, 83-86, 88-90, 91, 92, 94, 95-99
Hassan, Salah D., 3, 97n54
Hassanen, Nabra, 109-110
Heyer, Heather, 10n6
Hicks, Craig Stephen, 108-109
Hijazi, Ali, 163
Horowitz, David. *See* David Horowitz Freedom Center
Howell, Sally, 4, 212n28
Hurt, Charles, 58-59
Hussain, Amir, 36
Hussein, Saddam, 74

Ingle, David, 51

Jabarra, Khalid, 32
Jackson, Sherman, 208
Jebreal, Rula, 94n47
Jefferson, Thomas, 12, 14, 36
Jesus, 53
Johnson, Lyndon, 208
Johnson, Sylvester, 14-15
Jones, Terry, 73, 74
Joseph, Suad, 87

Kathrada, Ahmed, 214
Kay, Jonathan, 74
Kertzer, David, 131, 140n42
Khalil, Mohammad Hassan, 88-89
Khan, Dada Amir Haider, 5, 202, 205, 210-214
Khan, Elsheba, 53, 58
Khan, Ghazala, 2, 29n9, 55, 57-58, 92
Khan, Humayun, 3, 27, 33, 48, 49, 55-62, 92
Khan, Kareem, 3, 48, 49, 50-55, 62
Khan, Khizr, 2, 3, 27, 28, 29n9, 33, 36, 37, 55-57, 58-59, 62, 92
Khan, Sarah, 77n17
Khomeini, Ayatollah, 70
Kimmel, Jimmy, 72
King, Martin Luther, Jr., 204
King, Peter, 74
King, Steve, 112-113
Klein, Joseph, 75-76
Kristof, Nicholas, 83, 84, 86, 92, 97, 98
Kumar, Deepa, 87
Kundnani, Arun, 87-88, 96

Levingston, Steven, 72
Lewis, Bernard, 88
Lincoln, Abraham, 56
Lincoln, Bruce, 48, 49
Lopez, Consuela, 142
Love, Erik, 106, 130, 130n15, 131n16, 133
Lowe, Lisa, 89

Maher, Bill, 83-91, 92, 94, 94n50, 95, 96-99
Mahmood, Saba, 107, 117
Mahmoody, Betty, 113
Maira, Sunaina, 130

Mamdani, Mahmood, 70-71, 71n4, 71n5, 92, 151
Malcolm X (Malik Shabazz, El-Hajj Malik El-Shabazz), 5, 201, 202, 204, 205-210, 205n13, 213-214
Malik, Tashfeen, 115-117
Mangla, Ismat Sarah, 61
Manji, Irshad, 94n47
Marable, Manning, 205n13
Marvin, Carolyn, 51
Mary, 53
Marzouki, Nadia, 17
Massad, Joseph, 90
Massumi, Brian, 131n19
Mateen, Omar, 1, 116, 128, 128n6, 135, 136
Mateen, Seddique Mir, 128-129
McAlister, Melani, 52
McCain, John, 49n8, 50
McQuade, Barbara, 165
Mende, Donald, 161, 162, 163, 164
Menzio, Guido, 32
Merkel, Angela, 10
Militello, Stefano, 163
Miller, Stephen, 9
Mobasher, Mohsen, 4
Modamani, Anas, 10
Mohammed, Warith Deen, 15
Monnet, Agnieszka Soltysik, 51-52, 54, 56
Morrison, Toni, 198
Mosadegh, Mohammad, 171
Mueller, Kayla, 119
Muhammad, 18, 197, 199
Muhammad, Elijah, 15, 189, 201, 204, 205, 209
Muhammad, Ibtihaj, 33
Muhammad, Warith Deen, 154n18, 202
Mulkane, Joseph, 212

Naber, Nadine, 106n7
Namkai-Meche, Taliesin Myrddin, 109, 110
Nawaz, Maajid, 85, 94n47
Netanyahu, Benjamin, 76
Nixon, Richard M., 60
Nomani, Asra, 94n47
Nussbaum, Martha, 98

Obama, Barack, 1, 15, 17-19, 22, 49n8, 50, 59, 70, 153, 179, 180
Obama administration, 31
Obama administrative policies, 61
Odinga, Sekou, 214
Offendum, Omar, 79
Omar, Ilhan, 2
Owen, Wilfred, 51

Paul II, John, 21
Perkins, Alisa, 4
Piepenburg, Erik P., 77n17
Pitard, Dana J. H., 57
Platon, 53, 58
Portes, Alejandro, 179
Powell, Colin, 48, 49-51, 52-55, 62

Qaddafi, Mu'amar, 59, 70
Qudosi, Shireen, 119

Rai, Lala Lajpat, 212
Rana, Junaid, 4, 106n7
Rancière, Jacques, 38
Rashid, Hussein, 61
Raza, Raheel, 94n47
Reagan, Ronald, 153
Reagan Democrats, 150, 152
Rehman, Rashid, 97
Rice, Tamir, 194
Riley, Krista Melanie, 93
Robart, James, 169

Robertson, Pat, 74
Robinson, Brandon, 151
Robinson, Cedric, 202
Romney, George, 208
Roy, M. N., 213
Rumbaut, Ruben, 179

Saarinen, Eero, 152
Sadat, Anwar, 70
Sadiq, Mufti Muhammad, 188-189
Said, Edward, 70, 71, 71n4, 90, 202, 203
Salaita, Steven, 87
Salman, Noor, 116
Sanders, Bernie, 59
Sanjek, Roger, 131-132
Sarsour, Linda, 2, 4, 37, 61, 79, 118-120, 133
Schnitzler, Martin, 42
Shabazz, Betty, 214
Shabazz, El-Hajj Malik El-. *See* Malcolm X
Shakur, Assata, 204
Sheth, Falguni, 89
Shibly, Hassan, 41-42
Silverstein, Richard, 118
Smedley, Agnes, 212
Smith, Jonathan Z., 48
Smith, Paul, 162
Sobh, Hussein, 163
Soros, George, 119
Spellberg, Denise, 11, 36
Spencer, Robert, 74, 97n54
Spivak, Gayatri, 104
Stafford, Katrease, 72
Steele, Michael, 83, 84, 92, 97, 98
Sultan, Aisha, 61

Tapper, Jake, 1
Taqi, Sayad, 153, 155-156
Taylor, Michael, 162, 165

Tlaib, Rashida, 127-128, 127n2
Torres, Darwin Martinez, 110
Trump, Donald, 1, 3, 4, 9-11, 17,
    19-22, 20n33, 20n34, 22n37, 27,
    28, 29, 29n9, 33, 34, 37, 41, 50,
    56-59, 61, 62, 70, 71, 72, 76, 92,
    114, 128, 139, 140, 143, 153, 165,
    169-170, 178, 180, 185, 199
    Trump administration, 113
    Trumpsters, 150
Truth, Sojourner, 195
Tubman, Harriet, 195

Uddin, Nizam, 154
Um, Ji-Young, 53, 54

Volpp, Leti, 129n7

Walid, Dawud, 136, 136n37, 158
Wallace, George, 208
Wasserstrom, Steve, 9n2
White, Frances, 150
Wilson, Darren, 186
Wright, David, 27
Wylie-Kellerman, Bill, 139n41

X, Malcolm. *See* Malcolm X

Yacef, Saadi, 214
Yamani, Ahmad Zaki, 70
Young, Coleman, 152
Yousafzai, Malala, 84, 97
Yusuf, Hamza, 195-197, 196n4

Zakaria, Fareed, 95
Zias, Dimitrious, 32